DELICATE COURAGE

March 2012
Charlotte + Phyllis,
Wonderful meeting
You! May Love's Light
Always Be Our Guide
Peace,
Jim Geary

DELICATE COURAGE

*An Exquisite Journey of Love, Death, and
Eternal Communication*

JIM GEARY

iUniverse, Inc.
New York Bloomington

Delicate Courage
An Exquisite Journey of Love, Death, and Eternal
Communication

iUniverse books may be ordered through booksellers or by contacting:

iUniverse
1663 Liberty Drive
Bloomington, IN 47403
www.iuniverse.com
1-800-Authors (1-800-288-4677)

ISBN: 978-1-4502-5036-8 (sc)
ISBN: 978-1-4502-5037-5 (ebook)
ISBN: 978-1-4502-5038-2 (dj)

Library of Congress Control Number: 2010912266

Printed in the United States of America

iUniverse rev. date: 10/29/2010

For my parents, Martha and Joe Geary, whose unwavering support continues to grace my life.

For my more-outrageous-than-I-am friend, Chris Ingenito, whose loving care will forever be held dear.

And for my sweet angel, Jess Andrew Randall, whose delicate courage forever beats in my heart.

Contents

Acknowledgments

Each step in life has prepared me for the next. Each person has given me the gift of deciding who I am in relationship to him or her. In this, all have been and remain my teachers.

I am particularly grateful to those who have allowed me to witness their passing, for they have awakened the parts of me that have enabled me to keep experiencing a deeper love.

The clients, volunteers, and staff of Shanti Project and other AIDS service organizations throughout the world have inspired me with their courage and remain the primary heroes and heroines of my life.

In writing this book, I am grateful for the assistance of Chris Ingenito, Susan King, Carrie Campbell, Ed Dry, Bob Jamieson, Terry Moore, Ed Wolf, and the encouragement and prodding of my partner, Jeff Allen.

Author's Preface

The idea for this book began to form nearly twenty-five years ago. In 1974, I relocated from the Washington DC area to San Francisco, where I worked as a hospital attendant in oncology. It was there that I first learned of Shanti Project, a peer counseling group based in Berkeley that provided support for people with life-threatening illnesses and for their loved ones. The thought of volunteering for Shanti Project was appealing, but since I was already finding my work at the hospital rewarding, I decided it was not the right time.

After leaving the hospital three years later, I worked as a massage therapist and volunteered with a San Francisco grassroots group that was working to defeat the statewide antigay Briggs Initiative. This initiative sought to fire all gay and lesbian teachers as well as non-gay teachers with whom they openly associated. It was during this time that I met Mayor George Moscone and worked alongside Supervisor Harvey Milk; 1978 was also the year I began corresponding with a man who would become my coworker and lover of twenty years.

After witnessing the devastating effects on our city of the mass suicides at Jonestown, followed a few weeks later by the assassinations of Mayor Moscone and Supervisor Milk, I volunteered with Shanti Project. Less than three years later, I was privileged to form the first AIDS support group for people with AIDS and, as executive director, spearhead Shanti Project's development into one of the premier AIDS organizations in the world.

By the time I left Shanti Project in October 1988 to settle in Ormond Beach, Florida, I had been deeply affected and blessed by the thousands of clients, volunteers, and staff with whom I had worked and played. I started working on this book to share some of their courageous stories and to provide insight into the inspiring work of Shanti Project. While keeping true to that intention, the book has expanded to include the story of my twenty-year relationship with Jess Randall. After learning of our own HIV-positive status in 1992, Jess and I were fortunate to travel extensively. *Delicate Courage* includes insights on the remarkable journey that we shared, both prior to and after learning of our health challenges.

During the many years in which I worked with people with life-threatening illnesses, I had never experienced after-death communication with any individual. This was to change with Jess, who, within twenty-four hours of his passing, began a series of amazing and wonderfully comforting communications. The last three chapters of *Delicate Courage* highlight thirty-five of these communications, which I have chronologically interwoven with journal entries that I wrote following his passing.

It has now been over ten years since Jess let go of his physical form. I am now sharing life with another dear man who also had a long-term partner pass of AIDS. After dating for three years, Jeff Allen and I moved in together six years ago. From the onset of our relationship, we have created a place within our relationship to nurture our love in addition to the love that we carry for our former partners. Both Jeff and I are long-time survivors and continue to contribute to AIDS awareness in our community in numerous ways.

Delicate Courage is also a story of one man's integration of his sexual and spiritual natures, developed in part during the turbulent years of Woodstock and Vietnam. It is my hope that in reading *Delicate Courage,* you will be uplifted by the people you meet and the love that they shared. Their love is a love that beats within each of us, and a love that remains eternally ours.

Jim Geary

Chapter 1

Builder of Rainbows

My first near-death encounter was at the age of six. In the winter of 1957, my parents and I were living in Hyattsville, Maryland. While I was playing outside one day, two slightly older boys invited me to the nearby creek. Happy to be included, I followed behind them.

The creek was mostly frozen—except for the middle, where the water was flowing freely. My new pals pointed to an area of the ice that protruded like a small peninsula into the middle of the creek. The boys dared me to walk onto the ice jetty. Excited by their challenge, I took pride in how I ventured forward slowly, appraising the thickness and strength of the ice.

I inched forward.

Suddenly there was a loud thud from behind. The next thing I knew, I was submerged in freezing water. I tried several times to catch hold of the ice and pull myself out of the water. My eyes then closed as an embracing and comforting sense of calm gave rise to understanding that it was futile to struggle. Obviously, I was not in control. My attention turned from the freezing water to a bright light that permeated my being. I felt an immediate but inexplicable oneness with the light. My entire focus became an awareness of an unseen but indubitably present higher consciousness. I knew the Light was God.

I told God that I was not going to fight. If it were my Creator's will that I should die in that moment, I would not resist. I knew intuitively that it was pointless to panic. I was determined not to thrash about and lose the sense of inner resolve I was experiencing. I was not going to jeopardize my dignity. My choice not to panic was actually an attempt to gain control. By deciding not to outwardly struggle, I remained inwardly strong. From this very reasoned place, I informed God that I would lift my arm one more time; if it were God's will that I should live, then I would touch ice and pull myself from the water. If it were God's will that I should die, I intended not to lift my arm again. I had made the choice to accept what would follow as calmly as possible. I was not afraid, and, while aware that God was in control, I also felt on equal footing. This acceptance was not mere resignation; on the contrary, it was a feeling of being very much together, of being ready to look my Maker in the eye. I lifted my arm and touched the edge of the ice jetty. Grabbing hold of it, I pulled myself out of the water. It was like pulling myself back into the world. On the nearby ice, I saw a large piece of wood that the boys had thrown to crack the ice. My awareness abruptly shifted from the edge of eternity to two boys running and laughing as they made their way home. I marveled at how different their experience was from mine. They had no idea how powerful those timeless moments had been for me.

I find it curious that, as a young child, I could experience such profound awareness and yet not have the speaking skills to communicate it to anyone. How many children experience similar states of awareness yet cannot share or do not feel the need to share the significance of their experiences with others? Not until years later could I articulate the depth of this experience, despite its enduring clarity.

This first near-death encounter left me with a powerful understanding of how much of our experience lies within our control. And from this event came knowledge of the deep peace that comes from acceptance or surrender. I had also received insight into the type of relationship that I would have with God. From this point forward, I would never fear God. I would respect God as the ultimate boss, but I had discovered a power within myself which death itself could not overcome.

Martha, my mother, remarried when I was five. I have no memory of my birth father and know only the little my mother has told me: He was alluring and part Native American; he had a propensity for gambling and womanizing. In their second year of marriage, he got another woman pregnant. My mother divorced him when I was a year old, and for several years we lived with her parents before moving from Rhode Island to Washington DC in 1955. Mom was very loving and a champion of the underdog. She worked for the Department of the Navy as a liaison officer for several naval laboratories.

Joe adopted me soon after my mother married him. He came from a large, poor Irish Catholic family. He had grown up next to the railroad tracks in Hyattsville, Maryland, where the homeless were frequent guests at his family's kitchen table. Being poor left its scar on him. He often recounted the tale of one Christmas when his only memory was of a tattered teddy bear donated by a church. Dad held a number of different jobs, working in sales, amateur comedy, and as a postal carrier. I call Joe my dad because he is the only father I remember.

My new father was an alcoholic. He was very emotionally distant and jealous of the closeness that I shared with my mom. One day, after he spanked me, I screamed, "I hate you now and I'll always hate you!" When he left the room, I was astounded that an eight-year-old could feel such intense hatred. It seemed incomprehensible to say that I could hate someone forever, but I felt so much hurt at that time that I found it impossible to think of a day when I would feel anything else.

I was an only child and attended Catholic school. We attended church on Sundays but were not a particularly religious family. The only time I used the Bible as a child was when my mother was in agony due to chronic constipation. When she moaned in discomfort in the bathroom, I would run and get the Bible and place it by the bathroom door, along with every accessible statue of Christ or Mary that I could find. Doing this eased my sense of helplessness and made her pain more bearable for me.

I believe that a sense of spirituality was something that I carried with me into this life. As a nine-year-old, I would lie in my bed at night and have the recurring experience of the energy in my spine rising toward the top of my head. I had an intuitive feeling that if I could somehow force this energy to rise a little higher—to the very top of my head—I would instantly know everything. It was a frustrating attempt but also an exhilarating one. I wondered why God would bring me so close to experiencing perfect peace and understanding yet deny me that final merging. As much as I experienced my spiritual energy and nature in those attempts to raise my awareness, I also experienced my will power. I realized it would *not* be only through the grace of God that I would be given the gift of wisdom, but through my own attempts to attain it.

Around this age, I frequently lost things. After second grade, I was left alone in the morning to get myself ready for school. Frequently, I was unable to find my lunch money, house keys, or homework. Initially, I would try to remain calm as I searched for whatever I had misplaced. As my searching continued, a mounting feeling that God was testing me arose. My frustration and anger increased. Eventually, I would direct my anger at God. Using the harshest language I could summon, I would scream, "You goddamn bastard! You are obviously in control. Why are you testing me? I am only nine years old!" I would then begin to cry and say, "There, you got what you wanted. You forced me into resorting to anger and relying on you. I guess now you're happy!" Inevitably, after I said that, I would find what I was looking for. Usually it would be within sight of where I ended up after my tantrum at God.

At first, these experiences led me to feel that God was a bully, a perverse deity who found pleasure in reducing children to tears and paying Him homage. But soon, I started to view and handle these experiences differently. I realized that when I gave myself permission to direct my anger at God, my focus on God was stronger than ever. This intensity of focus resulted finally in my awareness of my link with God. I began to realize that when I remembered my relationship with God, things worked out. I came to understand that I could bypass my anger at God and surrender into the Spirit's pervading presence. It was not so much a case of God responding to me but of my remembering my connection to the Spirit, and as a result, my path became clearer.

As a child, I experienced very vivid and lucid images of flying. They always occurred in a neighborhood field at dusk. I would run for a few yards, then fall to earth. My ability to fly was directly related to my success in surrendering to God's pervading consciousness. As I fell, I maintained my complete focus on God, who always enabled me to glide for a distance of about eight feet before I safely landed on the ground.

When I prayed to God, I would often ask God to take my life then and there if I were going to do more harm in living than good, even if this meant that I would go to hell. Since I had asked God with all my heart, I believed that God would take my life if I were destined to cause more misery on earth than joy. When I found myself still alive, I was relieved. Apparently, though, I continued to doubt God's wisdom, offering my Creator the same option many more times!

I frequently talked with my neighbors about their relationships with their families and about my relationship with mine. Sharing information about family matters was a source of some contention with my mother. Mom had been raised not to share personal problems. In some ways, I was my mother's best friend. She confided in me at a very early age. My father's drinking increased my mother's desire to talk with me, which in turn fueled my father's jealousy. A psychic who I would visit years later told me that, as a child, I had been surrounded by people who often needed more than they could give. She said that to compensate for this, I concentrated on giving to others while putting my own needs on hold. It was a survival tactic, a way of coping with the reality of my situation. Learning to receive has been one of my major life goals.

My mother's parents, whom I called Nana and Dada, earned their living working in textile mills, spending most of their lives saving money and traveling little. My grandmother and I shared a particularly tender relationship. As a child, I was prone to terrible bouts of poison ivy. On several occasions, my face became so infected that my eyes were mere slits. I vividly recall Nana gently bathing me in warm water and covering my body with soothing, bright pink calamine lotion.

When my mother remarried, my grandparents moved from Rhode Island to a nearby apartment. Like many grandparents, they much enjoyed watching their grandchild grow and change. My mother somewhat painfully observed how Nana found it easier to express affection to me than she had to her. Nana's whole being radiated love and affection when we were together. In my grandmother's eyes I could see the pride she had for me. I often walked to my grandparents' house from school at lunchtime, where Nana would have my favorite foods waiting. If time allowed, Dada and I might play a quick card game of pitch or rummy. My grandparents frequently bickered, and it was hard to pinpoint the source of their friction. My grandmother seemed embarrassed by my grandfather. She would get irritated over the littlest things he did. Dada, on the other hand, idolized her. Maybe it was difficult for Nana to accept being loved that much.

Nana was diagnosed with breast cancer and had a mastectomy when I was eight. Years earlier, she had told her family that if she ever had cancer, she wouldn't want to know it. In 1960, cancer was not talked about as openly as it is now, and it carried some of the taboo that AIDS does today. It was common for people to attempt to hide a diagnosis as if it were something shameful. My grandparents made the difficult decision to move back to Rhode Island in 1963 to assist one of my great aunts. Less than a year after their move, Nana's cancer returned, and she was diagnosed with bone cancer. As Nana's illness progressed, her bones became brittle and sometimes broke. Her physician and her family would agree on what to tell her, so that she wouldn't realize how bleak her situation was. Nana readily accepted whatever explanation was given to her. According to what she was told, the cause was always one that could be treated. At times, Nana got depressed because she wasn't recuperating as quickly as she wanted. However, her hope for recovery was so strong that her optimism would soon overcome her despair. My grandmother's illness was a long one. She deteriorated slowly during the next three years.

I wanted to be with my grandmother as much as possible. During the critical times of Nana's illness, I was taken out of school and told that my grandmother's death was imminent. As we headed off, I would wonder if Nana would be alive when we arrived. When we'd arrive and see her, I was always thrilled to find that she hadn't died. I relished the "extra" time and the opportunity to share with her how much I loved her.

Nana spent much of the time in the hospital when she was sick. Often, I visited her by myself. Nana was in and out of comas during much of her illness. One time when I was visiting her, it appeared as if the end was near. She looked awful. She had been unable to eat for a number of days, and her tongue was so dry that it had withered beyond recognition. My grandfather and I decided that it was time to call my mother. By the time my mom arrived, Nana looked worse. Over the next few days, however, she began to rally. A few days later, she was sitting up and talking to us. It was so strange—I wondered how a person could look so close to death one day and converse with me the next. So many times, I readied myself for her death, only to be kissed and touched by her again.

Shortly before her death, I was with my grandmother when she had a vision of the Blessed Mother. She shared with me, in detail, what she was seeing. She told me that Mary was pointing the way to her mother and her sister, Peg, both of whom had died from cancer and were waiting for her to join them. If it had been possible, I believe Nana would have passed right then. Nana had no fear. She was crying, but in a state of joyous ecstasy.

During my last visit with my grandmother, she shared her remorse over her relationship with my grandfather. Nana said, "My one regret is not telling your grandfather that I loved him more often." I could see the deep hurt and remorse in her eyes. I left this last visit feeling overwhelmed, and I returned home to Maryland the next day. A few weeks later, I came home to find my mother talking on the phone. She was crying. When she hung up, she told me that Nana had died.

It was at the funeral that I communicated Nana's regret to my grandfather. She had never told my grandfather what she had shared with me. It was such a heavy responsibility conveying that message from my grandmother to my grandfather. At first, he was disbelieving. I am sure that he had badly wanted to hear those words throughout the years of their relationship. Perhaps it was easier for her to tell me. And perhaps it was even more powerful for him to receive her message through the fourteen-year-old grandson who they loved so dearly. By telling me her feelings, Nana made them public. If she had shared them directly with him, no one besides Dada would have ever known her regret. Now we all could forgive the part of her that withheld love. After I assured Dada several times that what she had told me was indeed true, he began to softly weep.

The admission of Nana's regret would serve as a powerful reminder to me throughout my life to openly express my love.

In 1964, several years prior to my grandmother's death, we moved to the small community of Beverly Beach on the Chesapeake Bay. Our new home was about forty miles east of Washington DC and about fifteen miles south of Annapolis, Maryland, where I attended Catholic school. The residential section of the community was segregated. The public beach and concession area remained segregated until 1968, when the owner was forced to integrate. Many African Americans lived just outside of Beverly Beach, behind the local store. The majority of their homes were shacks. Blacks were allowed in the store but a "Whites Only" sign forbade them from entering the bar.

I had a paper route and was proud to be the first newspaper boy to solicit subscriptions and deliver newspapers in the African American neighborhood. My friends predicted that I would never be able to collect payment. I was more concerned with the yapping dogs. Collecting the newspaper money was never a problem.

It was a great day when the beach was integrated. I encouraged many of my customers to come to the beach, but they were frightened and preferred to leave integration efforts to professionals from Washington DC. The owner of the beach was so biased that he closed the beach two weeks after it was integrated. A residents' association was then formed, which, of course, limited access to the beach to property owners and their invited guests.

Soon after Nana's death, my grandfather came to live with us, and he remained there until he died three years later. Shortly after his eightieth birthday, he had a stroke and was admitted to the hospital. After visiting him in the hospital the following day, I left my mother with Dada and went to a dental appointment. When I returned to his room, the curtains were pulled. Apparently the nursing staff had been watching for my return, but I had entered unnoticed. I was flooded with a prescient awareness before opening the curtains and finding him dead. As I approached his body to kiss him one more time, I felt an unexpected and spontaneous wave of peace and acceptance. My focus shifted to finding and comforting my mother.

I learned from Mom that a nurse, who was unfamiliar with my grandfather, had attempted to feed him, causing him to choke. My mother had been present when this occurred, which added to her trauma at the time of Dada's death and throughout her grieving period. Yet together we found comfort in knowing that he had lived a full and active life and that his physical suffering had been short. We notified my father, who was now sober and working for the National Park Service. He was attending a training seminar in the Grand Canyon, but he returned home immediately.

My dad had joined Alcoholics Anonymous in 1967. His alcoholism had brought on grand mal seizures, which resulted in several car accidents. Fortunately, no other individuals were ever involved and injury to my father was minimal. Dad adapted well to the AA program and soon found great reward in helping others maintain their sobriety. After becoming sober, he was promoted to manager of Ford's Theater in Washington DC. He has now been sober for over forty years, and we continue to be instrumental in each other's spiritual growth.

When my father stopped drinking, I was faced with the decision of what to do with my twelve-year reservoir of hurt and anger. Part of me wanted to hold him accountable for all those years of pain and rejection. Before I was able to forgive him, I was looking for a way in which he could compensate for those twelve years of unexpressed love and affection. Yet at the same time, I could feel my own ability to let go of my wounded feelings and forgive my father. In some ways it stunned and frightened me to think that I could let go of my resentment. It was awesome to feel that much power and to accept that I had that much control over my feelings. It seemed that only yesterday that I had said I would hate him forever.

Fortunately, I was blessed with the insight that the only result of holding on to my pain would be to experience more of it. For so long, I had identified with the part of myself that felt victimized. Now, I was faced with the opportunity to form a new relationship, not only with my father, but with myself. I wasn't completely sure I wanted to—I knew that once I did the victim part of myself would be gone forever. Once I released them, I would have no way of using my hurt feelings to gain anything, such as love, understanding, or support. There would be no one to hold me and say, "You poor boy, I can see how much you suffered." It seemed odd that it was now up to me, and not my father, to free myself from these years of hurt.

As I forgave my father, I asked God to help me release my pain. I released the part of me that wanted to be compensated for those years of neglect. In that moment, I accepted a new life of healing and happiness, for my father and for myself. I realized that by letting go of the past, I could begin to replace it with all the future joyful moments that life with my father would bring. Healing for both of us now centered on living one day at a time. It awes me how complete healing can be in such miraculous moments of awareness. When I forgave my father, it was amazingly thorough. I could feel the weight of my bitterness and pain exiting my body, and I felt myself being born anew. It would be five more years before he was able to verbalize his love for me, but we had embarked on a journey of mutual healing and respect that continues to increase with each passing day.

Shortly after my dad stopped drinking, I told my parents I was gay. I was sixteen. I tried to soften their shock by saying I was bisexual. In truth, part of me has always been and remains uncomfortable with solely identifying myself as gay. I would call myself bisexual except that the vast majority of my sexual experience has been with men. However, when I have been sexual with women, it has always been filled with play, tenderness, and heart.

I thought that bisexuality would be easier for them to accept. I even went so far as to try to convince my mother that everyone—including her—had bisexual potential. I would batter my mom with the query, "Now, Mom, be honest. If it was a choice between going to bed with Joni Mitchell and Richard Nixon who would you pick?" Mom would bite her lip, look exasperated, and blurt out, "Neither!"

I persisted, "But Mom, you have to pick one. Who is it going to be?"

"Well, Joni Mitchell. But I wouldn't enjoy it!"

My mom wanted me to see a psychiatrist. My dad's response was, "Well, as long as you are happy." Although his response flustered my mother, it was wonderful experiencing the feeling of being validated by my father. It made clear how dramatically my feelings for him had changed since those early years.

By the time I shared my sexual orientation with my parents, I had gone through a five-year struggle with self-acceptance. In eighth grade, a classmate circulated the rumor that I had performed oral sex on another boy. The boy whom I was accused of having sex with never refuted the accusation, since he gained attention because of it. I, on the other hand, was teased unmercifully for three years until I transferred to another school. I thought that my sexual desires would change after adolescence. I dated girls, but my fantasies always centered on boys. The midshipmen at the Annapolis Naval Academy, Georgia Congressman Julian Bond, Captain Kirk, and Donovan, a folk singer, were my usual fantasy subjects. I never have understood why people limit their fantasies to one type of person!

At one point, I thought of becoming a priest. However, the more I examined my motivation, the more I realized that I was trying to run away from desires which were natural for me. I also knew I wouldn't be happy as a priest unless I could be the pope. I would want to change things! I eventually decided that if God would send me to hell for loving another man, then there was something wrong with God, not with me. I further reasoned that any expression of love between two people couldn't be wrong in the eyes of God.

In the summer of 1969, a few months before I entered my senior year in high school, I saw an advertisement for a three-day music festival in a place called Woodstock, New York. For members of my generation, the list of performers was awesome: Richie Havens, Ravi Shankar, Joan Baez, Canned Heat, Creedence Clearwater Revival, Grateful Dead, Janis Joplin, Jefferson Airplane, Santana Blues Band, Sly and the Family Stone, The Band, The Who, Blood Sweat & Tears, Joe Cocker, Crosby, Stills & Nash, Iron Butterfly, and Jimi Hendrix. And that was just a partial list! I knew I had to be there! Since we would be departing on buses from Falls Church, Virginia, my parents fortunately thought that it would be a supervised event. So, at seventeen, I purchased tickets and headed off on an adventure that would help define a generation.

Because of unimaginable congestion, the buses were only able to get within eighteen miles of the concert grounds. We walked for most of those eighteen miles, catching an occasional ride for a few hundred feet when traffic was able to move. It was after midnight when I arrived at Woodstock to the mystical sounds of Ravi Shankar and the mass of people who would become my family for the next three days. An eight-months-pregnant Joan Baez held us gently captive as she spoke of her husband, David Harris, and a hunger strike he had initiated while incarcerated for resisting the draft. Her crystalline voice soothed us to rest on our first night.

The following morning, I awoke to an early morning yoga demonstration on the stage and the smell of mud and marijuana. Although I had experimented with marijuana and acid before attending Woodstock, I was probably one of the few who remained drug-free for the three-day event. Being there was such a natural high that drug use seemed unnecessary. Moreover, the daily announcements from the stage about bad acid and the few people in close proximity to me who had paranoid trips made it downright scary.

Woodstock happened during the height of the Vietnam War and there was much mistrust regarding the government and the military. Because of the much-larger-than-anticipated crowd and the lack of food and facilities, the event was quickly declared a disaster area. On the second day of the festival, the massive gathering came to a pronounced hush as a military helicopter flew directly in front of the stage, hovering above us. None of us knew what to expect, and for those who had taken mind-altering drugs, I can imagine it was even more alarming! After a few minutes, the helicopter's doors opened and young men in uniform began throwing sandwiches to a greatly relieved and grateful gathering. All of us joined in thunderous applause. A half-hour later, the helicopter returned, this time to shower long-stemmed carnations on the flower generation. It was such an awesome moment of healing as people's fear and mistrust gave way to a new way of seeing those in the military: a way that allowed us to embrace one another in the shared light of brotherhood.

Shortly after Woodstock, I moved from my parents' home to begin my freshman year at the University of Maryland. I became involved with a gay group on campus and began meeting other gay men and women. It felt wonderful to finally let go of my internal struggle of self-condemnation versus self-acceptance and begin to accept the truth of my sexuality.

I went through a year where I considered myself an agnostic, despite all my experiences that had pointed me in a different direction. Thinking as an agnostic provided me with an opportunity to decide for myself what was true. I had read some writings by Camus and Nietzsche and was fascinated with their ideas on existentialism. In my last prayer to God, I said, "Well, if you do exist, I know that you love me enough to allow me to explore this new way of seeing. I just need to find out what is true for me." Deciding to no longer define myself as a Catholic, Christian, or follower of any particular faith was difficult at first, but it was also tremendously exhilarating. It gave me the opportunity to really decide for myself what I believed. I came to understand how I had denied my true nature and optimal growth by trying desperately to fit into a belief system that I was moving beyond. In a similar way, recognizing how my own awareness of certain issues exceeded that of my parents, I was able to embrace the parts of myself that transcended the institutions in which I was raised. It was initially hard for me to accept my own answers and truth, particularly when my truth ran counter to the point of view of those in authority or in the majority. In a sense, by cleansing myself of what others were telling me I should believe, I was able to develop my own personal awareness of God's presence in my life. After my brief period of agnosticism, I said hello to God again. I now feel connected to God most when I live with the awareness that Spirit's presence is pervasive. My spiritual path continues to be largely a journey of valuing and accepting the innate worth of others and myself.

I began my freshman year of college in 1970, as the Vietnam War intensified. Although I was eligible for a student deferment, I had returned the draft card that I had been issued. I could have applied for conscientious objector status, but I didn't want to recognize the government's right to draft me at all. It was also disturbing to me that both conscientious objector status and student deferments were more available to the middle and upper classes. Moreover, the idea of giving guns to eighteen-year-olds, who often don't know what they believe, was simply beyond my comprehension. One night I had the radio on while I was studying biology. I heard a news story about Quakers who had assembled at the Pentagon to simply read the list of the war dead. As I listened to the reading of the names, I wondered, "What in the hell am I doing? Here I am studying about the miracle of life while thousands of men, women, and children are being napalmed. This is crazy! How can I justify devoting six to eight years to getting a degree while people are being annihilated *now*?" I decided that the best way I could serve my fellow human beings and myself was to direct my full energy to ending the war. The next day, I went to

Washington DC to visit the Quakers. In less than a week, I had left college and joined the staff of Catholic Peace Fellowship.

I lived and worked with them for two years. My job involved community networking and participating in nonviolent social action. One key demonstration that we organized was an ecumenical chain-in at the Federal Bureau of Investigation. We were protesting both the Vietnam War and the FBI's investigation of student groups. FBI director J. Edgar Hoover had denied allegations that agents were working undercover on campuses. However, our ecumenical group had been given copies of actual FBI reports that undercover agents had filed after investigating campus groups. The protest organizers wanted to ensure that the anonymity of the persons who supplied the documents was protected. Since I knew nothing about the particulars of where the documents came from, I was asked to distribute the reports while we were at the FBI building. After the press had time to read them, I was to collect them and leave them at the FBI building.

We had chosen Good Friday for the chain-in. Each of us was individually chained to a larger chain, which we had attached to the doors of the FBI. A small group of ten of us remained chained until Monday morning, when we were arrested for blocking the main entrance to the FBI. We attracted a lot of press and received a great outpouring of community support. One incredible coincidence was that directly across the street from where we were chained, there was a gay bar. During the three days we were chained, the bar owners brought us coffee and graciously allowed us to use their restrooms. I couldn't believe that right there on Pennsylvania Avenue, less than one hundred feet from the FBI, was a gay bar! Maybe those rumors about J. Edgar were true!

My parents came to see me on Easter Sunday. While my mother had previously joined me in several peace marches, this period was very difficult for her because it continued to challenge her to examine many of her own beliefs. My dad's alcoholism had also exhausted her. She wasn't quite ready to now contend with her gay, draft-resisting, law-breaking son. Yet, despite the fact that my choices and the way I have lived my life have often distressed my mother, her primary concern has always been my happiness. Most important, she never withheld her love.

FBI agents visited me after I was released from jail. They showed me pictures of various people who they thought might have been responsible for breaking into the FBI building in Media, Pennsylvania, and taking the reports. It certainly didn't make the FBI security system look very reliable if, as the agents suspected, the reports had been stolen from their offices by a group of priests and nuns! I felt that it was honorable to be involved in political activity during those years. The thought of possible imprisonment as a result of resisting the draft was scary. Yet I had come to realize that regardless of the potential consequences, standing up for one's principles is important.

Much has been said in recent years to acknowledge Vietnam veterans who returned home without a hero's welcome. Yet I remember the courage of tens of thousands of people who were willing to question their nation's leaders and who, because of their convictions, experienced tremendous parental and societal condemnation. I recall the bravery of Paul, an army private, who made the spontaneous decision to join us as he walked by our chain-in on his way to the USO. On Monday morning, Paul was arrested with us. All of us, except Paul, were released within twenty-four hours. We later learned that Paul spent six months in the brig and was dishonorably discharged. I feel tremendous pride for the many men, women, and children who knew that the Vietnam War was, in many ways, an atrocity and who courageously joined together to end it.

It was during this period that I met my first lover. I was twenty-one and getting tired of one-night stands and sexual contact without intimacy. I asked God, "Please send me a nice Catholic boy!" I wanted to meet someone who was sensitive and who possessed good moral character. A Saturday night dance was coming up at George Washington University; after some ambivalence, I decided to go.

I was sitting and watching people dance when I saw him. I felt instant electricity. He was so good-looking. His black, curly hair reminded me of Donovan. He was slightly less than six feet tall, and he had a very fair complexion and warm, sparkling brown eyes. I was so nervous that I could only look at him for short intervals. During one of my moments of feeling uptight and looking away, he disappeared. I thought, "Oh well, he was much too attractive for you, so it's just as well." However, a short while later, I walked out onto the balcony to get some fresh air, and I ran smack into him. There was something so familiar and comfortable about him. I felt at ease immediately. His name was Matthew. Without exchanging many words, we began to dance. As we danced, I felt incredibly safe; being with him felt so right. After leaving the dance, we went for a ride. Matthew told me he was twenty-one and a junior at the University of Maryland, where he was completing his major in drama. He was very proud of a number of plays he had directed in high school and college. Matthew had not yet come out as a gay man to his friends and family. He had been raised Catholic, was articulate, and had an innate, basic goodness that permeated his being. I could barely contain myself! As he was driving, I laid my head in his lap. It wasn't a sexual gesture but rather one expressing my feeling of immediate safety and trust. It felt so natural. I could rest with Matthew. I was home.

In the course of the next few months, Matt and I marveled at how our lives had crossed several times before. Most significant was that we had attended the same school in first grade, though we were in different classes. Upon learning this, I vividly recalled an incident that had occurred during first grade on the playground. I was playing by myself when I felt myself being drawn to the center of the playground. Once there, I found myself looking deeply into the eyes of another boy whom I had not seen before. After sharing a lingering and seemingly timeless hello, we smiled warmly at one another and went our separate ways. I had the distinct feeling that this connection was enough for then. I am convinced that this was Matt, whom I was destined to meet again fifteen years later. Matt and I also discovered that about three years before we met at the dance, he had come to Catholic Peace Fellowship for draft counseling in Washington DC, where I was working and living at that time. Furthermore, Matt's younger brother was a good friend of my cousin's while they were growing up. Matt and I were amazed at how our lives had been interwoven for so long. I believe this created the electricity I felt when we first met. Life had been preparing us for this moment. I started to appreciate on a deeper level how God was leading me.

That summer, I went to Europe for two months. I had planned the trip before meeting Matt and decided to go through with it. I wrote to Matt every day. While in Europe, I spent my time in France, Italy, and Greece. The French and Italian art was a source of constant inspiration, and the beauty of the Greek Islands deeply soothed my soul. In Genoa, Italy, I visited a cemetery that lies on gently rolling hills. It was the largest cemetery I had ever seen, but what startled me most was that each gravestone bore a picture of the deceased. There was also a separate section for children. The faces on the stones were filled with so much life and vibrancy. After walking around for hours, I sat and cried. "Who were all these people? How was I connected with them? Where are they now?" As I sat in that cemetery, four thousand miles from the United States, I wondered how and if I was connected to the billions of people living in the world. I felt more confused about life and death than ever. Suddenly, in the silence of that moment, I could hear my pulse inside my head and feel the pulse in my hands. I became aware of how every person's pulse on earth was beating in that moment with mine. I looked over the hills of graves and realized how each of these individuals had shared this sacred rhythm of life. I understood that in spite of all our cultural differences, struggles, and geographical boundaries, we all share this miraculous and continuous pulsing of life. In that moment, I felt my sacred connection with all living things, for even those who had died had shared this miracle. My tears of despair turned into tears of joy as I was overcome with gratitude for being part of this shared, sacred, and ongoing rhythm of life.

While I was in Europe, Matt came out to his family. His parents were very upset and wanted him to see a psychiatrist and a priest. Matt agreed to go with his parents to a priest who had a degree in counseling. As fortune would have it, the priest was gay and suggested that Matt's parents seek counseling! When I returned from Europe, Matt and I moved in together. Although his parents refused to meet me, we agreed to go to another priest who Matt's mom had thoroughly checked out. The priest stated the church's position on homosexuality and said that he felt we were destined to a life of ostracism and pain. Sensing that our meeting was over, I spontaneously asked him for his blessing. He obviously was caught off guard but agreed. I held Matt's hand and we knelt before him. After we left, Matt laughed hysterically as he told me, "Well, you don't get much closer to performing a gay marriage in the Catholic Church than that!"

While Matt completed his senior year of college, I worked as a recreational therapy leader at Hospital for Sick Children in Washington DC. I had charge of twenty preschoolers, many of whom had undergone much physical and emotional abuse. One little girl, Lena, had been placed in an oven when she was an infant. Her toes had been burned off and her hands were severely deformed. She wore hearing aids in both ears due to damage from the severe heat. Despite all her hardships, she had a very sweet disposition and smile. Lena typified most of the children I worked with. Matt began working with me on the weekends. It was wonderful sharing the children and finding ways to bring joy into their lives. They would all wildly cheer when Matt and I arrived, shortly after their breakfast, to take them from the nursing ward to the activities room.

After living together for five months, Matt and I decided to enter a Holy Union. The service was to be performed at Metropolitan Community Church in Washington DC, a ministry founded by the Rev. Troy Perry primarily to administer to the spiritual needs of gay people who felt ostracized from their own denominations. In hopes of healing the rift between Matt and his parents, I wrote to them a month before our service. I explained how hurt Matt was by their refusal to meet me and invited them to our Holy Union. Matt's parents refused to attend. My mother held off on making her decision until the thirteenth hour, but when my parents did arrive at the service, they performed the role of ushers, handing out programs to our invited guests!

Matt and I exchanged vows to be honest and to love one another as best we could, and we shared the following statements with those present.

Jim	*Matthew*
I am	*I am*
I am pulsation	*I am metamorphic*
I am in search of truth	*I am an heir of wisdom*
I am a man of reason	*I am a man of prayer*
I am a man of passion	*I am a man of need*
I am a fragile body	*I am a strong soul*
I am a part of all	*I am a singer of joy*
I am a dancer in the moonlight	*I am a lover in the daylight*
I am one who is ready to listen	*I am one who is ready to share*
I am a builder of rainbows	*I, too, am a builder of rainbows*

At our reception, one of my friends asked my father how he was feeling about our union. Dad chuckled, "Well, I look at it this way. It's not like losing a son but gaining two daughters!" That's my dad!

Matt and I remained in Maryland until Matt finished college in June 1974. We then decided to move to San Francisco. Having visited San Francisco once before, I had often thought of eventually living there. Matt also thought that San Francisco offered him the opportunity for work in the theater. Traveling with a dear friend, Helene, whom I had met in Greece, we took several months to cross the country. We arrived in San Francisco in September, eager to begin our new lives. The charm of the city quickly cast its spell on us. Since money was tight, Matt sought immediate work scooping ice cream at Baskin-Robbins, and I soon found work as a nurse's aide in a hospital oncology unit.

Chapter 2

City by the Bay

Sorrows are our best educators. A [person] can see further through a tear than a telescope.

Lord Byron

Working at the hospital was both challenging and rewarding. We had many terminally ill patients in the ward, and I offered to be assigned to them whenever I could. I was attracted to the degree of honesty that I found when working with these individuals. Dying doesn't leave much room for pretense. Even if patients and family members are uncomfortable with what is happening, it is difficult to avoid dealing with the reality of the dying process. Dying elicits authenticity. People are often more honest during this time than they have been throughout their lives. As a care provider to those who were dying, I found my own authenticity awakening as well. Since I was working in an area that I didn't know a great deal about, I tended to observe and listen more than I usually would, and I allowed myself to surrender to many new insights and sensitivities.

After working at the hospital for a year, I attended an in-service training provided by Dr. Charles Garfield, a psychologist who represented an organization called Shanti Project. He had founded Shanti Project in 1974 as a volunteer counseling agency for people facing a life-threatening illness and for their loved ones. Charlie chose the Sanskrit word Shanti, which translates to "inner peace" or the peace that comes from a fuller understanding.

Actually, Charlie had founded Shanti Project with Ram Dass. Ram Dass, formerly Dr. Richard Alpert, was renowned for his work with Dr. Timothy Leary in the late sixties and for his meditation techniques and seminars. Ram Dass had wanted to lead Shanti in a more spiritually focused direction, but Charlie wanted the project to provide services to a wider clientele. Charlie's focus prevailed, and Ram Dass decided to focus his energy elsewhere.

At the in-service training, Charlie talked in depth about his work with clients and why he had formed Shanti Project. When he had worked with cancer patients at the University of California in San Francisco, he had been appalled at how poorly equipped the medical staff was to support people with life-threatening illnesses. Charlie came to strongly believe that what people who were facing a life-threatening illness needed most was someone to listen to their feelings in a loving, nonjudgmental way. They needed someone who wouldn't recoil, over protect, or run away.

Dr. Garfield developed the idea of training volunteers who would then commit eight hours a week to work with clients who requested emotional support. Shanti Project was particularly interested in volunteers who either had experience being with people with a life-threatening illness or who had experienced grief in their own lives. Shanti Project sounded interesting, but I was already so involved in my work at the hospital that I had no immediate interest in volunteering.

After working at the hospital for several years, I sought new ways to connect with patients, and I decided to attend massage school. Providing nurturing touch to patients who were approaching death and who were often severely touch-deprived was very rewarding. I was drawn to doing massage full-time. Leaving the hospital to work as a massage therapist out of my home seemed like the right step. I advertised in local papers, and before long, I had a steady clientele. Matt and I were living near the Pacific Ocean, close to Golden Gate Park. Some days I had only two massage clients, which freed me to walk along the beach or sit in the park. The years when I worked as a masseur were very relaxed, and when I reflect on them, they still bring me a sense of freedom and calm.

Matt and I delved more deeply into Eastern spirituality. We studied the teachings of Paramahansa Yogananda, through the Self-Realization Fellowship and the teachings of Sri Ramakrishna and Swami Vivekananda, through the Vedanta Society. We set aside a specific area in our home for meditation, and our conversations about God provided a source of joy and unity in our relationship.

I loved the part of many Eastern religions that acknowledges that there are numerous paths to God. Also, I found that Eastern religions encompassed a broader approach to spirituality than many Western religions. They speak of God's consciousness pervading everything and say that our goal is to live with and in that abiding consciousness. Yet one problem I found in some Eastern religions is the belief that union with God entails a high level of sacrifice and discipline. I have long held that accessing the Spirit's presence within should be a relatively easy and natural process. If God is absolute love, then it never made sense to me that we should have to work hard to find that love. I had come to believe that God was fully present in my life and that it was God's will for me to know this.

One evening, I had an extraordinary meditation. I was home alone and decided to meditate on the couch in our living room. In this meditation, I was focusing on the area just above the center of my eyes when I heard a voice resounding in my head. It is hard to describe the voice without seeming to be crazy! The voice sounded as if it had emerged from within me, but it had an identity separate from my own. I had no conscious awareness of it being my voice on any level. The voice had only one thing to say: "You are ignorant." Over and over, the voice repeated this phrase. "You are ignorant."

Intellectually, I could accept this pronouncement. My mind reasoned that in comparison with the vast amount of knowledge that exists, I knew very little. The voice, however, was not appeased by this admission. In fact, the intensity increased as it repeated over and over again, "You are ignorant." I then began to get images of the many people I had interacted with in my life, particularly people to whom I thought I had in some way been helpful. As their faces flashed before me, I realized how little I knew about each of them. Previously, when I thought I had helped someone, I would sometimes credit myself with a job well done. I would attribute my helpfulness to my keen insight into a person's character or situation. But in my meditation, I realized that I knew practically nothing about these individuals. I slowly began to grasp my ignorance in thinking that I had known what was best.

Still, the voice continued, louder than ever. "You are ignorant. You are ignorant."

"All right already!" I protested. "What do you want me to do about it?" During this whole period my body was paralyzed. My head was tilted to one side and I was drooling. I felt completely unable to move. Suddenly, I became aware of time and thought, "What if Matt comes home and sees me like this? He will think that I'm dead."

The voice responded, "Maybe this *is* your death."

"Holy shit!" I thought. "I'm not ready to die, it's not fair! How can you be so cruel as to let my lover walk in and find me dead! It's not fair!"

I remembered that I also had plans the following day to meet my mother in San Diego. Why couldn't my death wait until I saw my mother one more time? I had never bargained so intensely. I had read about the stage of bargaining that people experienced when dying but I had never really understood it. Now I was desperately trying to postpone death. After all, I was meeting my mother, and I didn't want my lover to find me dead on the living room couch. If I could at least get to the bedroom, that would be a more acceptable place for Matt to find my body!

The voice persisted, "This could be your death."

I began to realize that if it was my moment to die, I couldn't do one damn thing about it. As soon as I began to surrender to this possibility, the voice became a very loud hum, which felt like it was directly over my head. As the humming increased, I was flooded with an extraordinary feeling of peace and the realization that everything would be fine. I accepted that God was with me and not against me. The vibrating sound increased, and I felt deep waves of serenity flow through me. After simply enjoying this sense of stillness for some time, I began to analyze the humming sound.

Some Eastern religions speak of a sound that can be heard in certain states of meditation. The sound is the "Om" sound, and it is considered to be a composite of all sounds that exist—the universal vibratory sound of creation. The vibrating sound began to decrease as I attempted to analyze it. On a certain level, I knew that my ego was latching onto the experience. It wanted to say, "Hey, look at you! Aren't you holy, hearing the Om sound!"

No matter how I attempted to focus on my oneness with the sound and disconnect from my thoughts, the distracting thoughts continued. The humming sound became louder when I was able to focus purely on it and not on my mental processes, which kept trying to interpret or explain the experience. As I identified more and more with my thinking self, I could feel myself being pulled back into my body. The ability to move my body returned. The sound was getting weaker and weaker. I eventually opened my eyes, and off in the distance, I could hear the muffled humming of the refrigerator. *How perfect!* I thought. *My mind is now reducing this entire spiritual experience into a reality it can understand—it's telling me that it is just the fucking refrigerator!*

By June 1978, I was beginning to miss working with people with life-threatening illnesses. I decided I would volunteer for Shanti Project. There was an extensive volunteer application to complete, an hour-long interview, and forty hours of training which was held over two weekends. Shanti Project's office was located in Berkeley, which lies about ten miles east of San Francisco. The project was comparatively small at that time—there were about sixty volunteers, most of whom were women. During much of my first three years of involvement with Shanti Project, I was the only openly gay male volunteer. The project was attempting to serve a wide geographical area that comprised five Bay Area counties. They had an annual budget of less than fifty thousand dollars, and about two-thirds of the project's funding came from foundations.

When I wasn't volunteering with Shanti or doing massage, I volunteered for the Bay Area Committee Against the Briggs Initiative (BACABI). Sen. John Briggs of Fullerton, California, had introduced a bill that, if passed by the voters of California, would have made it a crime for gay, lesbian, or bisexual teachers to be employed in California public schools. It was a horrendous bill, but polls indicated that it had an excellent chance of passing.

I started my involvement with BACABI by distributing information on busy street corners throughout San Francisco. I became so impassioned about defeating the initiative that I asked Matt if he would financially support us for the two months remaining before the election. Matt, who was now manager of Sutro Baths, San Francisco's only coed bathhouse, was happy to contribute in this way.

I soon organized a cadre of volunteers who staffed tables throughout the city and informed people about the initiative. It was very exciting to be reaching out to people about such an important issue. From our table efforts alone, we collected ten thousand signatures on a petition to President Carter, asking him to make a public stand against the initiative.

During this period I was assigned my first Shanti client. Hank was a San Francisco firefighter who had a very disfiguring form of cancer. He lived with his wife, Ann, and their two adolescent sons. Prior to Hank's diagnosis, Hank and Ann had become involved with a spiritual group whose principles were helping them to cope with Hank's illness. However, when I first met Hank, I found him to be somewhat gruff and withdrawn.

Initially, Hank and I spent most of our time together talking about his belief system and about how devastatingly painful both physically and emotionally his illness had become. His sons found it difficult to interact with their father, in part because of the way the cancer had eaten away Hank's face. Hank was very depressed by his sons' natural avoidance and because of his inability to be a parent to his sons in the way he had been. Although Hank's belief in an afterlife gave him a sense of hope and purpose, he found the actual dying process very trying. Daily, Hank watched his strong muscular body transform into a dysfunctional and grotesque sight.

Hank also shared with me his concern for his family's well-being after he died. Ann held a good job, but with two teenage sons, Hank was very worried about the family's financial welfare. Just after his diagnosis, Hank had bought a new car, which enabled him to secure a ten thousand-dollar life insurance policy. It was an unusual policy. The gist of it was that if Hank lived six months after the policy became effective, then his wife would be entitled to the payout. The six-month date was still three months away. The thought of Hank continuing to suffer and deteriorate for that length of time was overwhelming. The whole situation was very distressing for everyone involved.

I always wore my "Stop *Briggotry*" button, except when I visited Hank. I didn't know his politics, and I was concerned that a conversation about the initiative might create awkwardness in our relationship. After working with Hank for two months, I decided not to remove my button when I next visited. He noticed it immediately and asked me its significance. I told him about the initiative. Hank then asked me if I was gay. I told him that I had had sex with women but that my preference was men. Hank's response surprised me. He said that he admired my ability to risk relating to both sexes and that bisexuality was something that he respected. It felt good adding this new level of authenticity to my relationship with Hank.

As a gay person, I had experienced my share of prejudice and rejection. As a way of protecting myself from hurt, I had developed a pattern of guarding myself against homophobia—even when it wasn't present. Thanks to my interaction with Hank, I came to understand that the way others viewed me was often far less oppressive than I feared. I realized that releasing my fear of rejection, my own internalized homophobia, was as important as the need for some heterosexuals to overcome their discomfort and fear of homosexuals.

During the last two months of his life, Hank began to deteriorate rapidly and was forced to let go of everything during his dying process. Hank taught me more about this than anyone else. As Hank grew weaker, he felt proud of his ability to use a walker so that he could continue to reach the bathroom. A friend of Hank's did some construction on the bathroom door to make physical access easier, and I found an elevated toilet seat that made it simpler for him to use the toilet. He fought hard to handle his walker so he could continue to use the bathroom. However, as he became weaker, he required a bedside commode. He managed to use that successfully for two weeks before having to resort to one of the things he had dreaded most, the bedpan. During this period, Hank had to let go of many other things as well: He was losing his ability to read mail and pay bills. He eventually lost his ability to even sign his name.

I have heard many people say that if they got to a particular point in their illness, they would just give up and end their life. Yet I realized with Hank that what a person thinks he would never be able to bear is sometimes made easier and more tolerable by the gradual decline in his abilities. Hank's ability to cope and to adjust to his horrendous situation was astonishing.

During the last three weeks of Hank's life, Ann and Hank decided that it would be best for Hank to be hospitalized. They also wanted someone to be with him overnight. Hank knew that I had worked in hospitals and asked if I would do it. They insisted that this scheduled time be compensated and not volunteered. Because Hank had requested it, and because the hours involved far exceeded what I had committed as a volunteer, the project approved of me providing this care.

Hank had excruciating pain. Sometimes, his awareness of another person's presence in the room contributed to him feeling his pain more intensely. However, he refused higher doses of his pain medication, fearing that it would result in his dying before the life insurance policy became effective.

I think one of the reasons Hank had wanted me to spend nights with him was that I was able to be very unobtrusive when necessary. I could pick up on his mood quickly when I entered the room. Hank would shoot me a glance, and I would know that he didn't want me to interact with him but to just sit quietly. It was unnerving at times to be slowly walking toward him and see him writhe in agony. Hank was convinced that his pain level increased because of the physical presence of others.

One of the tasks I performed was to turn him every two hours. He had developed severe bedsores, and to prevent them from getting worse, he had to be turned. At times, this was an agonizing process. I found, however, that if I could maintain a sense of calm within myself and turn him as consciously as possible, it made the ordeal easier.

The day the insurance policy would become effective was more than a week away. When Hank wasn't experiencing intense pain, he was mostly comatose. I was torn. Part of me wanted Hank to continue living until the policy became effective. Yet when I saw how absolutely miserable Hank was, I wanted him to die. Hank regularly asked what day it was, and he kept calculating how many more days he needed to continue living. During the last week of his life, Hank experienced lengthy periods of apnea in which his breathing stopped. Hank might go forty seconds without taking a breath. One night, Hank's breathing ceased altogether. The effective date was still three days away.

I had talked previously with Ann to determine if she wanted the medical staff to attempt resuscitation. I knew that Hank had wanted them to resuscitate him, but now that he was comatose, the choice was left to his wife. For Ann, the choice was a simple one: Hank was simply experiencing too much agony to prolong his life any longer.

Over a minute had passed since Hank had stopped breathing. As I looked at Hank, I thought, *Well, you gave it your best shot. It's a statement of your tremendous strength and your intense love of your family that you have lived this long.* As I was leaving to get the nurse, I heard Hank take a breath. It was unbelievable. Hank continued living for another few days. He died two hours after the six-month insurance policy became effective. Hank had demonstrated the remarkable ability to actually control the moment of one's death. He had also helped me to realize that regardless of how prepared one may be spiritually, the dying process itself can still be horrendous.

With my increasing involvement with Shanti and BACABI, Matt and I began experiencing difficulty connecting emotionally. Matt seemed to be experiencing some conflict over merging his sexual and spiritual energies. He wanted to have sex less often, and when we lay together, he frequently wanted us to simply hold one another. I felt stifled.

We entered couple counseling, but our ability to communicate continued to deteriorate. I was still very much in love with Matt, but our disagreements and inability to emotionally support each other were more predominant. I knew that I loved him too much to stay in a relationship that was becoming ever more hurtful.

In my efforts to increase intimacy in my life and develop high-quality friendships, I joined a predominately gay men's organization, The Loving Brotherhood. It was through this organization that I met a man who was destined to transform my life more than any other.

In addition to holding retreats, The Loving Brotherhood published an international monthly newsletter that contained New Age-focused articles. It also printed the addresses of members who submitted a fifty-word self-description. Unlike many other personal ads, the focus was primarily on spiritual interests. The year was 1978, and Jess and I were among the first three hundred members. Members were encouraged to "be slow to say no" to other members wishing to make contact. My listing read as follows:

Jim Geary (home address and phone number), 26 5'9" 145. When my eye is open, I see myself as the universe. I treasure affection, warmth, children, nature, and an open heart. I am a licensed masseur and am more intuitive than rational. Peace.

Jess's listing has been misplaced over the years, but what I remember most from his description was the phrase, "masculine yet delicate with my feelings." Jess wrote to me first. At that time, he was still using his birth name, Bruce, which he changed legally to Jess several years later. Our early correspondence follows:

August 20, 1978

Dear Jim,

How does one open a letter to one whom they've never met?
Howdy.
I'm drawn to write you because of your description of yourself in The Loving Brotherhood and because,

come Oct 15, I'll be moving to the Bay Area, probably San Francisco, and it'll be nice to know a few people when I arrive.

I'm presently living in southeast Idaho, working for the fire service, feeding the Young Adult Conservation Corps, who are young adults building picnic tables, clearing trails, building fences, making signs, collecting seeds, etc.

My listing in The Loving Brotherhood doesn't really give much information. Besides teaching meditation, my life's love is cooking. I was chef in a vegetarian kitchen feeding 1,400 in Iowa for a year. I enjoy working with fresh fruits and vegetables most, although I'm experienced with roast duck, caviar, lobster, glazed salmon, etc. Making a full meal with candlelight and all is heaven for me. My life's work, I think, will somehow be in service to others, be it food or whatever.

My sister, Cathy, is in a relationship with another woman, having been with her lover Ginny for thirteen years. They just recently bought a home in Palo Alto, and I'll be helping them fix it up in October for several weeks.

I've visited the Bay Area ten times, always enjoying the magic of San Francisco. I've had a desire for several years to live in the gay community, taking part in the culture to whatever extent is comfortable. It's now time to follow my desire and make it happen. I'll be looking for a small, cozy, inexpensive place to live, come November, either in the city or on a good bus run, and a part-time job, maybe as a waiter in a ritzy restaurant.

I'll enjoy hearing from you and perhaps making some contact in future months. If I hear from you, great, if not, I appreciate you reaching out in your listing. Good luck. I think all our desires will be fulfilled in time. Sincerely,

Love, Bruce

P.S. I also cherish open hearts, full hearts, and my intuition rules my movements usually.

I replied to Jess's first letter on September 1, 1978:

Dear Bruce,

Thank you so much for your kind and loving letter; you write wonderfully and it was a joy hearing from you. The last few months have been especially busy for me, as I have been working against the upcoming Briggs Initiative. If passed, it would fire all gay teachers and teachers who openly support them in California public schools. It will be on our November ballot. If you would like to vote against it, fill out the enclosed registration card, and use my address as your residence, since you will be living here at that time.

I've also joined an organization, Shanti Project, which assists people with a life-threatening illness (cancer, etc.). I feel if I stay with it, I will learn much. I would love to get to know you better when you arrive and you would be most welcome to stay with me for a few weeks while you look for a permanent place to live in San Francisco. It is a lovely state and I look forward to meeting you. I am sending much love and peace to you, dear brother.

Jim

September 6, 1978

Dear Jim,

Thank you for the beautiful card and the even more heartwarming thoughts inside. Out of the five or six people I've written in the Bay Area, you shine out as a man with an open heart. So often, due I am sure to our culture, men are reserved, leaving the sensitive things to women; or they overcompensate and try too hard to be warm and loving. But somehow, mom or dad, or teachers, or church interfere, and men never quite learn the ease of it, the knack of expressing one's self. You came through loud and clear.

I was happy to hear of your political nature. I'm slowly watching myself drift that way, yet thinking I'm not harsh enough for the games played. But I'm drifting there. I'm sure with friends like you, my political side will be drawn out. Thanks for helping me to register to vote.

It looks like I will be in the Bay Area come October 15, although it may be as late as November 15. God, I hope it's October 15!

I'm getting so ready to dive into the city I love, and when someone writes, "I would love to get to know you better. It is a lovely state and I will look forward to receiving you. I am sending much love and peace to you, dear brother."—well, when someone so full of love writes me that, how can I not leave for California today!

I'm an interesting mixture of a strong, clear, dynamic, almost brusque, fast-paced food service administrator, along with (mostly off work) a delicate, loving, seeker who enjoys lazy days, sharing emotionally and sometimes intellectually in the most hidden areas of one's life.

I'm looking forward to cooking you some great meals, mostly vegetarian: spinach lasagna, pizza, broccoli with cheese sauce; soft candlelight and some Joni Mitchell singing for us. Cooking, I guess, is my first great love; there is something about being in service to people that I just love. I feel so lucky to have found my path at such an early age. I look forward to sharing stories of being chef of a kitchen that fed fourteen hundred people vegetarian foods.

What part of San Francisco do you live in? Where is it in relationship to Market and Powell, or Castro Street? You can tell I love the cable cars! If you hear of a nice, quiet, clean, tiny, inexpensive place, let me know. I'll send you a check to rent it for me.

This winter, I think I will work only part-time, really enjoying the gay culture. I'm looking forward to helping with the political campaign; perhaps joining a gay rap group—although I don't want to sit around and talk of problems, I want to celebrate the joy of life. Maybe hit the bars once or twice a month, the tubs occasionally, and just enjoy being gay.

I smoked dope just about every day for four years, but I haven't smoked any for about five years. I prefer a non-smoking environment, although sometimes I don't mind it at all.

Enclosed is a picture you might enjoy. I am so looking forward to my plunge into San Francisco and our blossoming friendship.

Much love to you dear brother,
Bruce
P.S. If you have the time and desire, send me more of your great energy. Idaho seems to be in the dark ages.

September 11, 1978

Dear Bruce,

What joy to receive such a full, open letter from
you. And what a glorious picture of you, you look
beautiful and powerful with the waterfalls rushing
behind you. I feel good writing you now and want
you to know that; perhaps it's always thrilling to
begin a new relationship and from the sound of your
letter I feel I can trust you.

One thing about your description of yourself in
the newsletter I wanted to comment on. I believe
you said you liked being masculine and masculine
men; perhaps you could clarify that in your next
correspondence. I, too, like masculine energy,
but I'm also quite in touch with my feminine side.
Physically, my body is muscular, but to some friends
I have an androgynous quality, and personally and
fortunately I consider myself a far cry from the
macho man image. I used to be physically attracted
to "masculine" men, but during the last year, I've
tried to let go of "my type" and be more open to the
individual person.

I don't know if I mentioned before that I am
primarily vegetarian (presently my diet includes fish
and eggs). I am anticipating learning much from you
in the kitchen. When I have time, I enjoy cooking
as well, but consider myself a basic cook with an
occasional flair.

Did I mention to you my involvement with Shanti
Project, the group that assists dying persons and
their families? Right now, and for the past few
weeks, I have been sitting midnight to dawn with
a forty-four-year-old man who is dying of cancer.
Shanti is a volunteer organization (eight to ten hours

a week), but Hank's wife asked me to sit regularly with him for pay.

When I first started sitting two months ago, Hank was at home; he could walk with crutches but he was confined mostly to bed. We shared some good discussions. His body is quite grotesque, abundant with bulging tumors. Hank recently told me how he marveled at seeing his physical body deteriorate, while at the same time feeling that he was consciously expanding, as he realized more and more that he was not his body.

I worked as a nurse's aide for seven years, but never before have I spent so much time with someone in such pain. At times, I can visualize the cancer eating away the cells, such an intense process.

I feel a need in my life for physical and emotional tender loving care. I have been in a lover relationship for five and a half years with a very sensitive and gentle soul, Matthew. We continue to live together and may or may not for some time. We had a union five years ago in the Metropolitan Community Church in Washington DC and share a unique spiritual similarity. Sexually, however, we haven't been doing so well.

For the last three years, we have had an open relationship but we rarely physically connect with others. We both can honestly say that jealousy has never been a problem, which a lot of our friends have difficulty understanding. We respect each other and want the best for each other and for ourselves. We are not afraid of losing the other, because the love we share can never be lost, even if we were to fall in love with another and move physically apart. Perhaps there will be a time when one person can fill all our needs, but in such a hectic and neurotic society, I feel it is unfair and probably unhealthy to expect that from one person.

I feel so often the desire to be held and kissed, to feel the warm vibrant love of some extension of myself, to let the anxieties of life melt away in the presence of loving union. There is too little touching, holding, surrendering, and what better way is there to realize who we truly are.

Take precious care of yourself, dear brother in Idaho. Breathe deeply and remember the glorious beings that we are. May all beings of the universe rejoice in unfolding it to you. May we meet in truth, beauty, and joy.

Peace, Om, and Love
Jim

September 18, 1978

Dear Jim,

I've been sitting here for about five minutes, pen in hand, wrapped in many layers of clothes, wearing four pairs of socks, a hat and scarf, a towel draped over my head, sitting in bed, warm, having blown my nose several times ... once again ... drenching the toilet paper. It is 7:00 PM, very silent. A plane is high above somewhere, the toilet is leaking, faintly in the distance I can see my breath, I'm sick in bed with a cold, my head is stuffy, I have a slight sinus headache, but massaging my face relieves that some. As I hate to take aspirin, I've been drinking orange juice, taking 10,000 mg of vitamin C, drinking Red Zinger, Sleepytime, and chamomile tea ... once again massaging my face ... I just put some Tiger Balm under my nose and above my brows. And so here I am, the pen is moving, and I'm on my way to writing you.

I stalled for a while at first, holding the pen, but not cognizing how I could relate to you my joy in receiving your last letter. No words seem to fit around my feelings; I can't seem to categorize, neatly put my emotions into linear words to fit on these lines. I'm one thousand miles from you, I'm sick with a cold, in a freezing trailer, there are six inches of snow on the ground, and we have no heat. You are probably in a fairly warm room, reading this letter, smiling. Yet through all the distance, I feel your heart reaching out, holding me, oh I did enjoy your letter so much. Having not yet met you seems unimportant.

To a Stranger

Passing stranger! You do not know how lovingly I look upon you,

You must be he I was seeking, or she I was seeking, (it comes to me as of a dream).

I have somewhere surely lived a life of joy with you,

All is recalled as we flit by each other, fluid, affectionate, chaste, matured,

You grew up with me, were a boy with me or a girl with me,

I ate with you and slept with you, your body has become not yours only nor left my body mine only,

You give me the pleasure of your eyes, face, flesh, as we pass, you take of my beard, breast, hands in return,

I am not to speak with you, I am to think of you when I sit alone or wake at night alone,

I am to wait, I do not doubt I am to meet you again,

I am to see to it that I do not lose you.

Walt Whitman

And you were so gracious to be able to read my listing, take in the "masculine message," yet see through all that and still perceive Bruce. I'm not sure I'm always so fortunate. I think I sometimes have missed the chance of knowing someone because my intellect very neatly puts one in a stereotyped slot, and then it's good-bye to him. I do it some in person as well as when reading a listing. You've helped me to once again move along a bit, freeing myself of all the bullshit that society, some friends, parents, school, church, my karma, have so completely clouded my brain with. That freedom, even just a bit more of it, feels good.

I think in my last letter to you, I described myself as having sort of two sides, one side is very successful, dynamic, clear, dependable, and can be a little gruff. This side accomplishes a lot and succeeds well in the fast pace of complicated food service ... Phew! A dog outside just got a skunk pissed! Last night it got into our garbage. Even with a completely stuffed nose, it smells strong ... This side is also enjoyed by some older ladies who perceive me as charming, kind, attentive; and my bosses, who perceive me as clear, focused, into details, dependable to the last, etc.

My other side is so quiet. I love just lying with my love, kissing ever so lightly, just floating in the warmth of it all. I treasure listening to the "waves" outside created by passing cars on wet pavement, quietly smiling, gently touching, and all of a sudden exploding into passion! I enjoy so much being allowed to dive into someone else's soul, having him share with me himself by speaking of secret thoughts. Nothing is more exciting, more compelling to me than getting to know, really understand, really see the person next to me.

Sometimes I seem almost demanding to people who are not used to baring themselves and their thoughts. I seem too inquisitive. I sometimes don't give enough space, enough room to breathe. In work, I'm ruled by reason; in love and in play I know no reason.

My love is so strong sometimes I tend to freak people out. I'm too open, too ready to move from being introduced to them, to being best friends, to loving, to desiring their love, all in a few hours. Many people desire more time; my emotions rule in love so strongly I can't hold back (I've tried).

When I meet someone who seems so rare, who opens so quickly, it just blows my mind. Here is a poem, which I love so much. I have met so many men who don't know the joy of being open.

Among the Multitude

Among the men and women the multitude,
I perceive one picking me out by secret and divine signs,
Acknowledging none else, not parent, wife, husband, brother, child, any nearer than I am,
Some are baffled, but that one is not—that one knows me.

Ah lover and perfect equal,
I meant that you should discover me so by faint indirections,
And when I meet you mean to discover you by the like in you.

Walt Whitman

Oh yes, another one which I send to you in
thanks, for seeing through my masculinity, or desire
for it.

When I Heard at the Close of the Day

When I heard at the close of the day how my
name had been received with plaudits in the capitol,
still it was not a happy night for me that followed,
And else when I caroused, or when my plans
were accomplished, still I was not happy,
But the day when I rose at dawn from the bed of
perfect health, refreshed, singing, inhaling the ripe
breath of autumn,
When I saw the full moon in the west grow pale
and disappear in the morning light,
When I wandered alone on the beach, and
undressing bathed, laughing with the cool waters,
and saw the sun rise,
And when I thought how my dear friend my lover
was on his way coming, O then I was happy,
O then each breath tasted sweeter, and all that
day my food nourished me more, and the beautiful
day passed well,
And the next came with equal joy, and with the
next at evening came my friend,
And that night while all was still I heard the
waters roll slowly continually up the shores,
I heard the hissing rustle of the liquid and sands
as directed to me whispering to congratulate me,
For the one I love most lay sleeping by me under
the same cover in that cool night,
In the stillness on the autumn moonbeams his
face was inclined toward me,

And his arm lay lightly around my breast—and that night I was happy.

Walt Whitman

The picture you sent is great. Perhaps I will make it to this Halloween party. Rereading your letter ... such a relief to share with you, your idea of going beyond body types and seeing the individual person, such a blessing, so rare! You are learning so much from the man dying of cancer. I think of that, occasionally experiencing myself to be somehow separate from my body. I look forward to hearing more of your MCC union with Matthew, of your "open marriage," of the lack of jealousy, of Shanti, and of your political work.

Your thoughts on love, so amazing, yippee, hurray, it is so nice to read a letter I may have written.

I look forward to perhaps someday having you meet my friends Katie and Johnny. Katie is a dear close friend and poet. We were occasional lovers, her drawing out my love for women, which only she was able to do, after so many months loving men, a truly amazing feat on her part! And Johnny, an artist, a man whom I fell deeply, quickly in love with, whom I introduced to Katie, that same night the three of us made love, and eight weeks later, they were married!

That was quite a trip for me. I seem to create such melodramatic plots in my life! Finally, six months later, I am finishing wading through the bullshit of jealously, of loneliness, etc. In the last months, we have sent tapes back and forth, with so much love it blows my mind. Johnny sent me a watercolor he did, Katie sent me wool booties she knitted, and in two weeks or so I will be with them again.

Jim, by sharing about my friends, you know me better. Oh to be in your arms! Yikes I'm freaking out! You said it best, "Oh to be in one's arms, to let the anxieties of life melt away in the presence of loving union." Oh, dear brother, you, too, take a deep breath. I should be in the Bay Area soon, come October 15 if not sooner.

I enjoyed my evening with you.
Love, Bruce

Shortly after receiving this letter, I called and talked to Jess for the first time. I found him very upset. He had been driving home the night before and hit an elk. He had gotten out of his vehicle to find the animal but was unable to do so. Jess loved wildlife and had a great respect for nature, in fact, when referring to God, he would often use the word, "Nature."

I had once met an eighty-year-old woman patient in the hospital, who was a member of the Theosophical Society. She shared with me how important it had been in her life to periodically lie on the earth as a way of grounding and centering. I suggested to Jess that he lie on the earth to feel his connection with Mother Earth. By doing this, it was my hope, he would realize that what had happened was not his fault. I encouraged him to ask Mother Earth to heal him and to visualize being held and comforted by Her and to imagine that She was doing the same with the elk that he had hit. It was such a tender way for us to connect in our first conversation. He would share this story with friends for the rest of his earthly life.

September 20, 1978

Dear Jim,

I totally love you! Thank you for calling. I felt so calm, so easy with you on the phone, as if we had known each other for many years.

I'm feeling much better now that it has been a few days since I killed the elk. I'm sorry to have dumped that all on you, but in talking with you, my spirits were lifted considerably.

I'll be leaving Idaho Sunday morning. Not a minute too soon.

I am looking forward to your next letter. In the next few days, I'm going to try and send you a cassette tape.

It's such a miracle to have met you. Each day is drawing me nearer.

Love, Bruce
PS. I lay on the earth, in the sun that day, as you suggested. It really helped.

October 8, 1978

Dear Jim,

I called today and got your recording, what a great message—out to save the world, our world.

I wondered at not hearing from you, but having heard the recording, I know you are spending your time fully and in the best way. You wonderful soul!

Jimmy, send me a note as to your thoughts. I'm feeling that I am destined to be a close, close man of yours—you of mine. Maybe time will bring us that fullness. Your last letter still warms my heart.

In any case we will be close friends and spend time together, enjoying the fullness we both have.
Is there anything I can do with the campaign when I arrive?

See you soon, Jimmy.
Love, Bruce

I picked Jess up at the San Francisco bus station about two weeks later. He was standing by the wall, off to the side of the front door as I entered the station. His warm, smiling eyes met mine as we saw one another for the first time. Jess leaning against the wall instantly brought back memories of Matt. On my return from Europe, Matt had surprised me by meeting me at the Port Authority Building in New York. Matt had also positioned himself against a wall, and I had been thrilled to see him. Intuitively I felt that my friendship with Jess was beginning a new chapter in my life, and my transference of these tender memories and feelings to Jess was bittersweet.

Jess and I kissed briefly. He looked younger than his picture, and I was able to observe his profile more in person. He had a Roman nose similar to mine, which I later learned was not one of his favorite features. Jess's now familiar voice was also comforting and reassuring. Our initial awkwardness was eased by our eagerness to be present for one another and my desire to respond to a phone call I had received moments before meeting Jess.

Joe, my massage client, was suicidal. Joe was a recovering alcoholic whom I massaged three times a week. He was the only client I had kept during the four months I worked to defeat the Briggs Initiative. I quickly filled Jess in on the details and swept him up into my drama. When Jess and I arrived at Joe's ninth-story apartment, it absolutely reeked of urine. Such a romantic beginning for our first encounter! Joe had been binge drinking for about four days. He pleaded with us to go buy him another bottle. I would have none of it. I told him that I would be happy to take him to the treatment center where he had been hospitalized several times before. He told Jess and me that unless we got him a bottle, he was going to jump out the window. I called the police and was informed that they would only come after he jumped! After another bout of pleading for a bottle, making coffee, and more threats of suicide, I told Joe that we needed to go. I said I would call him later to see if he would like me to take him to the hospital.

It was then a quick stop for a nutritious breakfast of coffee and donuts before I brought Jess to the campaign headquarters. From there, we proceeded to drop campaign literature at the infamous Pink Palace, which was a subsidized housing project in the city. Many of the apartment windows and doors were boarded over, due to acts of violence and vandalism. Jess and I and several other volunteers wrestled with our fear as we placed the "Vote No on Six" pamphlets underneath the doors.

After a few slices of greasy pizza for lunch, which we quickly gobbled, it was off to the airport where we illegally placed flyers on parked cars and skirted the security guards. About ten hours later, I brought Jess to my house, where he and I slept on a futon in the living room, as my lover Matt and his boyfriend, Ed, occupied our waterbed. So much for calming meditation, healthy vegetarianism, and candlelight dinners! Jess had entered the whirlwind of my San Francisco life.

The election was a few weeks away and I was working eighty hours a week passing out as much information as possible. We were still behind in the polls, but the gap was narrowing. San Francisco was pretty much covered, so we began venturing into the more conservative suburbs, dropping information door-to-door. Just a few days before the election, six of us, including Jess, were driving back to San Francisco when we heard on the radio that President Carter had encouraged Californians to vote against the Briggs Initiative. We all screamed wildly. Maybe our petition had done some good after all!

Halloween was always a festive time in San Francisco, and it was celebrated enthusiastically by many gays and lesbians on Polk and Castro streets. Although the Castro district was more of a hub for the gay community, the Polk Street Halloween celebration had a reputation for having more outrageously dressed revelers. We caught word that Senator Briggs, sensing that his initiative might be heading for defeat at the polls, had decided to come to the Polk Street Halloween festivities that night. Apparently, it was his hope to create an altercation between himself and the revelers and garner some press coverage that would affect the upcoming election. Jess and I organized a small group that went into all of the Polk Street bars and asked the staff to inform patrons that Senator Briggs was coming but to encourage all customers to remain inside.

San Francisco Mayor George Moscone and Supervisor Harvey Milk met Senator Briggs' motorcade on a side street just off of Polk. A group of us joined hands, creating a protective barrier between them and the Halloween revelers. I was so impressed with the persuasive strength of Mayor Moscone and the way he and Supervisor Milk convinced Senator Briggs that it was not in his best interest to attempt to walk on Polk Street. All of us had worked together to avert what could have been an ugly altercation.

On Election Day, the initiative was defeated by a three-to-two margin. We felt on top of the world! The people of California had been able to rise above their fears and misconceptions about gay school workers and to understand that the initiative was really about discrimination, stereotypes, and myths about gay people. Hallelujah, California! We celebrated that night at campaign headquarters with our openly gay supervisor, Harvey Milk, and Mayor George Moscone.

Less than two weeks later, we received news of the murder of Representative Leo Ryan and *San Francisco Examiner* photographer Greg Robinson in Guyana. Horrifying reports soon followed about the death by suicide and murder of 912 in Jonestown,

Guyana, where the Rev. Jim Jones had led his church members to set up a sanctuary. For over two years, Matt and I had lived only two short blocks from the Jones church in San Francisco, the People's Temple. It was from there that the Rev. Jones had led his flock into paradise. San Franciscans were stunned in trying to understand how nine hundred people could, for the most part, make a collective decision to kill themselves by drinking poison.

While we were still reeling in shock and grief over Jonestown, a few days later, Moscone and Milk were assassinated. They were shot and killed on November 27, 1978, in San Francisco City Hall by Dan White, a city supervisor. Thirty thousand of us walked that night in a candlelight march from the Castro to City Hall. Grief permeated the city. It was if the sky had fallen closer to earth and everyone could feel its oppressive pressure. It was painful to breathe. It was hard to open to life again. Sudden death doesn't allow time for good-byes or the opportunity to prepare. Many San Franciscans felt as if a large part of our guts had been ripped out, and we wondered if time could heal the overwhelming sadness and sense of loss.

Through Shanti, I began working with a fifteen-year-old girl whose boyfriend and some family members had died in Jonestown. Jeanette lived with the daily fear of hearing reports about hit men who had allegedly agreed to kill any living members of People's Temple. Jeanette's fear for her life and the lives of her friends made it difficult for her to experience her grief. In addition, the return of the bodies of her boyfriend and family members was delayed for weeks. Once the bodies were identified, the caskets were permanently sealed. Jeanette never was able to see the bodies of her boyfriend and family. It made the whole situation more surreal.

Mayor Moscone's and Supervisor Milk's caskets were sealed as well. As Jess and I filed past their caskets, I remembered how jubilant we had been only a few weeks before. Now, an assassin's bullets had silenced their bright spirits. I felt drained, exhausted from crying. I was numb. I tried to make sense of why so many gentle beings like Mahatma Gandhi, John and Robert Kennedy, the Reverend Martin Luther King, and now George and Harvey had all met the assassin's bullet. I grieved for humanity, gradually grasping that we commit so many horrendous deeds out of our collective ignorance.

My relationship with Matt was beginning to show more signs of wear and tear; he was becoming more disinterested in sex. Matt had tried very hard to find work as a theatrical director. I had seen a number of the plays he had directed, and I knew that he really had a gift. But directing never came together for Matt in San Francisco. It was difficult for him to let go of his dream. Matt was also keenly aware of how well my life was working. Matt would tell me that I had a sort of magic. What I think he meant by that was that whatever I set my mind to, happened.

Matt asked me to quit volunteering at Shanti and become his business manager. He was hoping that my magic would rub off on him if we worked together. It was one of the hardest decisions of my life, but I refused Matt's request. I loved him very much and so much wanted his dreams to come to fruition, and yet I felt myself being called in another direction. I told him that I needed to pursue my own goals of working more intensely with people with life-threatening illnesses.

I began to feel more and more convinced that things were not improving. The thought of leaving Matt was very painful. I still loved him very much. As our problems increased, it was difficult to avoid hurting one another. I had treasured our relationship so much and I didn't want to ruin it now. But our arguing increased, and it grew harder to resolve our hurt feelings. I was able to confide in Jess about the mounting problems in my relationship. Jess was great in that he never gave me any advice; he listened and validated my feelings but made it clear that I would have to do what I thought was best. Jess was also very fond of Matt.

It was very painful to learn that I could leave someone with whom I was still in love. Up until that point in my life, I naively thought that the reason I would leave a relationship would be because we had stopped loving one another. Finally, I decided that it was becoming too painful to continue living together; we were wounding each other too much. Matt loved me and did want me to stay, but he was unable to express his feelings and affection in the way I wanted him to. I told him I would be moving out at the end of the month.

About two weeks before I left Matt, I got a call from Shanti Project offering me a job as volunteer coordinator. They felt that I did excellent client work and was well-respected by the volunteers. I was thrilled. I accepted immediately.

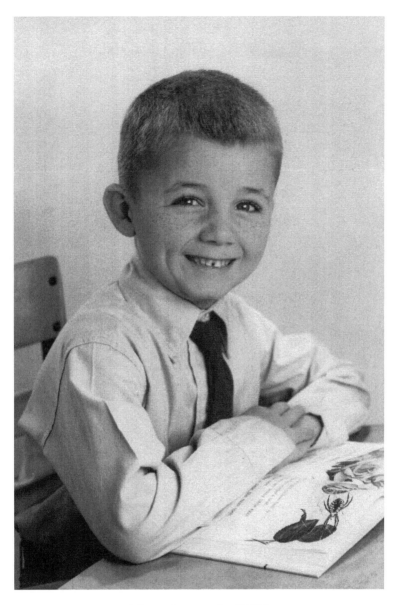

Me in first grade (1959)

"Nana," my maternal grandmother (1917)

My parents, Matt, and me at the reception
for our Holy Union (1972)

Marching against the Briggs Initiative (1978)
Me and Jess under "against"

Walter and Ruby (Jess's parents) (1965)

Jess (age four), as a Halloween leopard (1958)

Chapter 3

Dance, Dance, Dance

The most spiritual of acts is to be genuinely human at every moment.

Judith Orloff, MD

My office was a small room with a window that overlooked a garden. The sun poured in most of the day. It was important to me, in doing this work, to be able to look outside, part of my desire to connect with life's bigger picture. It is so easy to get lost in the world of grief and illness. A window provided me the perspective I needed when people's issues seemed overwhelming.

My responsibilities as volunteer coordinator were twofold: I received calls from new clients, and I supervised volunteers. During phone intakes, I asked potential clients why they felt that having a Shanti volunteer would be beneficial. Other questions were aimed at gathering information about clients' support systems, their coping mechanisms, and if they might feel most comfortable with a particular type of volunteer. Sometimes a volunteer's gender, age, spiritual affiliation, sexual orientation, or ethnicity was an important factor for a client.

Volunteers made contact with clients within a forty-eight hour period of the intake. I based decisions on which volunteer to match with a client on what the client had specifically requested and my own intuition. Through my interactions with volunteers, I had developed a sense of which clients each volunteer could most effectively assist. In most cases, the matches worked amazingly well. Volunteers often continued friendships with clients long after their Shanti client/volunteer relationships had ended. If clients had misgivings about their volunteers, they were told to call the office and request another volunteer.

Repeat matching processes were at times difficult for the volunteers. Oftentimes, the reasons that a client wanted a different match were beyond the volunteer's control. Perhaps the volunteer lacked sufficient experience, or the client had decided that the volunteer's sex or age was important. One client said he disliked his volunteer arriving at his door with a bicycle. The client thought this was very unprofessional. Another client, when asked why he wanted a new volunteer, sheepishly replied, "My volunteer, John, always takes his shoes off, and he has such strong foot odor." Informal peer counseling does have its drawbacks, and giving honest feedback to well-intentioned volunteers was not the easiest part of my job!

One thing that both attracted and frustrated me about Shanti Project was the project's lack of spiritual focus. My work with people with a life-threatening illness has always been immensely spiritual and has paralleled my own spiritual journey and unfolding. Many of Shanti Project's early volunteers were drawn to the project because of their attraction to the work of Dr. Kubler-Ross, Stephen Levine, and Ram Dass—individuals known for their spiritual and metaphysical leanings. Dr. Kubler-Ross had publicly spoken of her contacts with spirit guides and how they had assisted her in her work. I wondered occasionally if I lacked special guidance of some sort. Yet part of me was grateful that Shanti Project didn't expound any set beliefs about life after death. It enabled us to work with a diverse clientele. Even as I became increasingly fascinated with metaphysical and life-after-death issues, I continued to believe that by putting aside our own agendas and being open to the diverse beliefs our clients had regarding afterlife, we were providing an immensely valuable service.

Because so many clients were dealing with intense feelings, their friends and families frequently pulled away. It was necessary for the volunteers to open themselves to considerable emotional intensity as a way of empathizing and supporting clients in the way they needed. So much of what was asked of our volunteers was contrary to what many professional counselors and medical personnel are taught. Therapists, nurses, and doctors are often instructed to keep a professional distance from clients as a way to protect themselves and prevent eventual burnout. Yet I had found in my work with clients that when I did not get emotionally involved and attempted to suppress my feelings or those of clients, that was when I was at the greatest risk for burnout. It was when I protected myself from intense feelings that I ended up stifling them. Suppression of feelings can become a key factor in burnout.

In many ways, there was not a lot of difference between being a good friend and being a Shanti volunteer. I knew that when I was upset by a situation, I wanted support from friends who would open themselves to my pain. I wanted friends to allow themselves to be affected by my situation. I did not want them to drown in my feelings, but I did want them to emotionally grasp my feelings so that they could understand and respond to me in a supportive way.

For many clients' issues, there were simply no answers. Volunteers needed to be open to their own awkward helplessness so that they could more fully grasp the emotional frustration of their clients. Empathizing and opening up to the feelings of others required authenticity and a willingness to simply accompany others on their paths.

As a new staff member, I continued to volunteer with clients on a one-to-one basis. My involvement with one client forced me to face my own judgment around class issues. Mathur was originally from India. Mathur's wife, who had cancer, had recently returned to India with their two young children so that she could die on native soil. Mathur was financially unable to accompany his family, and he knew he would never see his wife again. He was deeply depressed, not knowing if his wife had even arrived in India or if she was still alive. With his wife and children gone, Mathur's apartment was suddenly a lonely and scary place. Mathur lived in a very poor section of San Leandro, California, and his apartment was sparsely furnished. Foam mats were used as beds. The only pictures were newspaper photos taped to the apartment walls. One day when Mathur was very depressed, I offered to spend the night. Mathur gave me a pad to sleep on with a tattered sheet. I was flooded with feelings of fear as I lay on his living room floor. I felt as if I could catch his wife's cancer by merely being in this impoverished environment. The newspaper pictures on the wall, sleeping on the floor, and Mathur's wife's disease had combined to create in me a tangible feeling of the fear of transmissibility. My feelings shocked me. Intellectually, I knew I was not at risk. Nevertheless, I felt immensely fearful and couldn't wait for the night to pass.

It was very difficult to share these feelings. In my position as volunteer coordinator, I rotated through the weekly volunteer support groups. I did this to observe group process, give feedback, and so that I could discuss later with group leaders how they might improve group interaction. I also used the groups to discuss my own client work and the feelings that I was experiencing. The feelings I had experienced with Mathur embarrassed me, though; I was ashamed of them. I wanted to hide my feelings not only from the group but from myself as well. My middle-class upbringing had not prepared me to feel comfortable in such poor surroundings. I was not proud of the part of me that wanted to get out of Mathur's apartment as quickly as possible. Yet I knew that I needed to share these feelings, and the support group listened and validated the feelings I was experiencing. In my work with Shanti, I learned the importance of honestly admitting my own thoughts and feelings regarding racism, economic status, and other attitudes that create separation. I realized that my prejudice was simply ignorance, which resulted from my lack of contact with people I viewed as different from myself. In order to free myself of prejudice, I first needed to understand how I was affected by racist, classist, and sexist conditioning, which influenced not only my thoughts, but my feelings and behaviors. I learned that when I identified prejudice in myself, or when someone else pointed it out, there was an opportunity to look closely at the roots of such prejudice. Since prejudice is often a result of ignorance, I couldn't expect myself to grasp or understand the subtlety of it immediately. I learned that it took a conscious commitment to become sensitive to the perspectives of others.

I also came to understand that unconditional loving is not devoid of thoughts that are judgmental. Unconditional loving is achieved though an ability to recognize judgments while still being able to connect with the true being of each person encountered. It is the nature of the mind to judge. My goal was not to prevent my mind from judging but to discover my reasons, subtle as they may have been, for wanting to separate myself from others. Through a deeper look into the way I interacted with and judged another, I found my deeper interconnectedness and began to celebrate the joy and awe of kindred hearts.

I found it curious that when I was feeling overwhelmed at work and hoped that the phones would not ring, they didn't. Sometimes I would be feeling emotionally closed down for a few days, and client intakes would come to a standstill. After I had worked through whatever was depressing me, the phones would start ringing. It also seemed that whenever a volunteer would request a particular type of client, a client would call who met the volunteer's specifications. This synchronicity helped me to maintain a reverence for the work of Shanti Project. Often, I felt as if the hand of God was guiding us.

Several months had passed without me working directly with someone who was dying. As a staff member, I thought that it was important to stay connected with the essence of our work. I felt that it was paramount that I keep pushing past my fear and continue to work with clients who seemed difficult to me. I realized that being with someone who was dying stretched me like nothing else. I was eager to experience this aspect of the work again.

A woman named Mary called the project to request a volunteer. She and her husband, Scotty, were in their late fifties, and Scotty was dying of cancer. Mary said that she was basically fine but that someone had suggested she call Shanti for some emotional support. After matching Mary with a volunteer, I got a strong sense that I would like to work with Scotty. I asked Mary if she thought her husband could benefit from a volunteer. She said no. Mary then said that Scotty was comatose and had not been out of bed or talked with her in two weeks. I pushed Mary a little, suggesting that having someone work with Scotty could free her to be with her own volunteer and to attend to whatever else was needed.

When working with members of the same family, I usually matched them with separate volunteers. Despite experiencing a similar situation, two people might experience very different feelings. Providing individual volunteers made it easier for each person to access and express emotions that they might feel the need to hide or protect from other family members. After Mary listened intently to my suggestion, she responded, "Well, if you want to see him, it is okay with me. But I don't think it will do any good."

Mary said that Scotty was very proud of his Scottish ancestry. It was the second marriage for both of them, and they had been married for ten years. Scotty had three sons from his previous marriage; they lived about thirty miles away. From what I could gather, Scotty and Mary enjoyed a close and fun relationship. Scotty wore a gold neck charm with the words, "Dance, Dance, Dance" set on top of each other. From their living room, they had a spectacular view of the Bay Bridge and San Francisco. Mary had a hospital bed in the living room. She had arranged for a night nurse to be with Scotty from midnight to 8 AM. At our first meeting, Mary left me alone with Scotty. I sat at the foot of the bed and thought of a story that I had heard from Ram Dass.

Ram Dass was visiting a friend who was experiencing intense pain and medical professionals were unable to do anything more for her. Ram Dass decided to sit at the foot of her bed and meditate. He entered a deep state of meditation. Suddenly, his friend, who was still writhing in pain, looked at him and said, "I am feeling such peace." Hearing Ram Dass tell this story had left me with hope that perhaps I could share some degree of inner peacefulness with my clients.

Scotty did not appear to be experiencing great pain, but since I could not decide what else to do, I thought I would meditate. After I'd meditated for about thirty minutes, Scotty opened his eyes and looked directly at me.

"Who are you?" he asked.

I nervously stammered, "My name is Jim. I am a volunteer from Shanti Project. Shanti works with people with a life-threatening illness and their families. Mary called and requested a volunteer. I am here to help you in any way I can."

Scotty listened attentively and said, "Well, I wouldn't want to trade places with you!"

Dumbfounded, I thought, *What does he mean by that?*

After uttering those few words, Scotty closed his eyes and drifted off. That brief but intense interaction would be the only time that Scotty would say distinguishable words to me in the week that I worked with him. It felt awesome. He was the one who was dying, and he told me that he wouldn't want to trade places! It didn't compute.

My next visit was two days later, on a Saturday morning. I had come early so Mary could do some shopping. When I arrived, I found Mary exhausted. Mary and the night attendant, Sarah, had been up most of the night while Scotty tossed and turned, tangling himself in the bed rails. Mary had decided that Scotty's position in the bed was just not proper. She worried, "What if Scotty should die that way?" I was mildly amused by the way we try to tidy the dying process and by our notion of how dying should be, and how we literally exhaust ourselves attempting to force it to conform to our specifications. I decided that it was best to keep these thoughts to myself.

Mary left, assuming that I would not allow Scotty to get twisted in the bed rails. I had the satisfying realization that allowing her husband to get twisted was precisely what I could offer Scotty in this moment. In less than five minutes, Scotty was in the most undignified position imaginable for a dying man. He slept, contented and undisturbed, for two hours!

Again, I took up my position at the foot of Scotty's bed. I had brought Kahlil Gibran's *The Prophet* and was reading the section on death where the prophet says, *"For what is it to die but to stand naked in the wind and to melt into the sun? And what is it to cease breathing, but to free the breath from its restless tides, that it may rise and expand and seek God unencumbered?"* I was feeling the calm of those words when suddenly Scotty opened his eyes.

Even though it had been only two days since I had first visited, he had lost his ability to speak. As before, he looked straight at me. He then lifted his arms, indicating that he wanted to sit. I cranked the bed to a sitting position, but he continued to move his arms upward. It seemed as if he was trying to communicate to me that he wanted to get up. I was nervous about getting him out of bed. I knew he hadn't been up for more than two weeks, and I immediately had thoughts of him falling and Shanti being sued. However, Scotty was persistent, and I eventually decided that I had adequate experience to help him out of bed. I first sat him on the side of the bed, hoping he would be satisfied in that position. But again, Scotty lifted his arms upward, indicating that he wanted to stand. I put my arms under his, wrapped them around his back, and lifted him to a standing position.

When Scotty was standing, he embraced me with an intensity I had never felt. As our bodies pressed tightly together, it felt as if Scotty was welcoming me into his heart, as if we had been the best of friends. Thoughts raced through my mind as a way of distracting and protecting me from the intimacy of that moment. *What does this mean? Why is he doing this? He doesn't even know me. Maybe he is going to die. I should call his sons. Maybe he thinks I am one of his sons. What if his wife walks in? What will she think? Maybe she'll think I am trying to molest her husband. Maybe Scotty is trying to molest me! That's it, he's a latent homosexual! Help!* It was all I could do to keep breathing.

Somehow, in this intense mental craziness, I became aware that I was simultaneously experiencing a different feeling in my heart. My heart was simply trying to open to the moment and not interpret it. It was simply trying to let the love flow between us. Scotty continued to hold me for about ten minutes. There was no way I could say anything to him. It was all I could do to free myself of the onslaught of thoughts that were desperately trying to distance me from the intimacy of that moment.

Some years later, I read that the Indian teacher, Rajneesh, distinguishes the ways in which Western psychology and Eastern spirituality view the mind. "The Western psychologist views the mind as something that is sick and can be cured; however, in the East, we realize the mind is totally insane and therefore we transcend it." Boy, if only I had read that before my experience with Scotty; I might not have felt so crazy!

Eventually, Scotty began to tire and I sat him down on the bed. I thought to myself, *Thank God that's over.* However, before either of us had a chance to catch our breath, he was raising his arms again. *Shit, here we go again!* I thought. When I helped Scotty to his feet, he embraced me again with the same intensity. In a way, it felt like he was squeezing the life out of me, holding on to his life as long as he could. This time, I was able to say a few things to him.

"It must feel really good to hold someone, Scotty."

"Uh."

"It feels good to hold you, Scotty."

"Uh."

"You must be frightened to be so sick, Scotty."

"Uh."

We repeated his sitting and standing one more time. As I put Scotty back to bed the last time, he quickly drifted off, leaving me alone to ponder the significance of what had taken place. I had entered this person's life only a few days ago, and now it felt as if I had just participated in something that the whole of our lives had prepared us to experience. I had taken a journey from my mind into my heart. In a very pure sense, it felt like I had made love with a total stranger.

The third and last time I was with Scotty was the night he died. I had called to check with Mary on how things were going. She said that the doctor had visited earlier and estimated that Scotty would not live more than another two weeks. Due to some odd circumstances, the Monday night volunteer support group I had planned to attend was cancelled. I told Mary that I would like to stop by that evening and visit Scotty. When I arrived and took one look at Scotty, I had a very strong feeling that he would die that night. I had been with enough people in their last few hours of life to recognize the breathing patterns indicative of impending death. Of course I never could be certain, but I had a strong sense that Scotty's time was very limited. I decided that I should share my feelings with Mary. I went to her bedroom door and told her that I would like to speak with her. I began by underscoring that I was not a medical specialist but from what I could see, I felt that it was very likely that Scotty would die that night. Mary collapsed, sobbing, in my arms. As I held her, I realized there was nothing to do except to hold her in her grief. Mary then asked me what we should do. I responded that I would like to remain as physically close to Scotty as possible. I suggested that it was often comforting to the person who was dying if they were touched in some manner. Mary said that that sounded like a good idea, so we both took up positions near Scotty. Later that night, the attendant, Sarah, arrived and joined us at his bedside. Mary found it difficult to believe that Scotty was aware of all that was going on around him. While we were seated at his bedside, she conversed mostly with Sarah. Mary told jokes and funny stories about her life with Scotty. Now my buttons were getting pushed regarding how the dying process should be! I was finding it hard to laugh at Mary's jokes. I wanted to focus my attention on Scotty.

I was seated toward the head of the bed. I spoke directly to Scotty. "Scotty, your wife, Mary, is here with you. We are planning on spending the night at your bedside." Mary watched me as I talked to Scotty. Eventually, she asked me if I thought Scotty could hear me. I told her that I did and that studies had established that during the dying process, the sense of hearing is the last to go. Mary nodded. Mary told us what she had planned for Scotty's funeral. She wanted him to be buried in his Scottish kilt. Mary said that he had liked to wear his kilt to local Scottish celebrations. I suggested that maybe Scotty would enjoy having it on the bed with him now. I thought that it might be comforting to him. Mary thought it weighed too much and that it would be uncomfortable for him to have it lying on him. I nodded, leaving the decision to her. After a few minutes had passed, she said that she liked the idea. She brought his favorite kilt and draped it over him. I told Scotty what we were doing, and he began to squeeze the kilt with his thumb and forefinger. We got the definite feeling that Scotty knew it was there.

Scotty began to lift his eyes upward; his breathing was very rapid. I told Mary that I was even more convinced that he was dying. Mary said that she did not want to call his sons without being sure. The three of us continued to touch Scotty. Mary and I were seated at the head of the bed and Sarah at the foot. Mary and Sarah thought he should lie flat, believing that it would be easier for him to die in that position. But Scotty kept rocking upward as if he wanted to sit. If I had been alone, I would have cranked the bed into a sitting position. However Mary insisted that we only raise the head of the bed a little. During the next hour, we must have cranked the bed a few inches higher every ten minutes. Sarah would crank it a few inches, and Mary would say, "That's enough." Ten minutes later, I would point out that Scotty was still trying to lift up, and Mary would approve the head of the bed going a bit higher.

Mary became increasingly uncomfortable with how much it appeared that Scotty was suffering. Mary said, "I hate to see him this way, and I wish it would be over." She asked me if there was anything she could do to make it easier for Scotty to die. Almost without thinking, I told her that it sometimes helped if you gave the person who was dying permission to go. "Perhaps you could let him know that it would be all right with you for him to die," I said. Before Mary had finished listening to what I was saying, she bent close to Scotty's ear and said, "It's all right Scotty, I'll be fine." A minute later, Mary glared at me and said, "You know, Jim, that was like handing him a gun and saying go ahead and shoot yourself." I looked her in the eyes, took a breath, and nodded my head in agreement. Mary was telling me exactly how it was for her. There was nothing to do except to accept how it had felt for her. Another few minutes passed. Mary said, "But you know, Jim, if I really put my heart into those words and told him that it was okay for him to die, I think it truly might help." I nodded. There was no way on earth I was going to recommend anything after knowing the effects of my last suggestion! Once again, Mary leaned over Scotty and said, "Scotty, it really is okay with me that you go now. I will be okay. Sarah and Jim are here with me. You can stop fighting, Scotty." It was powerful to hear Mary speak so honestly and directly. Mary was letting her husband know that she felt strong enough in that moment to continue living without him.

Mary then asked me what I thought of putting on some music. I said it sounded like a good idea and suggested playing one of Scotty's favorite songs. Mary said he loved the bagpipes, and she had an instrumental version of *Amazing Grace*. She turned the stereo volume high, and, as Scotty heard the bagpipes, he sat up straighter. The proud Scotsman died as the record came to an end. It seemed totally fitting that Scotty died wearing his kilt, sitting fully upright in bed, and hearing his beloved bagpipes.

My work with Shanti Project was very compelling and it helped to have something to devote myself to after leaving Matt. For the first months, Jess and I continued to see each other regularly, however his work and life in San Francisco was moving him in another direction as well. Jess had moved into an apartment in San Francisco that he shared with several other men. He was working as an office manager for the Institute for Food and Development Policy, a nonprofit educational group that was committed to raising awareness about the causes of world hunger. Dr. Joseph Collins and Frances Moore Lappe had founded the Institute.

Interestingly, Joe Collins and I were the only two of the five people who Jess had written to in the Bay Area who had responded to him. Jess had replied to an ad that Joe had placed in the national, primarily gay magazine *The Advocate*. Unbeknownst to Jess, Joe was also a regular massage client of mine. Jess often marveled that of the two individuals who responded to his letters, one was destined to become his lover and the other his employer.

Jess invited me to dinner in June 1979 and hesitantly conveyed the information that he wanted to pursue other sexual relationships. He awkwardly told me that he was now attracted to muscles, mustaches, and cowboy boots! There was such innocence in the way he communicated this, that, fortunately, I realized that his desires were about his own fantasies and not about any lack in myself. While there was a part of me that felt jilted, I was actually relieved, since my primary focus was my new job. And while I was attracted to Jess, our sexual relationship lacked a high degree of passion. I also realized that it would probably not be wise for me to enter into another primary relationship so soon. We decided to remain close friends; however, we saw little of each other during the next two years.

These two years were a sexually active time for both Jess and me. Prior to AIDS, the bathhouses were very active and he and I were frequent attendees. Jess tended to date men for longer periods than I. Most of my encounters during this period were for one night, or perhaps more accurately, a few hours. I always felt that I brought an open heart to my sexual liaisons but, while as a gay man I had learned how to connect sexually, emotional intimacy was another matter, not unlike the challenges that heterosexual couples face.

During this time, I recall a sweet date with Jess. He invited me to dinner at an upscale San Francisco gay restaurant. One of his regular dates had taken him there, and he was so impressed that he wanted to share the experience with a good friend. At the time, I think it was the fanciest place I had ever been, complete with linen tablecloths, candlelight, and a piano player. He was so excited to share it with me. Of course we had a full-course dinner, complete with a bottle of wonderful wine. I asked Jess why he had decided to invite me and he said, "Because I know that you haven't experienced anything like this before and I wanted to share it with you. I still see you as my dearest friend." I was touched by his sweet and thoughtful care for me that evening.

Almost a year later, at the San Francisco Gay and Lesbian Parade in June of 1981, I learned from a mutual friend that Jess had had a ruptured appendix and had been hospitalized for ten days. I couldn't believe how out of touch we had become and that I didn't even know about his illness. Shortly after the parade, Jess and I got together and made plans to move in together as roommates in San Francisco. The idea of maintaining a closer connection and friendship was exciting for both of us. We made the decision to take in a third roommate, Wendy, who was a volunteer with Shanti.

Jess and I continued to date separately and remained heavily involved in our work. We frequently had meals together and shared the details of our personal lives. At times, I found myself longing for more physical tenderness with Jess. But he kept the boundaries of our relationship more defined, so we rarely shared any intimate touching.

During this period, Jess was dating a few men who considered themselves part of San Francisco's A-gay group. This group was comprised of the city's jet-setters and its most attractive men. One guy whom Jess was dating had asked him, "Why on earth are you living with a heavyset woman and an androgynous man?" At the time, Jess hadn't told his friend to fuck off, and he was feeling guilty. A few weeks later, Jess came to me and said he felt he had let down Wendy and me. I told him that I understood. Jess was appreciative of my willingness to see through the various trips he would get into while continuing to value the deeper qualities that he possessed. The next day, he left the following note on my bed:

Dear, Dear Jim,

Things are happening so fast. I feel like I'm in a whirlwind, each day so full, so much to experience, so many battles, so many lessons, and so much beauty …

Somehow, I want you to feel my everlasting devotion to you … that feeling I have for you … that love, admiration, and respect.

And in these times when I feel things are happening too fast, when I'm feeling sort of numb, I want somehow for you still to know how much I cherish the delicate bouquets of life, of love, you hand to me. Sometimes, I feel so unworthy of them or I feel unable to accept your gifts.

In my lack of clarity and sensitivity these last few weeks, I hope you still see the true nature of me deep within.

I love you.
Bruce

A few months later, Jess decided he had enough of trying to fit into the A-group. He placed a personal listing, including our household phone number, in a predominately sexual gay publication. Fortunately, he specified that he only would receive calls between 7 and 9 PM. Since we all shared one phone, whenever Wendy or I answered the phone during those hours, we never quite knew what to expect. Several times, when Jess wasn't home, the callers would inquire about me. I was never as comfortable with phone sex as Jess, but sometimes I tried my best to accommodate!

Jess had one regular caller who would only identify himself as SIR. When Wendy or I would answer the phone and it was SIR, we would do our best to contain ourselves when telling Jess that he had a phone call. SIR actually wanted Jess to fly down to Los Angeles and spend an undetermined amount of time with him. SIR would let him know when it was okay for him to return. Jess actually seriously considered going. Jess could be very fanciful and impulsive with matters of the heart and regions south! Fortunately, after listening to Wendy's and my concerns, he made the decision not to go.

In September of 1981, Jess and I decided to demonstrate at the Diablo Canyon Nuclear Power Plant in San Luis Obispo, California. The plant had been built on a fault line and was the focus of much controversy. Both of our employers supported our decision to leave on very short notice. Jess had just returned from a

Radical Faeries gathering in northern New Mexico, where several hundred men had convened to celebrate their connection to nature and each other. (Radical Faeries is a movement that started in the late seventies to offer a new level of spirituality, celebration, and healing consciousness to the gay liberation movement.)

On our way to the plant, he wore around his head a wonderful, deep purple silk scarf with stars that glittered. It was gratifying to see him coming into his power and celebrating the many aspects of his nature.

The demonstration was very well-organized and anyone intending to sit in and risk arrest were required to participate in an all-day workshop on nonviolent civil disobedience. We were placed into affinity groups, and each group was given the task of choosing a name. Our group chose the name *Imagine*. Most members of our group, including Jess, had never been arrested. Jess had also been a conscientious objector to the Vietnam conflict, but, because of the lottery number assigned him, he had not had to face prison. For this demonstration, I felt great to have my best friend with me.

The first morning of the demonstration, workers arrived very early by bus, in hopes of getting through the gates before the demonstrators assembled. An affinity group, made up of all women, that had been selected to be the first group to sit in front of the plant's gates was still walking to the site. When one of the women in the group saw the employees' bus speeding toward the entrance, she made the spontaneous decision to lie down in the middle of the street. The bus came to a screeching stop, missing her by inches. Thus began three days and hundreds of arrests and a very effective protest.

I was the first member of our affinity group to be arrested. I decided to go limp. Since we were so tightly crammed in together, it was difficult for the arresting officers to move me. After I was carried through the main gate, I decided to cooperate and walk, since my point had been made. My arresting officer was very annoyed and bent my thumb into my wrist.

I pleaded, "Will you please stop bending my thumb? I am cooperating now."

"Oh, now you want me to stop, after you were such a big man in front of your friends," he chided.

I responded, "I am not protesting against you, but I feel I have a right to be here to protest what I feel is a potential danger to all of us." Hearing that and realizing that I did not see him as the enemy, he immediately loosened his grip.

We were jailed for three days in a gymnasium with bright fluorescent lighting. For meals, we were given white bread sandwiches with a dollop of peanut butter and an orange. I had an awful migraine headache for most of the three days, made worse by the almost constant dribbling of basketballs in the gymnasium. Jess was very sweet in securing a couple of aspirin from the guards, who were anything but cooperative to my requests.

Once we got to court, we were released on our own recognizance and informed that we would have to return at a later date for a trial. Several years later, the charges were dropped and the plant eventually closed.

A few weeks after the demonstration, Jess made the decision to come out to his parents. His parents, Walter and Ruby, were still living in Seattle, where Jess was born. They spent the winter months in Mesa, Arizona. Jess had many fond memories of his childhood. He had often accompanied his dad on their boat, salmon fishing, and he and his parents had enjoyed camping at many of the national parks. Walter had been a captain with the Seattle Fire Department. Ruby had worked for a number of years at a gas company. Both of Jess's parents were very craft oriented, making candles and sculpting stone and wood.

Jess was the youngest of three children: his brother, Jack, was eleven years older, and his sister, Cathy, was seven years his senior. Jack also worked for the Seattle Fire Department. Cathy worked as a quality control supervisor in a Palo Alto, California, pharmaceutical company. Jack had been a Green Beret, and Cathy had worked for several years with the Peace Corps in the southern United States. She had entered a relationship with another woman when she was in her teens. Her relationship continued to be a focal point of much consternation, particularly with her mother, Ruby.

Despite feeling that his coming out would be difficult for his parents, Jess felt that it was essential for him to be open about his sexual orientation. Jess asked me to help him write the following letter, and Wendy and I accompanied him to the mailbox. We hoped for a positive response, but more importantly, we were overjoyed at his self-acceptance, realizing that this act of self-love was a gift to each of us.

September 21, 1981

Dear Mom and Dad,

Thank you for the cute card. As always, I have too many pots cooking, and it is nice to regularly get your cards.

I was thinking that it would be good to open up to you about my life, so that you have a chance to work things through in your own heads and make a decision as to whether you still wanted to visit. I would like for you to visit me at my house, after reading what I have to say.

Your son Bruce is gay.

I'll fill you in on the gaps in all my letters and talks with you over the last ten years. Although I very much loved Robert, back in high school, we were never lovers. The first experience I had sexually with a man was in 1976 under very loving and supportive circumstances. I have known my uniqueness for many years, long before 1976.

Since then, I have had different lovers, although I have not yet connected with anyone in a long-term, committed way.

In 1978, as you may remember, I did political work opposing an antigay proposition in California. I vaguely recall sending you literature on that. In 1979, I flew to Washington DC and marched with two hundred thousand others for gay rights. I have been involved with a gay camping group, go to gay rap, and belong to a gay spiritual organization. The week before last, I went to the top of a beautiful mountain in northern New Mexico, with two hundred fifty other gay brothers for a political and spiritual weekend.

I live with a gay man, Jim Geary, and a straight woman, Wendy Brewton. I'd love to have you meet them both.

I just got out of jail! This last Tuesday, along with fourteen hundred other folks, I got arrested for failure to disperse at the Diablo Canyon Nuclear Power Plant. I pleaded no contest to a misdemeanor and was jailed for four days in a gym with five hundred men, all of whom feel as strongly as I do about the potential dangers of nuclear power and nuclear waste. The experiences at the power plant, the time spent in jail, and the week in New Mexico are among the high points in my life thus far.

As I have stated continually in the past, I love you both. I would love for us to become closer, for us to really open up to each other and support each other in all the growth and maturing that we have to do. The process of growth, I am finding out, is a never-ending one. I wish so much that we could be there for one another. One of my greatest fears is that you will both die without my having had the chance to hear stories of your youth, of your first loves, of your fears, of your real inner feelings, of your hopes and disappointments. I fear also that you will die never really knowing this wonderful being that you birthed and raised—your son, me.

On a lighter side, there is lots going on for me at work; I have many good projects there. There is a lot of closeness I'm feeling for my roommates, Jim and Wendy. The weather down here is great this time of year. I'm trying to grow a beard; we will see how it turns out! Cathy and Ginny are coming up to dinner next week. (I'm sure we will have a great discussion on nuclear power and civil disobedience!) I will be taking one hundred and twenty hours of training, focused on getting more in touch with my body, massage, dance, and healing techniques that you can do for yourself and others. These parts of my life I will go into greater detail at a later time.

I know I have given you lots to think about. I know that this reflection will be difficult for you. My thoughts and love are with you. And, although it is difficult for you now, I hope that this letter will bring us closer rather than move us farther apart.

Love, Bruce

Ruby's response to his letter was bitter. Jess would not see his parents again until a few weeks before his father died the following year. His father was not as negative and hurtful as his mother. Ruby would continue to voice her disapproval of his "lifestyle" in nearly every conversation that they had over the next fourteen years.

Two weeks after Jess came out and after his sister, Cathy, had written a letter to their parents as well, their father, Walter, secretly wrote a letter to Cathy in which he expressed his wish that things were different. Cathy shared this letter with Jess immediately.

October 7, 1981

Dear Cathy,

Just returned from the eye doctor, where Mom is having her eye test, so want to hurry this letter to you. I feel real sneaky doing it this way, but because of the way things are, things that I have let develop over the years, I don't have much privacy in letter writing or on the telephone. Wish things were different so I wouldn't have to feel this way. As much as you may wish to, please don't respond directly to me just now.

Yes, of course, I love you as I always have. So many thoughts flash through my head on this and I suppose that I don't always show this so well but I know that I love you and Bruce too. I can only relate my feelings and be honest, and, perhaps selfishly, I do wish things were different like you were happily married, perhaps with children, etc. But then this is forcing my wishes on you and I think you, as you have, should make your own choices for your life.

I know that I cannot always agree but I can try to understand and in this way give you your freedom of thought. In not agreeing, I can still love and respect you. Mother, on the other hand, sees and feels things differently and expresses herself very strongly. I can see where she has this right, but I do think she is not very tactful.

As for Bruce, I can say that I am disappointed but shall let him make his choices and shall try and understand even when I don't approve of his choice. I try not to be judging of others, as my track record is not so good in a number of ways. It is so hard for me when Mom is so bitter and negative. I have told her that she should act decently toward both of you and your friends, but I don't think that she will ever change.

Well, Cathy, keep yourself well, busy at work, free of stress and strain, and think for yourself. If you can do these things, I know you can be happy.

I will write again when we get to Mesa.

Love,
Dad

Ruby wrote Jess a short letter stating her disapproval, said that she didn't want to hear anything more about his lifestyle, and stated that she would remember him as he had been. Sensing Jess's disappointment over his parents' response and their decision not to visit, I left the following note on his bed.

October 8, 1981

Bruce,

You are Beautiful! Don't you forget it for one moment! My dreams of you are in the present and the future, not the past. I rejoice in all that you are and all that you will be. I celebrate and dance in my realization of your ever-unfolding beauty.

September 17: what a glory-filled, wondrous day, the day you decided to say *yes* to yourself! And yes to all your brothers and sisters! *Thank you,* dear brother. I *want* to know all about your life because I want to know *you!*—not images I have, but the real and ever-growing, ever-loving, ever-feeling child of the infinite that you are. What a wonder to know you! I love you.

Peace,
Jim

Chapter 4

Lesions and Age Spots

Life can only be understood backward, but it must be lived forward.

Søren Kierkegaard

During this same period, one of our volunteers was working with a gay man who had cancer. Steve Peskind said that his client, Bill, wanted to meet other gay men with a life-threatening illness. Steve and I decided that we would send out an announcement to all Bay Area oncologists announcing Shanti Project's desire to form a special group for gay men with a life-threatening illness.

It was October 1981 when Paul Dague, a psychologist at the University of California Medical Center, called to schedule an appointment with me regarding a dozen or so men that he was seeing. They had a disease called GRID (Gay Related Immune Deficiency). I had read a little bit about the disease in the local gay press. I was astounded that an institution as large as UC Medical Center did not already have a support group in place. I scheduled a meeting with Paul. I then called Steve, who was to be the group's co-facilitator, and told him it looked like we might have enough men to start the support group.

I was somewhat intimidated meeting Paul. Paul was a clinical psychologist and worked at one of the largest teaching hospitals in the country, and I had never even done a support group for people with a life-threatening illness. I wondered what Paul would think of me.

Paul told me that his hospital job entailed meeting with men who were being diagnosed with Kaposi's sarcoma, a rare form of skin cancer. He said that the men were very upset and he felt they needed more intensive intervention and counseling, but, because of insufficient funding, he was limited in what he could do. He asked me what my plans were, and I told him we planned to have an open, ongoing weekly group. We wanted to create a supportive place in which to explore feelings, exchange information, and form friendships with others who were facing life-threatening illnesses.

There was very little known about this disease in 1981. About twenty people had been diagnosed in San Francisco, all of whom were gay men. The Centers for Disease Control in Atlanta, Georgia, had conducted a study of fifty cases and released a profile that depicted those diagnosed as having had numerous venereal infections, using large amounts of recreational drugs, and engaging in what are commonly thought of as bizarre sexual practices. My own suspicions at this time mirrored these findings. This was the stereotype that was being perpetuated in the press, and most people, whether gay or heterosexual, accepted that image of the illness and its sufferers.

Paul and I took an immediate liking to one another. He had a sixteen-year-old daughter who lived with him. Paul was a very positive and animated individual. He was in his early forties and had bright orange-red hair. Paul worked part-time at the hospital and maintained a private practice as well. He had a keen wit and was very willing to admit what he didn't know. Paul had no idea where this disease had come from or why he was seeing so many young men diagnosed with it. As I left the meeting, I felt I had met a new friend.

The first person whom Paul referred to Shanti was a man named David. David was too weak to come to a support group. He was in the last stages of Kaposi's sarcoma and was planning to die at home. David was forty years old and had lived with his lover for two years. I decided that I would work individually with David. I wanted to find out more about the men who had this strange illness. When I knocked on David's door, I halfway expected to see chains and slings hanging from the ceiling and cans of sexual lubricant strewn all over the floor. I assumed that his conversation would be mostly one-dimensional and uninteresting. After all, what did a person who was a sex-crazed drug addict have to talk about?

David was nothing like I had imagined. He was a writer, had been married for twenty years, and had had his first gay experience only five years earlier. He was dominant sexually, preferring the "top" position when engaging in sex. There was a popular consensus at this time that only men who were anally receptive were getting the disease, so I was surprised by this revelation. But what really shocked me was that David was very spiritual. He had read numerous books on metaphysical thought that I had never heard about. David was an articulate man and made me feel absolutely comfortable.

However, David was also very sick. He was so weak that he couldn't even answer the door. With much difficulty, he was able to crawl from his mattress on the living room floor to the bathroom. He was on oral morphine for pain and was completely covered and swollen with lesions.

During our first meeting, David talked about his desire to make closure with people in his life and his decision to end his life when his physical deterioration worsened. I felt the pain of my loss immediately. Despite having just met him, I felt sad that our time together would be so limited. Together, we explored his feelings about his decision to end his life. David was very clear; he did not want to become incontinent and slip into a coma, only to have his lover and friends go through the ordeal of "caring for a vegetable." David told me that his ex-wife, his lover, and his doctor supported him in this decision.

I visited David frequently during the next few weeks. I explored with him his thoughts on afterlife and whether he felt that ending his life would have any spiritual repercussions. "I am not ending the life of my spirit, but merely helping the body to free the soul," David replied. As he looked at his swollen body, he continued, "Look at this. It should already be dead, but it just won't give up. My spirit already feels one with God. I'll need to help my body let go."

What struck me about David's words was that they emanated from a place of calm resolve. He wasn't angry or depressed but rather in a state of inner peace. David felt completely comfortable with his decision.

David and I decided to end our relationship about a week before he ended his life. He was at the point where he wished to focus his limited energy on those close to him. I was comfortable with this arrangement and felt that we had completed our work together. I thanked David for helping to free me of my stereotypes, and I wished him well in his life after death. David was gracious and quite appreciative of the small amount of time we had spent together. He had great respect for people who were willing to volunteer and to work with people who had a disease that struck terror into the hearts of many. His acknowledgement gave me new strength. As I left his apartment for the final time, I hoped that David's transition from this life into what lay ahead would be as smooth as possible.

I asked Jess and Wendy how they would feel about having the newly formed support group meet in our house. Each of us was a little nervous because the belief that the disease was somehow transmissible was gaining credibility. But Wendy and Jess both agreed to have the group meet on Wednesday evenings in our living room.

At our first support group we had three people, one of whom was Bobbi Campbell, a nursing student. Bobbi had recently returned from a camping trip and discovered a reddish lesion on the sole of his foot. It had been diagnosed as Kaposi's sarcoma. Bobbi was often referred to as the AIDS poster boy. Pictures of his foot lesions were prominently displayed on Walgreens' plate glass window in the Castro District. Bobbi was very excited about the support group because he very much wanted to meet other people with the illness. He knew a lot about the medical aspects of the illness and was able to answer many of our questions about the effects of specific treatments and explain how certain tests were performed. There was a consensus in the group that many people were being used as guinea pigs. In those early days, doctors wanted to biopsy every available lesion so that they could learn more about the illness.

The second person in the group, John, was a hair stylist and very soft-spoken. Like Bobbi, he had been diagnosed with Kaposi's sarcoma. John was experiencing strong chemotherapy treatments and was losing his hair. John was hopeful for a cure, but he realized that he was quite sick. His two brothers refused to talk with him, but he enjoyed a close relationship with his mother.

Bill, our catalyst for forming the group, was the sickest member. Bill had been diagnosed with lymphoma and was also undergoing heavy doses of chemotherapy. Even though we were unaware at the time that Bill's illness was also AIDS-related, he fit into the group just fine.

During the group meetings, Steve and I sometimes asked questions aimed at determining why group members were sick and we were not. Steve and I felt a little guilty about this. Our own fears of the disease made it very important for us to attempt to distinguish our behavior from that of the group members. We were hoping that we could find differences that would explain why they had the disease and we didn't. It would make us feel safe.

Steve and I would share a sense of relief when we heard something that seemed to distinguish a group member's behavior from our own. However, the group soon grew to eight men, and with each new man, our walls of defense slowly crumbled. It was terrifying. I think that Steve and I were among the first people to realize that this illness could happen to anyone.

These were difficult years. Every patient's doctor seemed to have a different explanation. At this time, there was no concrete, scientific evidence that the disease was sexually transmitted. Many doctors were not making recommendations that their patients use precautions when having sex. One man in the group, Jerry, was continuing to have unprotected sex fairly frequently. I shared my thoughts with Jerry that the disease might be transmitted sexually. I found myself praying that scientists would find out soon, so that we could begin to use that leverage in assisting people in making the necessary changes in their sexual practices.

My own sexual practices were also a concern for me. Since my breakup with Matt, I had been very sexually active. Like many other gay men in the city, I regularly frequented the bathhouses. During much of this period, I felt open to meeting someone and forming a relationship, but, in fact, I was still grieving over my separation from Matt. Putting a lot of energy into my work and having frequent sexual contacts were fairly effective ways of keeping my grief and loneliness disguised.

Many gay men face the problem of how to be intimate with each other. Even when we are attracted to one another, we have grown up in a society that does not support our being sensitive in our interactions with one another. For the most part, we have never learned to talk about our feelings. In San Francisco, I suddenly found myself in an environment that was fairly accepting of the gay lifestyle, but I lacked the necessary communication skills to develop intimate relationships with other men.

I went to the bathhouses for three months before I connected with anyone. I first needed to work through some issues of self-esteem regarding my body. Actually, the bathhouses were a great place to do this, because all we wore were towels! I would carry my towel and force myself to walk around naked, as an exercise in becoming more comfortable with my body. When men noticed me, I would freeze. I think that much of my negative body image derived from having rather severe acne as a teenager. I also thought my penis was too small. Like so many others, I had bought into false images of how we are supposed to look.

In some ways, I found my struggle to be comfortable when naked in a sexually charged setting to be out of sync with the rest of my life. I really liked being naked. One of the things I loved about California was the ability to go to a nude beach. There are few things that are as spiritually centering to me as feeling my body's gracefulness and harmony with nature when I am without clothes. Walking naked around the baths was an attempt to rediscover that unselfconscious, relaxed, and natural place within myself.

Most of the time, I tried to open my heart to the men with whom I connected sexually. But like myself, so many of my partners had not learned how to really communicate. I found an addictive quality to having frequent sex with multiple partners and, like most addictions, it had snuck up on me.

With my growing awareness of the devastating effects of this new illness, I knew I needed to make some changes. It was not an easy process.

I decided to start using condoms, go to the baths less, and cut down on my number of contacts when I did go. With the exception of poppers (nitrates) which I had decided to curtail, I was never into drugs, so that was one hurdle I didn't need to face. I found the most important thing was to be nonjudgmental and loving with myself. It was also important for me *not* to set my goals unrealistically high. Changing addictive behavior patterns is a slow process and it was important to set achievable goals. Safe sex practices had not yet been defined. Like many others, I did not even have the absolute knowledge that this disease was transmitted sexually to spur me on in my efforts.

There was increasing talk in the community that, even if the disease was sexually transmitted, you would only succumb to it if your immune system was really run down. This talk contributed to the mounting negative stereotypes. The hysteria level surrounding the disease was starting to rise.

Men in the support group began reporting that their roommates were asking them to move out. Funeral homes were refusing to handle the bodies of the deceased. Gay men were simultaneously coming out to their families as gay and revealing that they had a terminal illness. The survival statistics were very bleak then, and many of the men felt like they were being viewed more as a number than as a person.

Jess and Wendy experienced their share of hysteria as well. One night, I went into the kitchen and found my roommates boiling water to wash the glasses the men in support group had used during our meeting. Wendy asked, "Why do you stack the dishes your support group uses and ours together? You should keep them separate!" Jess had the whole cleaning system worked out: he boiled water for five minutes, and then he submerged the dishes for twenty minutes!

My mom and dad got into the act as well when they visited during the holidays. After support group, a couple of the guys said they would like to meet my folks. I knew Mom was nervous about the work I was doing, but she's always had the ability to be friendly, even while clenching her teeth. Bobbi went right up to her, held her hand, and said, "It's a pleasure to meet you, Mrs. Geary."

Mom said, "I am pleased to meet you too." After spending a few more minutes with my parents, I walked Bobbi and a few other guys to the door. When I came back into the living room, Mom had the lamp turned up and her forehead was sweating. "See those red spots on my hand! Right where he touched me! I've gotten that gay cancer!"

Dad said, "Martha, those are age spots!"

We all started to laugh.

While my parents and I remained separated by a continent, our connection had never been better. They were living in Alexandria, Virginia, and beginning to talk of retirement. San Francisco had become one of their favorite cities, and each year we would set aside a week to visit one another. They were understandably concerned about my involvement with people suffering from this strange new illness, but they were extremely proud of my pioneering efforts.

An evening in January 1982 found me sitting alone in a San Francisco bar on Polk Street. As I listened to the piano music, I looked at the faces of the many men joined in song and talking to one another. I suddenly welled up with emotion and began to cry, as I wondered how many of these men would eventually be diagnosed with this damn disease. I asked myself, *Why me God? Who am I to begin this task? There are certainly more qualified, capable people to move this organization forward.*

Quickly, the inner voice responded, *Why not you?*

As I began to accept that truth, I began to see my life as a series of patterns and events that had prepared me to be exactly where I was: I was a gay man. I had worked with people with a life-threatening illness for ten years. I held a key position in a project that had already served as a model for many similar groups across the country. I began to realize that I had been guided all along to be exactly where I was in this moment.

My tears of fear, grief, and despair gave way to tears of guidance, grace, and gratitude. I accepted the whole of myself more deeply that day than ever before. I walked out of that bar with an accepted mission and an increased awareness of my sacred link to my community and the awesome task that lay ahead.

In February 1982, I finished instructing at my second volunteer training. The training was very successful and we had thirty-three new volunteers who were very excited about beginning their work. Among them were five gay and lesbian volunteers who wanted to work specifically within the gay community.

I returned to the office following the weekend and found my three coworkers sitting in the main office area. I was exuberant from the success of the training and greeted them enthusiastically. Our administrator, Peggy, had a look of controlled intensity that I had not seen before. She said there was something on my desk that I should probably read.

In my office, I found a proposal that she had sent to our board of directors. The document stated that the project was nearing bankruptcy. It outlined how identifiable sources of funding had been tapped and stated that our operational expenses far exceeded projected income. It recommended the dissolution of the project and the liquidation of all office equipment. The dissolution was to occur in less than a month's time. In her proposal, Peggy suggested that the board could give the answering machine to the volunteers if the volunteers wanted to keep minimal client services operating.

My initial reaction to this document surprised me; it was as if a presence was guiding me to stay calm. There was a part of me that could easily have been outraged that Peggy had not talked with me before acting. But I took a deep breath and repeated several times, *Stay calm. Go and offer your support.*

I went back into the main area and could see that Peggy was prepared for any type of reaction. She took a breath of relief when I said, "It must be very difficult for you." I had no idea of what the board's response would be to her plan. The board was going to meet in two weeks to consider what action they would take. Peggy asked me to break the news to the trainees the following weekend.

I told the trainees that the board was considering dissolving the project and that there was not enough money to retain staff. I added that it was my strong feeling that somehow things would work out. There was just too much energy in that one training alone to let things collapse! The volunteers were shaken, of course, but we all had faith that somehow our vital services would continue.

When the training was over and I had more time to think about the situation, I decided that I would volunteer to remain on staff without salary. I knew two gay men who might be willing to help financially. My plan was to ask each of them for ten thousand dollars. One of them, Michael, was Jess's current boyfriend. The other man, Robert, was the beneficiary of the life insurance policy of a client of mine, Tim, who had died from AIDS. It felt very timely.

During the two weeks before the board met, I was dealing with my feelings regarding Tim's recent death. I had worked with Tim for about three months, and my time with him was most rewarding. Tim had been on a respirator in the intensive care unit (ICU) the entire time I had known him. Even though Tim was gay, I didn't initially identify with him. Before becoming ill, Tim had been a jock and had worked out daily at a gym. He had a very defined body. Tim was in a coma when I first met him.

Tim's lover, Chuck, had requested a counselor, as had Tim's heterosexual and somewhat homophobic brother, George. I felt challenged by George, so I decided to work with him as a client. George lived in Idaho but he came to visit Tim for weeks at a time. I spent considerable time with him. It was through George that I first met Tim, and I ended up visiting Tim nearly every day during the three months he was hospitalized.

The first few times I visited Tim in the hospital, I was uncomfortable. There were tubes everywhere. The respirator alone was intimidating enough—it had a tube connected to an opening in Tim's throat and was breathing for him. Tim's body was too weak to breathe on its own. Tim also had a catheter to collect his urine and one IV in his leg and another in his arm. All of Tim's limbs were restrained because he sometimes tried to pull the tubes out. For the first few days, I allowed myself to take the necessary time to get comfortable in his room. I grew increasingly relaxed about moving around the room without fearing that I would disconnect something.

Tim had been diagnosed with pneumocystis pneumonia, had massive herpes zoster on his back, and had sepsis (a blood infection). His doctor told us right from the beginning that Tim's chances of pulling through were one in a million. He told us that Tim could die at any time.

The nurses who attended to Tim were exceptionally caring, but, as is common in an ICU setting, hospital personnel are frequently involved with many painful procedures. I tried to provide Tim with touch that did not equate with pain or discomfort. I gently rubbed his forehead and held his hand.

I had done some work in the past with visualization, and I decided to try it with Tim. I did not know much about Tim's spiritual beliefs except that he was raised Catholic. Even though Tim was comatose and his doctor felt he was totally unaware of his surroundings, I talked with Tim, believing that, on some level, he could hear me.

Tim frequently had very high temperatures. I asked him to imagine himself standing under a cool and gentle waterfall that was softly cascading over his body, making him feel cool and revitalized. When he seemed agitated, I placed my hand on his chest and asked him to try to focus on his heart and the support that was all around him. I also explained to him what I had learned about his medical condition. I was sure that he must be terribly disoriented. Before he was hospitalized, Tim had not even been aware that he was sick. He had been working out at the gym and had suddenly become short of breath. The very next day, he was in a coma and on a respirator in ICU.

During the visualizations, I noticed a definite response from Tim. On numerous occasions, his temperature dropped and he became much less agitated. Even though Tim was still comatose and his eyes remained closed, his body relaxed with my touch.

I decided that it might be soothing to bring music into his environment. His lover, Chuck, gave me permission to record some of Tim's favorite music. I interspersed the music pieces with my voice. Between pieces, I encouraged him to relax and allow the music to flow though him, as it brought with it a sense of peace and healing.

The first time I played the tape, Tim reacted powerfully! He moved his head in the direction of the cassette player and squeezed my hand. When I wasn't in the room with him, the nurses played it frequently. Two days after he first heard the music, Tim came out of his coma.

I was delighted, but I was also anxious about what he would think of me. I thought, *What if I have been misreading his responses all along and he has really been thinking I'm a kook!*

When I came into his room, he recognized my voice immediately and looked right at me. I told him that I was the one who had been doing the "crazy" visualizations. I asked him if he would like to continue doing them. He communicated his willingness by closing his eyes and letting me guide him.

Tim's family and friends were having a difficult time trying to accept the abrupt deterioration of his health. Tim's lover, Chuck, completely fell apart when visiting Tim and refused to acknowledge any possibility of Tim's dying. Chuck said that the doctor was wrong and that Tim would show everyone. There was part of me that wanted Chuck to accept the possibility that Tim might die. I thought that if he did accept this likelihood, he would be better prepared to deal with Tim's death when it occurred.

I remembered that Charles Garfield had referred to denial as an effective form of "terror management." I was beginning to see firsthand that denial is the mind's natural way of protecting itself. Through denial, the mind is able to look at a terrifying situation in small doses.

I recommended to Chuck's volunteer that he explore Chuck's feelings about being the only one who really believed that Tim would recover. I also asked the volunteer to ask Chuck how he saw himself helping Tim recover. This approach seemed to be very effective in that it allowed Chuck to release his anger at others close to Tim who did not share Chuck's optimism. It also helped Chuck to focus on his feelings about their relationship.

Tim's brother, George, had had a fight with Tim three years earlier and was carrying a lot of guilt. George also did not like Chuck's emotional side and he referred to Chuck as a "milquetoast." My challenge was not to come to Chuck's defense, but rather to assist George in releasing his hostility.

After about two weeks, Tim's doctor told us again that Tim really should not be alive. His lab results were awful. We were told that we should be prepared for Tim to die at any time. Despite Tim's enthusiasm about our visualizations, I thought that maybe I should at least broach the subject of his death. I went in one morning and asked Tim, "Do you ever think about the possibility of not recovering from this illness?" Immediately, Tim turned his head away from me.

I felt terrible. I said, "Well, it's clear, Tim, that you don't want to talk about this. Do you want to do a visualization?" Tim quickly turned his head toward me.

About six weeks later, I again gave into pressure from his physician, who believed that Tim's death was imminent; I brought the subject up again. This time, I said, "Tim, do you ever get frustrated with trying so hard to recover? Do you fear that you might not be successful?" Again, Tim's head turned abruptly, giving me a clear indication that he did not want to even consider that possibility.

It was not until the night he died that Tim was ready to open himself to the possibility of dying. It had been three months since I had first met him; Tim was in renal failure and had not passed urine in over two days. His doctor said, with much certainty, that Tim's death was imminent. I walked in and said, "Tim, it doesn't look good, does it?" This time, my strong and positive friend turned his head toward me. Our eyes met and filled with tears. I told him that I imagined that he must be frightened and that he could try to focus on the white light we sometimes imagined in our visualizations. I then shared with him some stories I had heard from people who had died and later been revived: stories that included images like a tunnel, seeing friends and family members who had passed before, and merging into a warm white light or peaceful presence. I told him that all of the accounts I had heard were very peaceful and that many people said they did not fear dying after having gone through these experiences. Tim listened to every word and seemed to be greatly comforted. After a while, he slipped into a coma, and I went home.

I got a call about 3:00 AM, and was told that Tim's blood pressure had fallen so low they were unable to take it. I called Chuck's volunteer, and together we went to Chuck's house. I went in and told Chuck that the hospital had called and said they felt that Tim was very close to death. He said, "They have been wrong before. Tim is strong and he is going to make it."

I said, "I hope you're right, Chuck, but how would you feel if you were mistaken and didn't have this chance to be with him?" Chuck reluctantly got dressed; when we arrived at the hospital, Tim was very near death.

I told Chuck that it appeared that Tim was very close to dying. Chuck became overwhelmed with emotion. Even though Chuck was sobbing, George was able to be in the room while Chuck said good-bye. I was proud of the progress that George had made. George, who had remained fairly stoic right up until the end, was now able to be present with Chuck's strong emotion. George had earlier been able to apologize to Tim and make amends for the years they had wasted. He was able to open his heart to his brother and let his love flow.

I whispered in Tim's ear that I loved him, and I encouraged him to move into the light. Once again, he moved his head slightly toward me. A few minutes later, he took his last breath.

Tim had taught me so much about how to support someone in the quest for recovery. Even though I only raised the possibility of Tim's death twice in our three-month relationship, Tim had clearly not wanted to look at it. So often in this work we run into the temptation of thinking that we know what is best for our clients. Tim's time to deal with his dying was just four hours before his death. Those four hours were sufficient, and they were the right time for Tim to look more closely at his death. I feel blessed to have been able to spend so many days with him, helping him to visualize his heart opening, and to receive the love of all around him.

At the next volunteer meeting, the volunteers heard firsthand Peggy's recommendation to disband the project and my offer to remain without salary as the new director. Peggy felt sabotaged by my desire to stay and stated that she lacked confidence in my ability to secure funding. Yet for the volunteers the choice was a relatively simple one—they wanted client services to continue. I was unanimously elected as executive director. I felt humbled and filled with gratitude over the volunteers' confidence in me. They elected our new board two weeks later.

The new board was a working board and held meetings every two weeks for the first year and a half. There were some concerns among the volunteers that, now that I was director, the organization would become exclusively gay. "Not unless you abandon ship," I told them. I had no desire to create a gay organization. I did, however, want to get the project funded, and it seemed clear that AIDS was an issue that could do this.

The previous board had left four thousand dollars in outstanding bills. There was a mailing list of fifteen hundred donors who had contributed to the project. Jess had a wealth of knowledge regarding mailing lists and donor appeal letters. During his free time, he began volunteering at the project, updating the mailing list and sharing his skills regarding effective donor mailings. I was very gratified to be supported by Jess in this undertaking. In the past year, the donors had been inundated with urgent appeal letters forecasting the possible demise of the project. We wanted the first donor letter to capture our enthusiasm. We were thrilled that our efforts raised twenty-two hundred dollars.

The AIDS support group was increasingly concerned about the terrible stereotypes of people with AIDS that were being perpetuated in the media. I had the idea to put together a letter from people with AIDS to the community, which would provide an opportunity for the group to address these stereotypes as well as inform the community about Shanti Project. The support group was excited about reaching out to the community in this manner and began drafting the letter.

Jess and Michael were still dating, although it appeared that Jess was more romantically involved than Michael, who was a gifted artist and floral designer. Jess commented that there was a delicate quality about Michael that made him feel as if he had one foot in this world and one foot in the next. I called Michael and asked if he would pay for a full-page ad in *The Advocate*. Michael agreed to fund the ad. I told the support group and they were very excited about this opportunity to get their message out. From the onset of the disease in San Francisco, people with AIDS were instrumental in educating the community. Whether it was through community forums, speaking at hospitals and community organizations, or participating in Shanti Project training, people with AIDS led the way in educating and sensitizing San Franciscans to the psychosocial issues of the illness.

San Francisco's Department of Public Health was getting increasingly involved with AIDS. Initially, the health department coordinated its AIDS efforts through its office of Gay and Lesbian Health Concerns. Pat Norman was in charge of the program and was planning the first AIDS training for the health department staff. She called and asked me to speak at the training. I asked her how she had come to call Shanti. Pat said, "Well, from what I hear, Shanti is the only group that knows how to deal with the psychosocial issues that people with AIDS are facing."

As I prepared for my talk at the city health department, I decided I would begin with a visualization. I wanted to take the risk of accessing people's feelings. I asked everyone to close their eyes and to take a few deep breaths. I encouraged them to let go of all the facts and figures they had heard and to try and open up to what it might feel like to be diagnosed with AIDS. I then asked them to spend a few minutes considering how they might interact with a coworker or a friend who was diagnosed. Everyone seemed to appreciate having a chance to examine more intimately their feelings regarding AIDS. After the short centering exercise, I shared with them what I was learning from my work with the AIDS support group.

I highlighted how I had initially wanted people with AIDS to be different from me; I talked about my fear in realizing that they were not. I told them I had met individuals with AIDS who were vegetarians, practicing meditation, in monogamous relationships for many years, and who had healthy self-images. I emphasized healthy self-image because I was beginning to hear an increasing number of people attributing the cause of the illness to people's lack of self-love.

I stressed how unfortunate it was that the press and the majority of people seemed more fascinated by what gays do in bed than in how the disease affects those diagnosed and what we could do to protect ourselves. I finished my presentation by focusing on some key psychosocial issues, such as a person's reaction to initial diagnosis, who to tell, how to decide on treatment options, coping with the reactions of family and friends, dealing with our own grief, living with illness, and our attitudes about dying.

Pat impressed me greatly. She shared a few closing thoughts regarding the potential political consequences of the illness. Her thoughts were well-formulated and she had a far-reaching awareness of what the political ramifications could be. Pat spoke about the need to ensure client confidentiality, the importance of not labeling AIDS a "gay disease," and the blood bank issue. There was increasing talk at this time of trying to ban anyone gay from donating blood. The problem with this action was that it assumed that everyone who was gay was at risk for the virus. This assumption did not recognize that gay relationships and lifestyles have the same degree of differences as heterosexual relationships. This action would have also led to a witch-hunt mentality and many people's personal lives could have been shattered. I appreciated Pat's ability to separate from the hysteria and to rationally decide what was the most effective and humane response to many of the difficult issues we faced.

After the training, Pat came over and introduced herself. Pat said she had liked my presentation and would like to have lunch. I reported to the board that the speaking engagement had gone well and that it was encouraging to have our work recognized by the city. I also told them that I felt I needed to physically move into the office rather than continue commuting from San Francisco.

I had a very strong feeling that if the project was going to survive, it would require me to make an even deeper commitment. I felt that the success of my goals depended on my willingness to physically merge with the project. I was already working twelve-hour days and commuting from San Francisco. While the board was concerned about my need to separate from Shanti and take care of myself, they agreed that this "marriage" of my energy and that of the project was needed.

It was harder leaving Jess and Wendy than I thought it would be. They had both given me so much support throughout this time and I had come to care about each of them greatly. As I pulled away, I shed tears as I once again opened to saying good-bye to those I loved, moving forward into a world of unknown tomorrows.

Chapter 5

Phoenix Rising

The supreme happiness of life is the conviction that we are loved.

Victor Hugo

I claimed one of the project's office for my personal space. There was also a kitchen, so I was able to cook meals. I was collecting unemployment, so I had to attempt to find work. Since it was my intention to eventually be on salary again with Shanti, I developed a knack for inquiring about work at places that would not hire me. I figured that, in some ways, I was the recipient of the State of California's first AIDS funding!

I tried not to answer the phone after office hours. However, I did listen to the callers on the answering machine before deciding if I wanted to pick up. It was difficult to set limits when some of the callers were so distraught. One day in June, a man called after hours from San Francisco. He had just been diagnosed with AIDS. He had worked for the Pacific Gas and Electric Company for twenty years. There was a quality in his voice that really drew me in—he sounded slightly hesitant and nervous, yet there was a

gentleness and vulnerability in his voice as well. He had absolutely
no idea what Shanti was or really why he was even calling; a nurse
at the hospital had suggested that he call. His name was Bobby
Reynolds.

Bobby told me that he was going to be treated with
chemotherapy and that he had some concerns about the drugs'
side effects. He said that he lived with his lover, Mark, and that
Mark seemed to be handling things fairly well. Bobby had a sister
who lived near San Francisco who was pregnant. His sister was
afraid to see him.

He was not sure that he wanted a volunteer, but he was
interested in coming to our support group. I encouraged clients
who came to support group to work individually with a volunteer.
I did this because support groups often bring up many feelings,
and I wanted to ensure that group members had someone to talk
with after meetings. Bobby decided that he would try working
with a volunteer and that he would come to the next support
group.

Bobby had considered becoming a Jesuit priest but opted for
accepting his sexual orientation instead. Bobby's hair was graying
and he had a very soft manner of speaking. He was a little square
by San Francisco standards—he didn't enjoy bars, dancing, or
partying. This was due in part to hypoglycemia, which he had
before his AIDS diagnosis. Bobby and his lover, Mark, liked
to play pinochle and they were both members of a gay softball
league. Mark and Bobby had been lovers for four years. They
had a primarily monogamous relationship but occasionally they
engaged in sexual play with a third partner.

There was such ordinariness about Bobby. He was not politically
active and viewed himself as a shy person. I was very much taken
by Bobby and wanted him to take part in our upcoming volunteer
training. "This is who people need to see," I told my friends.
"Bobby looks like the guy next door. People will look at him and
say, 'That could be my brother, my son, or me.'"

I told the board that I felt that we needed to dramatically increase our presence in San Francisco if we were going to receive city funding. At this point, most of the diagnosed cases of AIDS in the Bay Area were in San Francisco, and 98 percent of the AIDS cases in the city were in the gay and bisexual community. We also needed to increase our number of San Francisco volunteers. I wanted to specifically bring more gay men into the project, and I wanted to be able to match gay clients with gay volunteers, if that was important to them. For many clients, the volunteer's gender or sexual orientation did not matter. Many gay men, though, were more comfortable with volunteers who were women, finding it easier to share their feelings with them, just as heterosexual men did. I wanted our clients with AIDS to have as much choice in selecting a volunteer as our non-AIDS clients.

The gay community was just beginning to respond. We had sixteen gay men in the upcoming training and an additional thirty trainees who were primarily heterosexual women. In getting Bobby to consent to come and speak at the training, I had emphasized the fact that we had sixteen gay male volunteers who wanted to help people with AIDS. I didn't mention that there would be forty-six trainees in all, plus ten facilitators. When Bobby arrived, he was surprised, to say the least. Bobby never missed an opportunity in what was to become our five-year relationship to remind me of how I had pulled a fast one!

I was very excited about the training because my friend Paul Dague was going to attend. Paul and I had had lunch a week earlier, and he had decided that although he wasn't able to make the volunteer commitment, the training would help him deal more effectively with his feelings. Paul shared that, at times, it was overwhelming for him to deal with the increasing number of people he was seeing as a hospital psychologist. Paul was frustrated that there was so little information to give to newly diagnosed clients. Paul also confided that he felt he was becoming a hypochondriac. He recently had a small sore on the back of his ear and practically had to force his doctor to biopsy it. Paul's doctor was sure that there was nothing to worry about.

I was eager for Paul to participate in the training so that he would know more about how we specifically trained our volunteers. On the first night of the training, I was surprised that Paul was not there. When I got home, I called to see if anything was wrong. I couldn't believe what Paul told me: the sore on the back of his ear had turned out to be a lesion. The results had come back positive for Kaposi's sarcoma. Paul had AIDS.

I absolutely fell apart on the phone. I was so overwhelmed with my own fear and grief that I just started to sob. I told Paul that I was sorry but that I couldn't be there for him at that time. He understood, and we agreed to talk later. Paul's diagnosis ripped away another layer of my denial. I had come to see Paul as my peer. Now Paul was one of them. Would I be next? I was shattered. Paul appeared so healthy. What was this goddamned disease and when would it stop? The whole situation suddenly seemed much more frightening. Paul's diagnosis forced my increasing awareness that an AIDS diagnosis could happen to anyone.

Bobby was the first person with AIDS to present at our training. He was wonderful. Bobby came to me and said, "Sixteen gay men, huh?" During his talk, he was willing to talk about anything, no matter how personal or difficult it was. Bobby talked about how other people with AIDS affected him when he went to the clinic for treatment. He saw men with more advanced cases of the disease. He mentioned one man in particular, Alex, who had lesions covering his entire face. Each time Bobby returned to the clinic, Alex's condition had worsened. Alex's face was eventually so swollen that his eyes had become mere slits. It was increasingly difficult for Bobby to talk with Alex. Bobby said that, after seeing Alex, he would go and look into the bathroom mirror and wonder if his face was one day going to look like Alex's.

Bobby talked about his decision to write a letter to all of his friends informing them of his diagnosis. He said that it was easier doing it that way than ending up having to support them when he told them in person of his diagnosis. I could identify with what Bobby was sharing because of my recent reaction with Paul. Bobby also shared the helplessness and hurt he felt regarding his relationship with his sister. Bobby had enjoyed a special relationship with his five-year-old niece. Now, because of his sister's and brother-in-law's fear, he was not permitted to see his niece. Bobby had arranged for his sister to talk with his doctor, but she was still uncomfortable being around her brother. Bobby felt lost as to what to do and how to cope with his feelings of hurt and anger. As was the case with the hundreds of volunteer and community training sessions that were to follow, firsthand accounts immensely moved the trainees.

After the training, we worked on the letter to the community from people with AIDS. The support group was empowered by writing it, and we were all excited about distributing the flyers and using the letter as an ad. The full-page ad that we ran in *The Advocate* netted over four thousand dollars in donations. We were finally able to pay off all our outstanding bills. We organized a group of volunteers one weekend and walked door-to-door in the Castro District of San Francisco and distributed the flyer. We received a number of letters from people thanking us for the work we were doing, and many people indicated that they would like to be volunteers. The letter read as follows:

A Letter to the Community from People with AIDS

As people with AIDS, we would like to say that there is nothing pleasant about rejection. In the last year, we have been ostracized, blamed, and damned by many throughout the community. We have been denied funeral services, medical treatment, housing, and employment. We have been shunned in public and isolated because of fear and hysteria. We have been forced to fight for our lives by demanding federal and local funding that would have been offered automatically to a more socially acceptable minority. We have had to undo the harm and hurt inflicted upon us by false stereotypes that depict us as less than human and as immoral people. The "moral majority" has told us that AIDS is the wrath of God. Even within the gay/lesbian/bisexual community, there have been frightening attempts to scapegoat us and deny us our freedoms. What is needed at this time is less prejudice and divisiveness and more compassion and unity.

People with AIDS are ordinary people. We are your sons and daughters, brothers and sisters, friends, co-workers, and neighbors. We developed AIDS because an unknown agent has attacked our immune systems. Despite the media's often-sensationalistic attempts to depict AIDS as a disease resulting from the gay lifestyle, AIDS has affected men, women, and children regardless of their sexual identity. AIDS does not discriminate on the basis of age, race, religion, or sexual orientation.

We know the fear of AIDS. We understand how frightening AIDS can be, and we understand the fears about how it might be transmitted. We encourage and support people to learn what is known about AIDS and not become paralyzed with fear. We suffer when uninformed people spread fear and misinformation. In fact, everyone in the community suffers. It is important for you to know that medical experts agree that AIDS is not casually transmitted. We need your caring and support more than ever. We aren't helpless, but sometimes we need help. Having us over to dinner and giving us a loving hug is no risk to you and good medicine for us.

Shanti Project provides us good medicine. Volunteers attend to our emotional needs and support groups offer a safe place for us and our loved ones to receive support.

Shanti Project is in need of donations to continue offering these vital services and in need of volunteers to meet the needs of the continuing crisis in our community. We encourage you to contribute in whatever way you can. By giving of yourself, you can make a difference.

We want to thank the many people and organizations who have given of themselves to help nurture and support us. This expression of love contributes to everyone's well-being.

We wish health and love to fill your lives.

All the members of the support group signed the letter.

Pat Norman and I continued to get together for lunch, sharing our concerns about how AIDS would impact the community. The more Pat talked, the more I continued to be fascinated by her perspective on AIDS. I found myself both enlightened by and in agreement with many of her stands. On an intuitive level, I knew it felt right to be with her. What I did not know was that Pat had been asked by the Department of Public Health and San Francisco Supervisor Harry Britt to identify what community agencies could help deal with the emerging AIDS problem.

At the end of lunch one day, Pat asked me point-blank, "So, how much do you need to do what you want to do?"

My eyes rolled a bit and I said, "What?"

"How much do you need? Ten, fifty, two-hundred thousand, what do you need to put yourself on salary, hire an office manager, and operate your services for a year?"

It was hard to believe what I was hearing. I stuttered out a figure of fifty thousand, which at the time seemed like a million. Pat said that certainly seemed reasonable and that I should write up a proposal.

"A proposal," I gulped.

Pat offered to help me with the wording and showed me copies of contracts that the department had with other agencies. Pat concluded by saying that Supervisor Britt wanted to sponsor a recommendation to Mayor Dianne Feinstein for city funding.

I left Pat, feeling dazed, and I began putting together my first budget. The idea of such a large sum of money coming all at once boggled my mind. And it seemed that I had walked right into it without being aware that it was there. I told the board about my meeting with Pat Norman and told them that it was my feeling that if we moved the project's office to San Francisco, we would have a better chance of becoming a city-funded agency. The project had been based in Berkeley for seven years, and there was considerable emotional attachment to keeping it there. I pointed out that even apart from city funding, I thought that the funding climate in San Francisco was more favorable.

Paul Dague called and invited me to the musical, *Showboat*. I had not seen Paul since his diagnosis. I felt that his invitation to the musical was his way of showing me that he was focused on living life and enjoying it. Paul and I had lunch soon after the musical. He had decided to try a macrobiotic diet. Part of the diet regimen was to chew each bite of food fifty times. I tried it with him for about five minutes and thought I would go crazy. He was also considering going to Mexico to try amino acid therapy. He was very hopeful about his full recovery and challenged a lot of people around him who viewed AIDS as a death sentence.

Both Paul and Bobby regularly attended our support group, which was now being held in a community center. Our group was fluctuating between fifteen and twenty men. Bobby's lover, Mark, also felt that Bobby would recover from AIDS as quickly as he developed it. Mark didn't want an emotional support volunteer, nor did he wish to make use of our family, friends, and lovers group. Mark, like Paul, felt things would be just fine.

The board voted to move our office to San Francisco. The new office building had formerly been a convent, and it was full of dimly lit passages and small mysterious rooms. Entering the building at night was a little scary. On several occasions, some of the other offices in the building were vandalized. The building manager pretended not to notice when he spotted my bed in an adjoining office. He liked the idea of someone sleeping in the building, even though I had slept through the break-ins.

The possibility of city funding looked more and more promising. I had submitted a proposal for fifty-seven thousand dollars, which included salaries for a full-time director and office manager, as well as operational expenses for one year. The mayor and the Board of Supervisors were considering proposals from a number of different agencies. Another community group that was very active from the onset was the Kaposi's Sarcoma Foundation (now known as the San Francisco AIDS Foundation). The foundation was primarily involved with community education and helping people with AIDS utilize available social services. The Department of Public Health played a key role in convening all community-based groups and mapping out a comprehensive strategy for addressing the epidemic. This early convening of community and city groups circumvented turf wars and duplication of services.

We received word in November 1982 that Mayor Feinstein had approved our proposal. Yet, by the time all the administrative steps were to be completed, we would not receive our first check until the following March. I was being asked to meet more frequently with the health department to develop a city response to the epidemic and to speak at city agencies and hospitals on the psychosocial impact of AIDS. I needed someone in the office full-time. By December, we had secured enough funds through other fundraising efforts to hire an office manager. It felt a little odd putting someone else on salary first, but the project didn't have the funds to support two positions.

My personal life had been put on hold for some time. It had been almost four years since I had left Matt. I had become so involved with my work that I didn't know how I would fit in a personal relationship. Moreover, the idea of bringing someone home to sleep on the office floor was not exactly a turn-on! I was lonely, however; I went out and attempted to meet people, but I frequently felt invisible. I would think, *Why doesn't anyone see me? Why can't they see that I am a really nice guy?* I also found that just being involved in Shanti was enough to scare people away. Many individuals knew of our increased focus on AIDS and desperately wanted to avoid looking at the issue. Also, some of my difficulty connecting with men was due in part to my nonconformity in dress and attitude: I simply did not mirror the Castro clone look, i.e., short hair and a mustache; I enjoyed wearing colorful, loosely hanging clothes, and I had gotten my ear pierced and enjoyed wearing an assortment of fun, dangling earrings. It saddened me that my own self-acceptance increased my rejection from within "my own" community. Yet I was not willing to compromise myself to attract another.

It was during the February 1983 volunteer training that circumstances forced me to take a deeper look at myself and what I wanted in a relationship. Jess had been accepted into the training, and while he had always been supportive of the work I was doing, he had never indicated any interest in working with people with a life-threatening illness. Jess had recently come through a very difficult period. His father, Walter, had died six months before the training. His mom had invited each of her three children to spend a week with their father in Mesa, Arizona, shortly before his death. Jess was very moved by this time spent with his dad, massaging his cancer-ridden body and feeding him small bites of watermelon. Jess opted not to attend his father's funeral, primarily because his mother remained so disapproving of Jess's sexual orientation. He knew he would feel uncomfortable not being himself around family and friends.

Jess suffered a major anxiety episode following his father's death. I spent several nights holding him while he was too anxiety-ridden to sleep. Jess's relationship with his lover, Michael, had ended a year prior. Jess was very much in love with Michael, and the end of their romantic relationship was a tremendous loss for him. Jess's sister, Cathy, had recently ended a seventeen-year relationship with her lover, Ginny. Jess was feeling a deep lack of stability in his life and decided to enter therapy.

During the training, two of the facilitators told me that Jess was having a difficult time. They felt that Jess was in love with me but didn't know how to express it. I thought Jess was probably infatuated by my training persona. I was at my best when I did training. It was such an opportunity and exercise in letting go of fear and opening my heart. I met with Jess the second weekend to find out more about how he was feeling. Jess said that while it was true he had experienced a deeper sense of me as a result of the training, he had also come to realize how I had been by his side during many of the difficult points of his life. We decided to get together after the training and talk further.

It was an intense evening. I reiterated my belief that he was awed with the part of me he saw in the training. I added that I didn't think we were the right types of partners for each other because our sexual attraction was not sufficiently charged. If anything, my muscles had sagged, I looked awful in a mustache, and, although I had bought a pair of cowboy boots, they looked more comical than macho! Jess assured me that none of that mattered and that he was attracted to me and wanted to begin dating again. I was skeptical and afraid of being left by him again. Despite my apprehension, we began to see each other more frequently. Even though I had had sex with literally hundreds of partners, I was still sexually inhibited. Jess had a very healthy sexual self-image and showed me that sex could be erotic, emotionally healing, and fun. I found myself gradually allowing my heart to open to Jess.

Jess also remained somewhat uncertain of the type of relationship he wanted with me. Some of his ongoing questioning is reflected in the following letter.

April 1983 (Tuesday evening)

Dear Jimmy,

I just spent most of my fifty minutes with my counselor talking about you, and I was thinking that I would like to sit down each night and write my thoughts. So much is going through my head. I want to try and be as open and honest as possible in these lines. I want to let you in as far as I possibly can. Hopefully, focusing some each day will help me sort through my many emotions and feelings for you.

Let's see ... what is it that I really want from you? What do I want to give you? What is it that draws me to you? Why have I desired you to be in my life? What pulls me toward you? I want to hold you and be held by you. I want to lie with you. I want to go on picnics. I want to confide in you, and I want you to confide in me. I want to feel special when I'm with you. I want you to drop by sometimes unannounced. I want to be with you when you need healing, when you are feeling weak. I want to go on trips with you. I want to feel close to you and needed by you.

Slow down a bit ... focus.

You are very dear to me. It's your heart, your expanded heart. It's your spiritually seeking nature. It's your zaniness. I love your laughter. I love so much your emotions, your bubbling, attuned, alive nature.

Since last fall, really since last June or so, I started missing you, feeling a void.

Let me see ... get to the center of my thoughts.

Jimmy, if I could have it all my way, if I could have you in my life just the way I wanted, leaving your desires out of the picture for a moment, I would like to be in contact with you on a very profound level. The training really brought this home to me. I want to be inside your heart, under your skin.

It seems so natural, of course—let's be roommates again. Office manager ... I would love that role so very much, daily contact, support, nurturing, and a regular input.

Lovers, loving, sex. That came along. I don't feel real passion for you. I don't yearn for the sex. It's the company, it's the hugs, it's the tears, it's the holding, squeezing, it's the flowers, it's movies, it's picnics, it's sex too—sometimes. Being physical with you has opened up our love; it has opened our hearts. It's very profound for me.

I'm afraid. Afraid to not have sex, because if we say we're not lovers, then somehow I'm afraid we'll be less special. That the opening of our hearts to each other will be less.

I loved staying after the Shanti meeting, staying behind, and being inside with you as the doors closed. I loved going for a drink, bringing you to my apartment. I loved the tea, the candles, the "spooning." The sex, it's okay; it'll get better as we explore. I loved you in bed with me as we woke. I liked sharing the photo album stories.

I'm changing so fast. Imagine the changes in the last six months. Where will it lead? I don't want the bars, the baths. I don't want to connect promiscuously. I don't want sex without caring and love. I don't want to be on cruise mode. I don't want a lot of pornography or masturbation.

I want to be held, rocked, and nurtured.

My heart is very full; since November, since my counseling, since the training—that was the ground work—but then you looked into my eyes, we realized our love for one another, I opened, opened, and I'm feeling very full.

(Friday noon)

I've gotten in touch quite a bit in the last week through Mark, my counselor, and Bob and Ed in my Shanti group, my gay men's support group, and with Steve and his lover last night. (This all sort of came to a head, or came up through the Shanti training.) More than sex, more than "a relationship" right now, what I am craving most, and it is scary to get in touch with, is my desire to be held in a non-threatening, non-sexual, no strings manner. In a way like Dad and Mom used to do when I was young, till the age of six or so. I want to be cuddled, petted, stroked, held, nurtured without any motive other than to just be there in that moment. I've gotten so in touch with this huge void, this lack of nurturing, which has been building for so many years. Even with Michael (longest to date), it was never safe, completely absolutely, unconditionally safe. Maybe with Michael, after the orgasm we would be in a state of stupor or glow, maybe a bit of time here or there, maybe for a few minutes hiding under the covers, but mostly there was always some underlying "effort."

What I began discovering during the Shanti training was that through all the many hours of sex, of cruising, of the chase, was that the nurturing, the total unconditional, effortless, loving, stroking, holding, rocking, nurturing space has not been there except for fleeting moments since early childhood. (Oh, how I long to be rocked in a rocking chair.)

I don't know how long this nurturing will go on with Bob and Ed, if it will at some point become sexual. Last night, Steve and Stephen began to open up emotionally, but it felt so good to be close without the "tension" of the sexual energy. We held each other, and then I covered them up with a blanket, blew out the candles, and left them after several hours of hugging. Maybe new men will come along to hold me.

Anyway, so at least for a little while, I am in a quandary of feeling like "nurturing, rocking, and safeness" and "sexual, passionate energy" are not necessarily to be found in the same person. (Actually I think it is possible, and that just old ways and old tapes from past lovers are coming up.)

Thank God I have come as far as I have. I'm so glad to be moving in with Scott. I feel like I am discovering a whole new way of relating, which the Radical Faeries spoke of, which Scott and Ed and I have done, which was there in the Shanti training. I feel like I want to write a book, or somehow take men on the journey I have started. When I spoke for fifteen minutes in my gay men's group, about my need for nurturing, going all the way back to childhood, it was electric in the room. It brought up so many issues for everyone—lots of tension around the idea of the "sex energy" not providing the nurturing we all need so much. Yet, still, we go after sex because it's the only safe way to climb into a man's arms.

Back to Jimmy now.

Something very powerful has occurred since Friday night when you and I had sex. My heart chakra has really opened up. I don't ever recall having the feeling of my heart being as big as a basketball. It's warm, from about my navel to my upper chest. Lots of chills and energy up and down my spine ... more silence. When I think about Jimmy, chills shoot up my spine.

In terms of love, whatever that is, I don't feel any changes really. My love for you, Jimmy, has been unchanging; it's so strong and a constant feeling. We have gone through so many changes, yet looking back, you have been on my mind in a constant way over the years. It's almost, these days, a devotional love ... too strong a word ... let's see ... focus.

What have you been experiencing? You have called late several times. Things are different for you in the last week. Share with me your thoughts.

I want to be in your life
I want your love and devotion to me
I'm afraid
I'm afraid of your need for lots of sex and the focus I am feeling on me about "relationship"
I want to keep letting go, letting you in
I want to go slow, slow, slow
I'm afraid of the pace I am feeling. I'm afraid of you reading these pages and shutting down from me.

I'm feeling a huge sense of power welling up inside of me. It is coming from this glowing heart. I want, in maybe six months or a year, to start workshops for gay men in how to be safe with each other. It feels like such a warrior feeling.

Jimmy, I love you so profoundly.

I was deeply touched by Jess's letter, but his uncertainty about the type of relationship that he wanted didn't help allay my fears. In contrast to my relationship with Matthew, I felt that I had to gradually grow in love with Jess. I also felt that because of my six-year relationship with Matthew, I had achieved a level of maturity that Jess was still seeking. I continued to share with him my fear of rejection, but the delicate and tender parts of his being continued to pull me closer despite my uncertainty.

I received my first paycheck in March 1983, and Jess was there to help me move out of the office into my own apartment. I had lived in the project's office for ten months and had let my personal life take such a low priority that it took me two months to unpack once I moved.

The demands on the project for increased services were mounting daily. The Kaposi's Sarcoma Foundation (K. S. Foundation) and Shanti had identified an increasing number of people with AIDS who were in need of housing. The idea of creating a residence program for people with AIDS was gaining momentum. The need for practical help for people with AIDS, such as cleaning, shopping, cooking, and transportation services was becoming more apparent. Bobby Reynolds told me that there was a need for some support services at the outpatient clinic at San Francisco General Hospital and there was talk about the possibility of opening an AIDS inpatient unit.

Shanti had an immediate need to hire a volunteer coordinator and someone who could coordinate direct mail and finances. Even though we had just received fifty-seven thousand dollars from the city, plans were underway to ask for an additional two hundred and fifty thousand dollars in July. Jess applied for the position of finance manager. He was interviewed and hired by Sam Mills, our board president, to avoid bias in hiring and potential charges of nepotism.

There was growing excitement about having a Memorial Day candlelight march. Bobbi Campbell, Bobby Reynolds, and a board member with AIDS, Gary Walsh, worked with our staff and the K. S. Foundation in organizing what has become an annual and international event. We agreed that we wanted the march to be a time to honor and grieve for those who had died and to support the living. We also wanted to use the march as an opportunity to bring media focus to the increasing toll that AIDS was claiming on our lives.

In 1983, I had no idea that in the next five years Shanti Project would increase its paid staff to seventy-five, its volunteer body to seven hundred, and its annual budget to over three million dollars. In many ways, it was important for me not to plan too far ahead. In the early years, it was particularly difficult to project the actual number of people who would require services. I tried to limit myself to planning for a maximum of eighteen months ahead.

Over the next five years, I would question my commitment to Shanti a number of times. I would need to open myself to suffering in ways in which I never had. My character would be exalted and degraded. The project's staff and board would need to accept that Shanti was no longer a small family but an internationally respected model, and, as such, would have to confront its unconscious desire to remain insular and comfortable.

Terminations of employees, disgruntled volunteers and staff, staff substance-abuse problems; and the diagnosis and deaths of many staff, board members, and volunteers were yet to be experienced. Yet, despite how difficult the ensuing challenges were, the work nourished and stretched me in ways that compelled me to continue.

Jerry was one individual who challenged and stretched my beliefs to the core. He was a member of our support group, and, because of his unique personality, I decided to work with him individually. Intuitively, I felt I had something to learn from him. He was a lonely forty-five-year-old man who was diagnosed with Kaposi's sarcoma in 1983. Jerry never had a primary relationship, but instead he had a few "fuck buddies" that he would occasionally get together with. He lived alone with his beloved cat. I don't know why I was so drawn to Jerry. He was fairly reclusive and not fun to be with. He had more than seven hundred lesions on his body. Jerry had found a certain brand of makeup at Macy's that concealed most of his facial lesions without appearing caked.

Something about Jerry made him different from the other men in the support group. Part of it was that he was older, but it had more to do with his attitude. Unlike other group members, he had found nothing redeeming about having AIDS. He wasn't particularly interested in the political ramifications or in becoming a spokesperson regarding the illness. He seldom exhibited emotion—except when he told the younger guys in the group that at least he had lived to middle age and that he simply couldn't imagine how he would cope with the illness if he were in his twenties.

After Jerry had been coming to group for a few months, I offered him a massage. Jerry's most steady buddy had abandoned him soon after his diagnosis. Jerry was feeling bitter, and he was yearning for physical intimacy. He was apprehensive about having a massage.

I brought my massage table to his house and worked on him for well over an hour. I felt a wave of fear come over me as my hands glided over his back. I had experienced a similar level of fear the first time I had used a client's bathroom, and the first time someone with AIDS prepared dinner for me. I had felt fine about eating food that was baked, but a salad prepared with loving hands ignited an unreasonable fear. Even though I knew, intellectually, that I was not going to get AIDS from a toilet seat or a salad, I needed to own my discomfort before I could release it. As I looked at Jerry's back, I took a couple of deep breaths into the knots in my stomach. Each time I exhaled, I tried to release some of the fear I was feeling. My fear began to dissipate. Jerry seemed to enjoy the massage.

Jerry's best friend, Bill, lived in Los Angeles. Bill was very upset by Jerry's condition and personally uncomfortable with AIDS. Yet Bill assured me that Jerry was his best friend and that, however difficult it got, he was committed to supporting his friend through the entire process. Shortly before his death, Jerry decided to vacation with Bill in Los Angeles for two weeks. About ten days after he had left, I received a call and was told that Jerry was having trouble breathing and was being flown to Stanford Hospital in Palo Alto. Jerry's doctor immediately began treatment for pneumocystis pneumonia. Jerry had a lot of faith in his doctor, Margaret. Over the next few days, Jerry got progressively worse. Margaret kept trying different drugs, but nothing worked. I had an increasingly sinking feeling that Jerry was dying. I knew that

Jerry wanted to be at home with his cat when he died. He also wanted to believe that his physician could reverse the situation.

The night before he died, I told him that it had been four days since he had been hospitalized and that it appeared to me he was getting considerably weaker. It seemed a likely possibility that he was not going to respond to treatment. I asked Jerry what he thought. Jerry said that he wasn't ready to accept that he was dying. He had faith in his doctor, and she hadn't indicated to him that she had given up hope. I told him that I hoped he was right and asked him if it was all right for me to talk with her. Jerry said he would appreciate it. I went out in the hall and told Bill about my conversation with Jerry. Bill said that Margaret had talked to him earlier that day and said that there was nothing else she could do for Jerry. I asked him why she didn't communicate this to Jerry and Bill started to cry. Bill and Margaret both thought it was better to spare Jerry this information. Bill said that he had called Jerry's sister in Colorado and that she was expected to arrive in the morning.

I could understand their desire to protect Jerry, but I felt that he wanted to know; I thought that if Jerry knew there wasn't anything left for Margaret to do, he might like to go home. Bill didn't know how we would get Jerry home. I suggested that the hospital could have an ambulance drive him home, and I offered to stay with Jerry until we could arrange attendant care. I told Bill that I would tell Jerry about my conversation with him. Bill didn't want to be present, but he agreed that it was best that Jerry should know. When I explained to Jerry what I had learned from Bill, he said, "So that's how it is." He indeed wanted to return home. Margaret came by later and agreed to make the necessary arrangements. Jerry seemed pleased that his sister would be arriving in the morning.

Jerry was in an isolation room at the hospital but there was an extra bed. I told him that I would spend the night. I pushed the two beds together and lay next to him. He had a very fitful night. At his request, the nurses kept increasing the amount of morphine.

I asked Jerry if he realized that, at a certain point, the level of morphine could switch from easing his pain in breathing to actually making it impossible for him to breathe. He said he understood. I assured him that his decision was okay with me, but that it might mean that he would be unable to go home the following morning. Jerry nodded.

Although he had been raised as an Episcopalian, Jerry didn't have a spiritual belief system. I asked him what he thought might happen after he died, and he said, "I don't have any idea if anything will; I have always been an agnostic."

Jerry was too weak to care about covering his lesions any longer, and with his high fever, his makeup began to run onto the pillowcase. As I lay with my friend, I counted seventy-seven lesions on his face alone.

I felt so helpless and angry. I couldn't see any purpose in it at all. I asked myself, *Why do people have to suffer so much? Where in the hell is this compassionate God who supposedly cares for us?* As I watched Jerry get increasingly sicker, I realized that he would never get home to see his cat again. It felt so unfair. Jerry's doctor, Margaret, arrived early in the morning and remained with Jerry until he died, just a few minutes before his sister arrived. As he closed his eyelids in death, I saw three lesions on his eyelids that I had not included in my count. I muttered, "Jesus Christ! Couldn't you even spare his eyelids? What type of a monster God are you?"

During the six months following Jerry's death, I experienced a profound sense of betrayal. My entire belief system collapsed; I didn't believe in anything. There were no pieces to put together. Up until that point in my life, I thought I had things pretty well figured out. I thought I understood the reason people suffered; I had read a number of books on karma, and as I understood karma, things occurred to people in this life that were a result of something they had done in a past life. "It's their karma" people would offer, to explain why a whole group of people were experiencing starvation. I now realized that these same people might conclude that the reason Jerry got AIDS was because he had done something horrible in a past life for which he was now making amends. I felt like such a fool for having believed any part of that crap. I began to question whether the reason people believed these things was to protect themselves from feeling the suffering of others—and, in a sense, their own.

I recalled how, years earlier, I had seen the bloated bellies of Biafran babies on television, but I hadn't in any real sense been open to the reality of their suffering. And, despite experiences working with the dying, I began to see how little I really looked into the face of suffering and allowed myself to experience my own pitiful helplessness.

I thought I believed in a loving God. Where the hell was He/She? I didn't want to hear that metaphysical jargon about how God has given us free will and that it isn't God, but us, who create suffering. If I had any power to stop Jerry's suffering, I would have used it. Shouldn't the creator of the universe be more powerful and compassionate than I was? There was just no satisfactory explanation: God's testing us? Testing us? Fuck! I could find no reason on earth to allow someone to suffer as much as Jerry had. If it was a test, and God so loved us, then why didn't He/She solve it for us? Why not stop this ridiculous merry-go-round of pain and suffering?

I felt like such a fool, so naïve. I was so angry that when I left the hospital, I took the laminated picture of Jesus that was on my dashboard and repeatedly bit it. I didn't want any part of this God crap. I had been fooled long enough.

Friends were at a loss as to what to say to me. Fortunately, most simply listened, allowing me to express my sense of betrayal and confusion. Gradually, I came to realize that much of the grief I experienced with Jerry was my own unexpressed, accumulated grief. Like many, in the process of growing up, I had suffered hurt and merely buried it. Now it was unearthed.

I'm sure that a lot of my collected grief accumulated from growing up in a racist society. Living in Maryland, I had heard the word "nigger" no less than fifteen times a day. I had been the only one in my circle of friends who objected to its use. All of my friends heard their families using it. I recalled that I had had a picture of Dr. Martin Luther King Jr. in my bedroom with a passage he had written about brotherhood and nonviolence. Dr. King's brilliance was clear in the words of that passage. Still, my friends couldn't get beyond the black face on the wall to even read his words. Some of my neighbors had actually expressed happiness when Dr. King was assassinated. Of course I challenged and edified, but what had I done with the part of myself that simply ached in seeing mankind's inhumanity to one another? Where was my pain, which grew with my knowledge that many wish to persecute and kill that which they don't understand?

I had felt similar grief about the people being napalmed in Vietnam. I realized how a part of us clearly endeavors to dehumanize the enemy. Using labels such as gooks, kikes, niggers, and fags can quite effectively allow us to deny that we are dealing with individuals. We become so governed by our fear and desire for separation that we condone annihilation or second-class citizenship for others.

In one of our Shanti training sessions, we had two Native American participants. They wanted to learn as much about AIDS as possible so they could take the information back to the reservations. Listening to them, I got in touch with another layer of grief that I hadn't uncovered: I opened to the personal grief of acknowledging that an entire people's land had been seized, their natural ways ridiculed, treaties ignored, and thousands of people slaughtered.

I thought of the many hours I had spent watching killings on television, rooting for the hero; a pastime that I had used to numb myself to violence, sadness, and the sacredness of life. Again, what had I and others done with the buried part of ourselves that continued to be affected by the suffering of others? Where does grief go that results from the many ways we summarily dismiss and falsely judge our brothers and sisters? Now, Jerry's death was helping me to realize that I must first recognize my own accumulated grief in order to release it.

I heard many say that they feared that if they opened themselves to their grief, they would fall apart and never recover. But how long, as individuals and as a society, can we keep adding layers to this well of unexpressed hurt and pain? With AIDS, I found I could no longer avoid dealing with my feelings. It hit me in my gut and knocked the lid off a well of grief that had accumulated over a lifetime.

In the months following Jerry's death, I saw more clearly that I had grown up in a world in which I was conditioned not to see individuals. By not seeing individuals, I had attempted to numb myself to the devastating effects of racism, poverty, war, and disease. Yet for the world to become a more united and loving place, I knew I must begin to see individuals. This seeing was painful. I had to be willing to have my core beliefs challenged as I continually opened to others' suffering. However, it was by seeing life as it *is* that I found myself and clearly saw my connection to others. It was ironic that through my willingness to open myself to another's pain, I gradually began to experience a greater degree of intimacy and joy than I had ever known.

My heart is now full with the pain and joy of feeling. There still are times, however, when I want to deafen my ears from hearing and shut my eyes from seeing. It is overwhelming to witness parents who reject their children who have AIDS; communities where people carry signs that declare "no AIDS children in our schools"; prisons that isolate inmates with AIDS from the already too few social and rehabilitative activities that are available; and countries that ban entrance to people with AIDS.

In the months following Jerry's death, I didn't easily replace my belief system with another. I didn't want to again put faith in something merely because it made the world in which I lived more bearable. What I came to understand, through Jerry's death, was that the dying process could indeed be extraordinarily painful. Jerry did suffer; he didn't view his death as one big joyous reunion with his Maker. Jerry resigned himself more than accepted death.

Yet what I came to eventually claim was the true capacity of the human heart. Even without any answers to comfort him, I had remained with my friend. However pitiful it seemed, I had supported him through his inglorious dying process. I remained, even though my concept of God abandoned me. Through this process, I had discovered the magnitude of the human heart. Perhaps our greatest lessons are learned when the questions themselves become meaningless and all that remains is our own humanness and how we choose to be in that moment.

I still don't have easy answers to some of the questions I asked myself then. I have found, however, new depths in my ability to love without any sense of reward, moral duty, or pride. I have discovered the place within me that can look in the face of suffering and see it—not obscure it with belief systems or platitudes, but simply see it and remain with it.

I have also found that now, when I grieve, I grieve more authentically. My grief has more to do with the present moment that I am experiencing and less to do with a lifetime of repressed guilt and feelings. Now, I take my grief one day at a time. It is bearable that way, if I also allow myself to open to the joy that life holds each day as well.

People often invalidate their grief by comparing it with others' grief. For example, a trainee might say, "I don't know if I can do this work because I have never grieved." The problem here is one of definition and comparison, not of an unfeeling person. All of us have experienced profound grief, which we would know if we just listened to the murmuring of our hearts. Recapturing the magnificence of the heart often rests in the ability to accept one's own grief and to realize that each of us has always felt deeply about the suffering in the world. If the problem lies anywhere, it is not in our inability to feel but perhaps in being overloaded with feelings of grief at an early age and not knowing how to express and eventually release them. So many people have now convinced themselves that they are unemotional or unfeeling. The opposite is true: our wholeness lies in our ability to recognize this and to reclaim our awareness of our sacred connection to all living things.

Chapter 6

Connecting the Dots

Those who say it cannot be done should not interrupt the person doing it.

Chinese Proverb

In 1983, Rick Crane and Ed Power of the San Francisco AIDS Foundation approached me to talk about the need for some type of long-term residential housing for people with AIDS. They were receiving more reports of people with AIDS who were being asked by their roommates to move out. The hysteria level was very high in San Francisco: Numerous mortuaries were refusing to handle the bodies of the deceased. The technical crew of a major radio station announced that they would walk off their jobs after learning that the station's management was going to have Bobby Reynolds and Reggie Williams, both of whom had AIDS, on their radio program.

Rick and Ed both thought that Shanti was the ideal organization to administer a residence program. I supported the idea, and the board agreed. Rick and Ed assisted in our preparation of a proposal, and their support did much to align our agencies in a common purpose.

In forming the residence program, we wanted to create a homelike atmosphere where residents could live in safety—and continue fully living their lives. We stayed away from creating a hotel-like atmosphere, preferring to keep the concept simple and cost-effective. We learned that if we provided no direct medical services and kept the number of residents in each home under seven, we would not be required to become a licensed residential facility. This was key, because licensure would have been costly and would have taken the project in a direction that we felt was far beyond our original purpose and design.

The next major task was to decide who could direct this project. I thought of Helen Schietinger, the nurse at the Kaposi's sarcoma clinic and knew she would be perfect. Helen was well-respected in the community for her knowledge of AIDS and was well-liked by our clients. Helen had a very secure job at the UC Medical Center, though, and imagining that she would leave it to join ranks with the Shanti Project was beyond my wildest hopes.

I took her to lunch and told her about the new program, adding that I thought she would be perfect in the position. She called me the next day to let me know that she was definitely interested. I was elated. Helen was the third staff member hired, a decision she and I would never regret.

Our idea was to find four- to six-bedroom houses in areas of the city where there were large gay populations and that had easy access to public transportation. Shanti staff would not reside in any of the homes but would facilitate weekly house meetings. Rents in San Francisco were prohibitive for people on disability or general assistance; however, we felt that it was important for residents to pay rent, primarily as a way of staying empowered and maintaining a sense of contribution. Residents would be charged 25 percent of their income to live in the residences. If residents had no income, they would not be required to pay.

Eventually, we located a gay landlord who had two available five-bedroom houses in the vicinity of our project's office. They were newly renovated and seemed perfect. We received word that the mayor supported our plan, so we eagerly signed the rental agreement.

Seven others joined Helen, Jess, and me as we gathered at the new location to have a simple house-blessing ceremony, where we asked for continued guidance in the administration of the program. As we walked through the houses, we left a daffodil in each room, asking the universe to make these rooms places of healing and comfort. Little did we know that our residence program would expand to twelve similar facilities during the next five years.

With AIDS manifesting as such a debilitating illness, increasing numbers of clients needed practical assistance. Shanti's emotional support volunteers often provided practical help as well, but the need for volunteers to provide ongoing basic assistance, such as grocery shopping, cooking, transportation, and housecleaning, was becoming apparent. I developed the idea of establishing a practical support program, based on the same model as our emotional support program. Volunteers were required to attend twenty-two hours of training and make a similar time commitment to clients.

We hired Randy Chelsey to be our practical support director. Randy was a licensed therapist and had served on our board of directors and as an emotional support group leader and volunteer. She brought a wonderful combination of counseling and administrative skills to the position.

In the next five years, the number of practical support volunteers would grow to well over two hundred, providing eighty thousand hours annually of free service to over four hundred clients.

Also at this time, the city indicated readiness to fund an AIDS inpatient unit at San Francisco General Hospital. There was some concern that the creation of the ward would be seen as expressing the need to isolate AIDS patients. The ward was not created for this reason, but rather to provide a setting in which people with AIDS would receive the best care. Cliff Morrison was hired by the hospital to head up the new unit. Cliff had been a Shanti volunteer and very much wanted Shanti volunteers on the unit.

Cliff met with me and said that he expected to take some flak from the hospital's psychiatry department, which he thought would object to a community agency contracting with a city hospital to provide services. Cliff was right, but the health department decided to go with Shanti. After all, at that time we had more experience in working with people with AIDS than anyone. We also had the support of people with AIDS, who told the health department that they didn't need psychiatrists but welcomed the idea of peer support. From the city's perspective, we were far more cost-effective. Once again, we were on our way to creating a model program.

Linda Maxey was hired as the Shanti counseling coordinator on the AIDS unit. Linda was a registered nurse, a former volunteer group leader, and a board member; she was ideal for the position. She had the responsibility of hiring two part-time counselors and supervising an additional part-time counselor who worked in the hospital's outpatient clinic. In five years, the original eight-bed unit expanded to twenty-four beds. There were often an additional ten patients with AIDS on other wards in the hospital who used the services of our counselors. The size of the staff increased to nine, with coverage offered seven days a week, including several evening shifts.

In 1983, Shanti Project had given birth to three programs that would become internationally acclaimed and modeled. We moved the project forward into providing a range of services that would interweave and support one another. Patients and their loved ones at San Francisco General Hospital had daily access to intensive counseling. On discharge, the patients had the security of relying on the services of Shanti Project's emotional support and practical support volunteers. Emotional support volunteers helped our clients make the adjustment of moving into a Shanti residence, as they faced the difficult realization that they could not afford their own apartments any longer. Once relocated, clients were assured assistance with housecleaning, shopping, and cooking by our practical support volunteers.

Each program started as a mere thought and eventually progressed to reality, with the help of thousands of volunteer hours and a dedicated staff and board. Shanti Project was stronger and providing more services than at any time in its nine-year history. There was a power afoot in Shanti that transcended any obstacles. A need was defined, the challenge accepted, the intention pure— and the rest manifested. Yet our growth was bittersweet, for while we were happy that we could create what was needed, we knew that our expansion was indicative of an increasing epidemic, an epidemic that, inwardly, we kept hoping would end.

With the intensification of administrative duties, I was finding it increasingly difficult to connect with clients and friends. In many ways, being executive director was a solitary position; I was not at liberty to talk freely with staff, volunteers, and clients. However, despite the enormous and rapid growth of the project, I continued to facilitate the weekly support group for people with AIDS. Facilitating the group kept me in touch with the essence of the work and provided quality time with those I cared about most.

My friend Paul Dague continued to try everything to cure himself. He experimented with vitamin therapy, interferon, diet, visualization, positive thinking, and a host of other traditional and alternative therapies. Those close to him were in awe. However, it seemed highly unlikely he could cure himself. Yet Paul was so enthused about whatever he was trying that sometimes I found myself sharing his optimism.

Shanti staff and volunteers had a retreat to which Paul was invited. Paul looked grotesque: he had lost all of his hair, and his face was terribly swollen and covered with dark purple splotches. A group of us were getting playful one afternoon and began throwing each other into the pool. I wanted to throw Paul in, but he had his socks and tennis shoes on. Others were concerned about getting him wet. After briefly weighing the pros and cons, we decided to go for it. Paul loved it! He told me later that he had been feeling left out, reminding me how important it was to keep challenging the limitations we place on people with a life-threatening illness.

I had recently learned from Paul's volunteer that Paul had decided to go to the Philippines. He had arranged to be treated by a prominent psychic surgeon. I thought, *Oh lord, it has come to this!* I had recently finished reading a critical expose on psychic surgeons of the Philippines. The book outlined in detail the various tricks and scams a number of "healers" used. I was very skeptical of Paul's journey and debated with myself whether I should give him the book. I decided against it. After all, maybe Paul had found someone wonderful.

I did, however, feel the need to say something to Paul. I told him that I was inspired by his optimism. I was aware of how much faith he had in his ability to heal himself, far more than anyone surrounding him. Paul smiled and said, "Jim, I know that I will very likely die from this disease. My body is not responding to the various methods that I have been trying. My trip to the Philippines is a long shot. But, Jim, I am having one hell of a good time trying to bring about a cure. I am living life more fully, and with greater awareness of my inner ability to manifest what I want, than I ever have before. I feel fully alive!" I was speechless.

Paul went to the Philippines and was treated by his psychic surgeon. He returned to San Francisco and died a few days later. After his death, I became aware that Paul *was* healing as he died—up until his last breath, he was healing the places within himself of limitation and hopelessness. He was continually expanding himself as he went through the dying process. Paul's moment-to-moment consciousness was pregnant with the feeling that he had the ability to move mountains. Even though his body didn't respond as he had wanted, he had succeeded in experiencing the immense power of his mind and spirit. Paul's body was dying but his mind and spirit were continually being born anew.

Before meeting Paul, I had viewed healing as an end result. I thought that in order for a person to have a successful healing, that person's body must regain its former healthy state. Paul helped me understand that healing is a process of becoming "more." He taught me that if we approach each moment as an opportunity for self-discovery, even though the body may wither, the mind and the spirit can simultaneously flourish.

Many persons ask, "How can you support a person in recovery when you know that he is going to die?" I have found that the first thing to admit is that no one knows absolutely when someone is going to die. I can believe that someone is not going to recover but I cannot know for certain. In working with people who were trying to cure themselves, it was important that I remain keenly aware of my own unknowingness. There have been countless documented cases of remissions for life-threatening illnesses, and many physicians who have told loved ones to prepare for a quick death have continued to care for the patient years after the initial prognosis. Moreover, why would anyone want to risk depriving someone of the exalted state of consciousness that Paul achieved? In working with people like Paul, I learned that the best approach was not to break through what I considered someone's denial, but to see the encounter as a gift, an opportunity to learn more about my own healing potential.

Dave Lawson was another close friend who maintained a very positive attitude throughout his illness. I held an image of Dave as the bull in a matador's ring. Dave had been physically very strong before his diagnosis. He had nodular Kaposi's sarcoma, in which the lesions protrude significantly. If Dave bumped himself the wrong way, a lesion could drop off. The circulation in his legs was very poor, and his legs were frequently swollen. Yet, no matter how much life knocked and jabbed at Dave, he kept plugging away.

One day, Dave shared with me a special vision. He told me that he imagined himself standing before a huge door that had an incredibly brilliant light spilling out from its sides and base. In the vision, Dave approaches the door and slowly opens it. As the door opens, his body is bathed and saturated with radiant light. Once he crosses the door's threshold, his body is restored to perfect health. As I listened to Dave, I realized how little I opened myself to knowledge of my own state of health. How many moments did I pause and acknowledge my wellness? When I don't feel well it is hard to concentrate on much else besides my discomfort. However, when I feel well, I take it for granted. Dave taught me that we all have the ability to step through his door into a consciousness of our awareness of vibrant health. Dave, whose body had been racked with pain and sickness, was able to envision a state of health of which I was barely aware.

Many of our clients, in coping with their illness, used positive and metaphysical principles. Although I personally believe in much of what I understand of metaphysics, I think that having only a little metaphysical understanding can be a bad thing; for example, the belief that we entirely create our own reality. Some people interpret this to mean that people create disease through their thoughts. While it seems clear that our thoughts play a significant role in the state of our health, to tell someone that his sickness is a result of his not thinking loving thoughts can do much psychological harm.

When I heard one metaphysical teacher who I had followed and respected for many years speak at a workshop about AIDS, I was appalled. She said that the reason people contract AIDS is that they are too attached to sexuality. She said that if people were willing on a spiritual level to give up their obsession with sex, AIDS would disappear. I challenged her by pointing out that the number of sexual experiences differed dramatically for people with AIDS and that one acquired the disease through means other than sexual contact. Her reply was that everyone, regardless of how they come to contract the AIDS virus, is attached on a deep level to obsessive sexuality. What surprised and disappointed me was that nobody else in the room questioned her; I guess that would have rocked our collective state of higher consciousness.

Undaunted, I continued by saying that I thought she was misrepresenting people with AIDS. She replied that it was obviously my issue, and that I myself should stop being so sexually obsessed. I told her that I did not have a problem with integrating my spiritual and sexual natures. I added that many of the people with AIDS whom I had the great fortune of knowing were among the most spiritually caring people I knew. I then asked her about her own sex life! She smiled and thanked me for sharing. Thanking a person for sharing is often a polite New Age way of saying, "I still think you are an asshole, but I want to move on." I left the seminar a hundred and fifty dollars poorer, but richer in my own ability to recognize and confront guilt and blame, even when I am speaking to a so-called enlightened being!

It is easy to misuse metaphysics as a defense system. Some people are so afraid of looking at their own fear that they adopt a metaphysical mindset as a way of not dealing with difficult issues. One metaphysical minister in San Francisco, upon learning that two of his friends had been diagnosed responded: "What part of you doesn't want to be well?" I see such masked terror in many of those who subscribe to positive thinking. They grasp at this belief system as a way of protecting themselves from the possibility of getting AIDS, and as a way of insulating themselves from the many other painful realities of this world.

A number of well-respected pioneers in the field of death and dying and metaphysical thought, including Dr. Elizabeth Kubler-Ross, Louise Hay, and Stephen Levine, began offering workshops for people with AIDS. Many of our clients attended these workshops and found them to be very valuable. Others felt that the workshops were too process-oriented; they wanted a more social and recreational focus.

Bobby Reynolds and Dale Hansen, our two board members with AIDS, identified the need to offer a recreational activities program for people with AIDS. Bobby, Dale, and a close group of other friends had been getting together at one another's homes over the months to play pinochle. Bobby and Dale thought that there must be a lot of people with AIDS who get bored in the daytime and would welcome a chance to socialize. They invited their good friend, Ron Carey, to meet with me to discuss their ideas. The initial meetings led to the creation of a new program, the Persons with AIDS Activities Program, affectionately referred to as the "fun squad."

Events were small at first—a special holiday party or an afternoon of board games. We then began planning picnics and field trips, and we began scheduling at least one major event every month. Fun squad members approached various movie houses and theaters to arrange for free or discounted tickets. We eventually hired a program coordinator to organize the events and produce a monthly *People with AIDS* newsletter. We also began to have regularly scheduled weekend retreats.

We felt that Wildwood, the Russian River resort where we had our staff and volunteer retreats, would be ideal. The resort sat on top of a mountain, surrounded by picturesque valleys. The panoramic view of the valleys and surrounding hills was breathtaking. The resort also had two hot tubs and a swimming pool. There was a redwood grove where people could sleep in tents in the warmer weather, as well as cabins, which could accommodate fifty. The staff maintained beautiful gardens and was available to cater meals.

Never having created a retreat for people with AIDS before, we were nervous about what to do with sixty people for the weekend! I knew I didn't want the weekend to be workshop-intensive; I wanted attendees to have time to relax, play, and enjoy one another's company. I wanted our retreats to be fun, and, as much as possible, a setting in which to forget about AIDS, or at least not have it be the focus of constant conversation.

Jim Skiba, a Shanti volunteer, offered to take on the logistics for pulling the weekends together. The retreats were frequently the first time that participants had been together outside a hospital or clinic setting. It was also likely the first time that a person acknowledged, in a large group situation, that he had AIDS. Attendees often commented on the freedom that they felt in not having to worry if people knew or not. So many participants desired to develop friendships and relationships with others after their diagnoses. At the retreats, they met others who shared a similar diagnosis as well as a desire to connect. It was very exciting to watch people rediscover affection and reclaim intimacy with one another.

All the workshops were optional. One popular workshop, on intimacy and sensuality, was primarily experiential and ran for two hours. The session started by asking participants to form two concentric circles facing each other. The inner circle remained stationary, while the outer circle kept moving one person to the right. As participants stood facing each new partner, the facilitator instructed them to interact in a specific way. As a person continued to move from partner to partner, the interactions become more intimate. At varying points, participants might be instructed to softly make eye contact and share a smile with their partner; outline with their hands their partner's body; gently touch their partner's face; explore their partner's hands and arms; place their extended palms on their partner's heart; hug their partner. Participants were instructed to take turns, while the person who was being touched was asked to keep his eyes closed. This exercise was a great way to interact quickly with a large number of people, effectively helping people to loosen up and feel more comfortable with both touching and being touched.

Next, we paired partners and asked them to take turns responding to such questions as, "What would you like to receive from and bring to this workshop?" "How can you bring more intimacy into your life?" or "Share with your partner a sensual fantasy." After both partners responded to all the questions, they were asked to form groups of four. Each person was then invited to share with the small group three qualities that he felt made him a sensual person. Participants were then instructed to share with each group member something sensual or intimate that he could envision doing together. Responses included taking a walk in the woods, singing, sitting by a fire, watching the night sky, massage, and a host of other sensual pleasures. The questions occasionally made people uncomfortable, particularly if they couldn't think of anything to say to other group members, or perhaps worse, if others couldn't identify anything they would like to do with them! However, the exercise helped people break out of the rut of thinking that, to experience intimacy and sensuality, they needed to be with Mr. or Ms. Right.

Afterward, we would have one member of each group lie on a pad and be massaged by other group members. We played soft music, and each person was massaged for ten to fifteen minutes. People were given the option of removing clothes to their individual comfort levels.

The workshop ended with what we called the "car wash." Participants formed two close lines facing one another. The person at the beginning of the line, with eyes closed, slowly began to pass through the two lines. The stationary participants massaged the person as he passed. After the first person passed the first three people, the next person slowly followed. The exercise ended when the last two people forming the original line walked through.

During the summer months, the pool was the center of activity. Many enjoyed listening to music, playing cards, or applauding the last dive of some daring acrobat. If the weather was cold or rainy, people played board games, snuggled up near the large fireplace, or organized an impromptu talent show. A walk out to "Julie Andrew's Point," which provided a panoramic view of the valley and distant hills, was always popular at sunset or at night when ten thousand stars held us in a trance.

We also invited three people to do professional massage for each weekend; they were usually booked solid by the first evening. Weather-permitting, massage was offered right under the redwood grove. We also frequently offered some type of art workshop. Body painting was very popular. Or, as some participants were sure to joke, "Connect the spots!"

To close the weekend, Bobby Reynolds had the idea of renting a helium tank and giving each person two balloons. On one balloon, participants were asked to write something that they would like to let go of, and on the other, something they would like to take home. People were then invited to share what they had written. On the count of three, over a hundred balloons lifted upward. It was always such a gift to see the changes in people's faces by the end of the weekend. As Jess and I made our way down the mountain at the end of each retreat, we often wondered who would not be able to attend the next one. For many, these retreats were their last. Our sadness was eased somewhat by knowing that we had shared the healing gift of laughter and play with so many dear souls and given our all.

Several years later, I had the good fortune to facilitate the first "Healing Weekend for People with AIDS" in Columbus, Ohio. The Ohio AIDS Coalition had heard of our people with AIDS retreats and wanted to offer their clients a similar program. The Ohio State Department of Health co-sponsored the weekend. Fifty-five people with AIDS participated, and, with the exception of one heterosexual male, the participants were all gay men. The retreat was held at the Radisson Hotel in Columbus. Retreat organizers did not anticipate any difficulties with the hotel staff. I was, however, concerned about the response from the hotel's other guests. At the close of Friday's session, a few of the guys decided to go to Bowties, the hotel bar. About twenty of us were enjoying the safety of sitting together in one of the bar's alcoves. There was a cabaret singer, and the dance floor was hopping. A number of us wanted to dance. It was particularly difficult shifting from the caring and openness of the "Intimacy and Sensuality" workshop to feeling inhibited and guarded in a heterosexual dance bar. I spoke up. "How long will it be before gay people can dance together in any bar without being asked to leave or risking violence?"

Suddenly, Sterling, a participant in our retreat, said, "I'll dance with you if you want to!" I could not believe that Sterling would get up and dance.

After my initial shock, I said, "All right, let's go for it!" We were not on the dance floor more than thirty seconds before three additional couples with AIDS joined us. No one on the dance floor said anything derogatory, and we did not notice anyone leave. In fact, several heterosexual couples danced even more enthusiastically as they shared warm smiles with us. We closed the bar three hours later, with everyone forming a circle and joining the cabaret singer in "That's What Friends Are For." I was "blown out." After all, this was Ohio, not San Francisco! There was tremendous healing that night. We had supported one another in removing the psychological chains we placed on ourselves and on others, chains that often hold us back from expressing our beauty and the joy of living. This was one night when we fully celebrated one another and rejoiced in the beauty of ourselves.

Jess and I rarely were able to take out-of-town trips together, but sharing with him these wonderful encounters when I returned brought us joy. We continued to grow more comfortable with one another and our relationship. The following entries from our journals reflect the changes we were undergoing toward the end of 1983.

July 31, 1983 (Jim)

Things are perfect. I get to write on the first page of our new journal, and Jess is making his delicious guacamole. We have had a wonderful weekend at Wildwood. Last night, I experienced a most extraordinary event as I was floating on my back alone in the pool. As I gazed up at the stars, my body began to experience waves of healing electrical currents. Surrendering to the All, I could feel my body being recharged, realigned, and reborn. As I floated in the arms of the universe, trusting completely in the Mighty Unknown, the forces of God were healing me. Oh, sweet Spirit, to surrender to you completely, to realize that all is your grace, your gift, and the sacred energy of life. To know that all is you, and that every expression of beauty is part of the One Prevailing Light, which reverberates, resonates, and resounds throughout all creation. Sweet Sound of Life, awaken us to the constant humming of your heart. Blue-white aura, release your glow to illuminate the dark night. You and you alone inhale, exhale, and are Breath Divine.

July 31, 1983 (Jess)

We're home now, just dropped off Bobby, and we're moving around the house in our usual way, preparing to have sex. Jimmy's singing a song now and lighting candles.

I saw Jimmy's aura last night. It was on Julie Andrew's Point (a majestic spot at Wildwood which offered a panoramic view of the mountains and stars), lying on a bench looking up at Jimmy's face. I saw this white-blue light around his head, extending maybe two inches out from his head. I didn't say anything right at that point, as I thought our friends might think I was hallucinating. I told Jimmy about it later, very profound—but normal too. Looking up at the stars was so powerful.

Friday night, as we all looked up into the heavens, David and Sam told us universe stories and shared their knowledge of the various constellations. We all had realizations, breakthroughs of some sort regarding our knowledge of the heavens.

Bobby was crying in the backseat as we were driving home and singing "You've Got a Friend" by James Taylor. Bobby is such a dear man, and I feel so much love for him.

I am enjoying so much my time with Jimmy. We give each other space in a group but still connect when either of us desires. It's nice to see Jimmy with other people. He so often brings people joy. He was so kind to a man named Paul. Paul hadn't been sleeping well and was very tense. Paul came out of that tense place because of Jimmy's kindness and love.

It's time for lovemaking. It's so nice to be looking at Jimmy now, soon to be kissing.

August 10, 1983 (Jim)

Last night, as Jess and I were making love, and everything seemed right and perfect, I had an insight to what the astral plane was all about. I remembered reading that on the astral plane, you can materialize whatever you want. I realized that what I had wanted for so long, I lay embracing in the form of Jess. In that moment, I realized that we had brought the astral plane to earth. I then began to laugh at my naïveté, in thinking that I couldn't experience the astral plane on this planet. How I so often distance myself from what I believe exists, thinking that the state of attaining and being is so different from what I am currently experiencing. In those moments last night, Jess and I transcended, and what was seen as only something to be experienced after death or by leaving the body was being realized while in the flesh, the here and now, in the arms of my earthly astral lover!

Christmas Eve 1983 (Jess)

It's December 24, early in the morning. Rain, lots of rain, gutters full, wires dripping, furnace whirring, presents under our tree, pine smell, Jimmy's sleeping.

Baby, I'm feeling so happy now. I'm feeling at home, blessed, content. We have had quite a number of amazing conversations over the months. Some have been painful, some scary, some easy, and some so full of light.

I truly do feel like I am on a wonderful path with you to enlightenment. You are such a precious being. Being with you, in several senses of that word, has really helped me burst through so many barriers, roadblocks, and the blurred vision inside my mind that keeps me so separate from life itself.

I'm feeling so much more alive now, so much more awake. There is now such a sense of movement for me. It's like being in a convertible car, floating on an air cushion, going down a warm country road. I am one with the beauty, the smells, the sun in my face, the light in my mind, and the feeling of God. Dear God, I feel so alive.

I want to thank you for so much. It feels so wonderful to be thankful. Listen to each line … take it to heart.

I'm thankful for your love of life.

I'm thankful for your love of me, Jess, this body, spirit, heart, personality, this being, this Godhead.

I'm thankful for your beautiful eyes that twinkle.

I'm thankful for your clarity, for the God in you that sees the God in me.

I'm thankful for your patience.

I'm thankful for your laughter.

I'm thankful for, dear God, your patience, your ability to let me doubt myself, to be scared, to drag my feet, to be sick, to be weak.

I'm thankful for your acceptance of my dullness and insensitivity, which sometimes overshadows my days.

I'm thankful for your parents, for their support of us.

I'm thankful for my job, which came through the God in you, from your indescribable strength and unwavering devotion to mankind.

I'm thankful for your work and devotion to nonviolence.

I'm thankful for your cock and your sensuous butt, your mouth and thighs, and all the times we have made love.

I'm thankful for all the life we have packed into ten months.

I'm thankful for making love on the beach, in Monterey, in Santa Cruz, at Orrs Hot Springs, at Wildwood, over the phone, on the kitchen table, kitchen chair, rooftop, curtains open, curtains closed. I treasure the times we made love in the morning, evening, night, fast, slow, hot, warm, safe, mirrors, fucking, sucking, sighing, crying, screaming, moaning, laughing, stoned, enlightened, beams of light, fucking into the heart, eyes, no eyes, such pure fun. Oh God, all the memories.

Baby, I hope that we can work on your needs too. I'm afraid of confronting you, of bringing you out at times. I think it is because I sense such a delicate nature inside of you. You are very self-contained and strong, but I know that there are areas in your mind and heart that you want to work on. I can see at times what it is that you need to work on, to open to … Busting you open doesn't feel right. How can

I help you to feel like a flower, blooming, delicate, and opening?

I know it is vital for us as a team, as lovers, for us both to be growing. What can I say, what key can I use to open you up? How can I help to melt you in the areas that you need to grow in?

I love you so much. I truly do see the gift you have and the gift that you are. Thank you for sharing that gift with me. I love you so much more than anyone else, at any time, in my life.

Merry Christmas, Baby!
Jess

Chapter 7

Swimming in Molasses

Courage is like an exquisite white cat coiled against a bank of snow. When the creature finally moves, there is a startling moment of disbelief followed by delight and gratitude.

Carol Pascoe

Jess was a godsend at work. He brought a wealth of practical knowledge, amazing drive, and an innate sweetness, which endeared him to all who knew him. He was always more than willing to perform duties beyond his job description, which greatly benefited the growth of the project. With the ongoing help of Matt, who had now grown to be our mutual dearest friend, Jess began the process of computerizing the project. He was in charge of purchasing and bought twenty desks from United Way for five dollars each. After conducting research, he purchased a van for client transportation and a thirty-thousand-dollar Xerox copier that we used to print our volunteer training manuals. He worked closely with each department head in developing their projected budgets, and he calculated the rather complex cost per unit of service that was required by the health department. His accounting system was held up as a model by the health department for other city-funded agencies.

Jess helped me immensely in deciding the best format and style for my quarterly donor appeal letters, which, in 1988, were regularly yielding over one hundred thousand dollars per mailing. He was instrumental in negotiating a ten-year lease on a ten-thousand-square-foot office that we moved into in 1985. The office was remodeled to our specifications and was large enough to accommodate our bimonthly volunteer and community training sessions. Jess also found time to organize logistics for numerous holiday parties for staff, volunteers, clients, and project supporters. His financial acumen and organizational expertise were key in raising the project's annual budget to over three million dollars. Jess was the backbone of the project, and his finance department staff soon grew to five.

Early in our working relationship, we had a few things to define. For the first three years that we worked together, I was Jess's supervisor. At first, Jess wanted me to be both a boss and a lover at work. If I expressed irritation over something that Jess hadn't done, he wanted to talk about his feelings. It wasn't working out. I needed to be able to voice my disappointment without having to deal with his expectation of me to make him feel better. I told him that he would have to take care of his wounded feelings himself. Jess was somewhat shocked by my decision, but he made a one-hundred-and-eighty-degree turn. This experience gave me another clear example of the importance and benefits of honoring my truth.

Jess and I moved in together in September 1983 and were officially lovers. We had embarked on a growing intimacy and trust that would deepen with each passing year. Jess's wonderful, uninhibited sexuality continued to be a source of healing for me.

Sexuality, intimacy, and spirituality—and their relationship to AIDS—are such charged issues, and they continued to be a major focus in our supports groups and in the lives of our clients.

I found that everyone had such deep-rooted and personal views that it sometimes made communication difficult. When sexuality is connected with intimacy, it can become even more confusing.

In coming out as a gay man, it was important for me to integrate my sexuality with my spirituality. On a spiritual level, I had to ask myself if it was truly okay to live as a gay man. I also knew that even if I answered yes to this question, I would still live in a world where the majority of people would say no.

Love has always been my personal proof of God's existence as a transcendental force. During most points in my life, I haven't needed more than this. The experience of love in my life has been so glorious that I cannot accept that a universe created by mere chance could lead to such a transcendent emotion. When I think of the ways in which people are capable of caring for one another, I am no longer able to attribute the magnificence of that to happenstance. People who consciously put their own lives in danger to protect the life of another confirm my belief in a state of awareness that transcends mere survival. This ability, this magnitude of heart, is my proof of something far greater. If I could experience this place within me at various times in my life, then it followed that there is a state of being that can always reside in that place of heightened awareness. I experience this state of heightened consciousness as God's unconditional and perfect love abiding within.

My past thoughts of a punishing God kept me from surrendering into and continually receiving the limitless abundance of God's unconditional love. When I first began to deal with my sexuality, I was still stuck in societal judgments, and I felt that I needed to turn away from God. It was a choice I was willing to make. If God disapproved of the love I felt, then I would be content to go my own way.

However, in certain Eastern practices, I had come to learn, lovemaking is a path to the Divine. When Jess and I made love, I frequently viewed him as a living embodiment of the Divine. Sometimes when we made love, I visualized myself being held by

Jesus, Krishna, or a master of another faith. When I was younger, I also made it a point to look at religious pictures if they were visible when I was making love. If it is really okay to be gay and sexual, then I should have no hesitancy in making love joyously in front of the Goddess Herself, I thought.

When viewing another's sexuality, focusing merely on the physical acts of sexual expression, it can be easy to lose sight of the transformative power and the internal emotional and spiritual connection that is transpiring. By viewing sexual acts from this limited perspective, it may be easy to see certain acts as vulgar and degrading. However, I have come to believe that unless we enter the hearts of those who are involved in sexual ecstasy, we cannot possibly know the depth of the emotional or spiritual connection that is being celebrated and realized.

For my own well-being and emotional health as a gay man, it has been vital that I throw off the chains that others would place on me and trust my direct connection with God in determining how to lead my life. Happily, I can now say I have no fear of God. I can honestly state that I have given up any feelings of shame about being gay. When I think of that joyous day of standing face-to-face with my Maker, my only thought is *Hi Dad or Hi Mom! It is great to be home again!* The fact that I do not feel shame does not mean that I do not feel grief. It's hard to imagine a greater pain than knowing the absolute holiness and perfection of something and seeing how it is despised, ridiculed, and misunderstood by a majority of others. My heart aches when I read about the high rate of suicide among gay teens, when I hesitate to touch my lover in public, or when I see the many ways that gay people compromise their innate spirits daily. For a person such as myself, whose life is about being authentic, it is very difficult to be in situations where I turn from my natural inclinations. It is not a matter of flaunting my sexuality but the desire to express it in the fullness that others are welcomed to express their love and affection. I do this for my own emotional healing, as well as for the collective spiritual evolution of our planet.

Even within the gay community, there were still some who
saw AIDS as a sign of God's wrath. The newly found sense of gay
pride and liberation was still too fresh to offset years of hearing
that our essential nature is sick. Because of society's condemnation
of forming natural loving relations with members of one's own
sex, many gay men had repressed their desires when growing up.
After eventually moving to a more sexually permissive city like
San Francisco, they frequently had sex with numerous partners
but often with very little intimacy. Some men held guilt about
the numerous and somewhat impersonal sexual contacts they
had had, and an AIDS diagnosis added fuel to their feelings of
low self-esteem.

Part of me wanted to grab them and say, "Don't be angry at
yourself!" In many ways it is society as a whole that produced such
a large degree of anonymous sexual activity in the gay community.
If we had been raised in a society that valued and praised the
beauty of gay sexuality, then the expression of our sexuality
would have been very different. But I knew that I couldn't get
clients to feel differently about themselves by merely offering
an explanation. As difficult as feelings of self-hate were to hear,
I knew that I needed to listen, hoping that by doing so I could
help people to eventually be able to release themselves from their
ingrained mental patterns and experience more self-love.

Still other gay men expressed such fear of contracting AIDS
that they became celibate or greatly reduced the amount of
intimacy in their lives. It saddened me to see so many clients
and others close down because of fear. I think that, with many,
it's not just the fear of AIDS that caused them to isolate but
the fear and difficulty of forming relationships based on honest
communication. There are few things as healing as physical
intimacy, sensuality, and sexuality. These are among the most
glorious gifts God has given. People with AIDS are no less entitled
to these gifts. Not only were our clients facing the fear of a life-
threatening illness, they were also dealing with the isolation that
results from having a sexually transmissible virus. For those clients

fortunate to find it, the gift of loving intimacy and informed, safe sexual contact was miraculously healing—physically, emotionally, and spiritually.

Jess and I had found such healing in our relationship. Jess frequently and tenderly told our friends that the closest he felt to Christ Consciousness was when we were making love. After living with Jess for five years, I knew that regardless of how our relationship continued to evolve, as with Matt, Jess and I would always be best friends.

In primary relationships, I have been blessed with not being a jealous person. This is not to say that I don't experience envy! When an attractive person showed interest in Jess, I would humorously assert, "What am I, chopped liver?" Yet my truth remained. If Jess met someone with whom he could truly be more fulfilled, then I would want him to be with that person. I have come to believe that if a decision is right for one person in a relationship, then it will be ultimately right for the other as well. It would be impossible for Jess to be moving in the direction of his highest good without me having the opportunity to do likewise.

Part of this security stems from my awareness that my source of happiness is within myself. Working with so many close clients and friends who have died has reinforced this awareness. I know that, no matter how many times I witness death, within me is a constant spring of new life and the ability to once again feel joy.

Jess and I occasionally were intimate with or dated other people. Jess regularly dated a man named Richard for about six months. The three of us never spent much time together, but Jess did have him over for dinner on several occasions. Eventually, Jess began seeing Richard two nights a week, but he made the decision to come home to sleep. I told Jess that I was fine with him seeing Richard two nights a week but that I wanted to be certain that he viewed me as his primary relationship. What I meant by this was that if I felt particularly vulnerable or upset by some personal issue on one of the nights he was going to see Richard, I would want Jess to reprioritize and spend the evening with me.

This admission on my part led him to confide that seeing Richard two times a week, while maintaining a full-time relationship with me and being so involved at work, was really more than he felt he could handle. He decided to end his relationship with Richard. It turned out to be a timely decision in that Richard was becoming very emotionally attached to Jess. Richard was even fantasizing about Jess leaving me, which was never a possibility as far as Jess was concerned. This experience helped us both to see how difficult maintaining an open relationship could be.

Different people have told me that if their partner had a boyfriend or a girlfriend they wouldn't want to know. I have heard others say that they could handle it as long as their partners didn't bring the other person home. I prefer to have things out in the open. What matters most to me in a relationship is absolute honesty, a commitment to not intentionally hurting one another, and a willingness to take risks in developing deeper levels of intimacy. Jess and I had a relationship where we could communicate whatever we were feeling—not with the expectation of being rescued but as a way of maintaining our own emotional health. Jess and I gradually developed such a relationship, and it did take constant care, patience, and a commitment to always telling the truth.

I was Jess's first long-term relationship. During our first years, each time Jess and I quarreled about something, he was terrified that I was going to leave. Over time, he began to understand that our love could withstand an occasional argument. At the beginning of our relationship, Jess was emotionally needier. He had many issues to work through: his father's death; his alienation from his mother; wanting to please everyone; financial struggles; and becoming more self-reliant. During much of our first three years together, I felt like a mentor waiting for him to catch up.

About three years into our relationship, Jess went through a difficult bout of depression. His former lover, Michael, was dying of AIDS. Jess was also becoming discontent with some aspects of his work at Shanti and his life in general. He was continuing to have a difficult time setting limits with family and friends. Conversely, I was feeling great—except for his depression. I was very enthusiastic and joyous about living each day to its fullest. I wanted to be there for Jess with his depression, yet, over time, I began to feel stifled because the support felt so one-sided. I finally told him that I was no longer willing to conceal my excitement about living in my attempts to help him with his depression. I know it is next to impossible to be with someone who is feeling great about life when you feel depressed, but Jess had been depressed for nearly six months, and I was beginning to feel that my reality was getting lost in his. I also realized how prone we are to focus on depression rather than joy. There is a part of me that feels that it is my moral duty to come to the aid of someone who is depressed. Yet what I realized during this period was how important it is to also support a person in his joy. I understand that it is certainly easy to focus on things that add to our feelings of misery. It takes a great deal of strength to find that silver lining. What I needed was support in living my life in a happy and joyous way. I told Jess that I was willing to spend time with him talking about his depression but that he in turn would have to spend time with me discussing my enthusiasm about life. It was a difficult balancing act for us both, but it worked. It was also crucial that Jess made the decision to get therapy during this time. It was helpful for us to accept that I didn't have to sacrifice my own experience and that it wasn't my role to be Jess's only source of support.

Therapy was immensely helpful to Jess. He found that a lot of his depression stemmed from his emotionally abusive relationship with his mom and his difficulty in finding effective ways to release his anger and hurt. He worked for several months with a wonderful woman, Irene, who had worked extensively with Dr. Kubler-Ross. Irene had Jess beat a phone book with a rubber hose for an extended period while he voiced his anger. Jess ended up sobbing. She then ended their session by giving him a body massage.

Our growing spiritual bond also helped with Jess's depression, in addition to increasing our intimacy and strengthening the foundation of our relationship. We began a study group based on *A Course in Miracles*, which I remained involved with for six years. The Course material comprises a workbook with daily lessons, a manual for teachers, and a text, which tackles everything from the nature of ego to new interpretations of the crucifixion and the Last Judgment. The Course defines miracles as natural and everyday occurrences that take place when Spirit is guiding us. Miracles are insights by which we remember truth when all around us is confusing; they are pauses in which we know that we are the sons and daughters of a living God. One thing that I have found personally transforming about the Course is its basic message, which reminds us that we are always faced with a choice to love or to fear.

During this period, I went through an intense time of fear. There had been much press coverage stating that the conversion rate of people exposed to the HIV virus to eventual AIDS diagnosis was much higher than previously thought. Although the US Department of Public Health later disclaimed these reports, some doctors actually predicted that the conversion rate was 100 percent.

Jess and I had decided not to take the AIDS antibody test. In the mid-eighties, there were not a lot of effective medications for the virus. Many clients were being overmedicated, which, in retrospect, we know was partly responsible for the high morbidity rate and the rapid decline in their health. I knew that there was a high likelihood that I was positive, but not knowing for certain was helpful to me at the time. Not knowing allowed me to focus my attention on my work and keep a positive attitude. Jess and I were already engaging in what was defined as "safer sexual activity." We decided that if we knew we were positive, it would only serve to make us identify more with being sick. I was, however, alarmed by the conversion rate reports, and I found myself becoming increasingly fearful. A metaphysical principle says, "That which one resists, persists." I had found this to be true—and it can be applied to both grief and fear. *What if Jess or I am next?* I thought.

At this time, two of our neighbors were diagnosed within a few weeks of each other. We were living in a three-unit apartment building on the outskirts of San Francisco. Jess and I had heard our downstairs neighbor coughing for some time. I asked his roommate how things were going, and he replied, "He has it!" A week later, I was coming home from a fun weekend at the Russian River, and my other neighbor told me that his lover of four years had been diagnosed. I realized that I had previously viewed my home as a sanctuary, a place to escape from the world of AIDS. For the first few weeks after learning about my neighbors' diagnoses, when I came home and reached for the doorknob, I felt like I was entering an AIDS residence.

Jess and I were sharing a three-bedroom apartment with our close friend and fellow staff member, Robin Rose. Robin was the counseling coordinator on the AIDS unit at San Francisco General Hospital. She had a nine-year-old son, Sam. Jess and I had wanted to bring children into our lives for some time. When Robin's relationship with her lover ended, we decided it was a wonderful opportunity for us to live together. When I thought of how unnatural it seemed for a nine-year-old to have two persons with life-threatening illnesses living in a three-unit building, I got increasingly depressed. I wondered, *My God, how is Sam going to handle it if Jess or I am diagnosed?* Sam had recently told his mother that he worried about her getting AIDS. Sam knew a number of our friends who had died from AIDS, as well as friends who were currently diagnosed. Yet the thought of Sam having to deal with Jess's or my diagnosis completely overwhelmed me.

A week later Jess, and I attended the San Francisco Gay Games celebration. Gay athletes had come from all over the world to participate in competition. As we sat on the benches enjoying the festivities, a friend whispered in my ear that the founder of the Gay Games, Dr. Tom Wadell, had recently been diagnosed. Tom had given so much to the community, and he had written many articles on the importance of taking care of oneself. I became increasingly anxious as I began to imagine everyone eventually being diagnosed. It all seemed so ominous. The more I attempted to avoid what I was feeling, the more it increased. I had hoped that by not talking about it, it would go away. I was afraid to talk about my feelings for fear of where they would lead.

We were having an emotional support training that weekend, and I was concerned about bringing so much of my fear to the training. It didn't seem appropriate to expose the new volunteers to my mounting terror. I had images of having a breakdown the first night of the training and needing to be carried out. Part of me knew that I needed to talk about what I was feeling, but the thought of doing so frightened me even more. I decided to take the risk by first talking with the men in the AIDS support group. I was hesitant to talk about my fear of being diagnosed, since all the group members were already living with AIDS. I thought that the last thing they would want to hear about was my fear of contracting AIDS. I was so embarrassed by my feelings. Part of me felt I was being melodramatic. I felt guilty taking time to talk about my fears, when I weighed them against what the group members were dealing with on a daily basis. I thought that they might find my concerns silly. I had no logical reason to think they would react that way; I had frequently used the group for my own personal support, and the members were always there for me. Despite some members' concerns that if they talked about painful emotions or fears, that would give the emotions and fears more power, I had come to accept that the expression of intense emotions was not negative but healing. I believed that no matter how painful the feelings I expressed were, by opening myself I could begin the process of releasing their hold on me. I decided to take the risk. The group was immensely supportive and actually welcomed the opportunity to give me support. At the group's end, I was still feeling fearful, but I felt better for having reached out. I knew I needed to continue.

After the training, I continued to talk with my friends about my fear of being diagnosed whenever I was aware of it. If someone asked me how I was doing, I answered honestly. Later that week, during our *A Course in Miracles* group, I again talked about my fear. I was surprised to find that everyone in the group was dealing with fear issues. Other members talked about their fear of diagnosis or the diagnosis of friends. They said that many of their friends were dealing with similar feelings. In an odd way, it felt wonderful that I wasn't alone. I began to realize that the reports about the conversion rates had produced a similar fear response in many others—we had all embraced the thought of eventual doom. After talking for a while longer, we closed our eyes to meditate and pray.

I had this image of San Francisco with a heavy fog completely covering the city. The fog was the manifestation of our collective fear. As I looked more closely, I realized that the fog had no substance, in the same way that our fear had no substance. I understood that my fear was not solely mine to begin with, but rather an oppressive, jointly held thought that was hovering in the collective mind. Suddenly, I felt incredibly strong and in touch with my own transformative power. I began to visualize myself breathing in the fog of fear that covered the city and shooting it upward, through the top of my head, toward the heavens. An hour before, I had been feeling terribly self-absorbed, without a glimmer of my ability to heal or extend myself. Now, in my visualization, I was feeling totally connected to everyone and the Source, and I actually felt myself being used as a channel to release an obsession with our collective fear.

Shanti participated in the annual San Francisco Gay, Lesbian, Bisexual, and Transgender Pride Parade. It was always a festive occasion, and we received a lot of support from onlookers. As executive director, I always had the honor of leading our contingent. I used this opportunity to celebrate the uninhibited side of my nature. Jess enjoyed wearing his leather chaps and leather armband, while I preferred to have my face painted with rainbows, wear a colorful Hawaiian sarong, and carry an amethyst crystal wand. We used the wand at the beginning of our volunteer training. Seated in a circle, the volunteers held the wand as they introduced themselves to the group and shared their hopes and fears of becoming Shanti volunteers.

My reason for dressing so colorfully was to help dispel the myth that working with people with a life-threatening illness is terribly depressing. While it is true that the work stretched me to embrace my helplessness and sorrow, it also heightened my awareness of the preciousness of each moment and my desire to live joyously and fully. I wanted to share this message as I marched in the parade!

One year, we had received several serious death threats prior to the parade. Jess and Andy Bowlds, our wonderful and dedicated Information and Referral Program Director, had informed the police department. The police assigned us undercover officers to march in our contingent, while other officers were strategically placed on top of city buildings to spot any potential threat.

Prior to the parade, I informed the several hundred volunteers, staff, and clients who were marching that year of the threats we had received. Considering that these same people had courageously risen above their fears in working with an illness that at the time brought terror into the hearts of so many, their response shouldn't have surprised me. Such was the bravery and commitment of our group that not a single person made the decision not to march. Fortunately, there were no snipers. However, midway along the parade route, we came upon a boisterous group of fundamentalists carrying blood-red letter placards which bore the messages, "Homosexuality is an abomination," "You will burn in Hell!" and "Repent, Repent, Repent." A protective circle of parade marshals had surrounded the fundamentalists, separating them from an equally vocal group of parade supporters who were chanting, "Shame on you!" The situation was highly charged.

As I looked at this confrontational situation, with each side attempting to drown out the other, I realized that I did not want to once again give away my power because of how other people viewed me. I wanted to own and celebrate my beauty as a healer and a child of the Infinite Light. I began to do a very centered, ritualized, fairy-like dance. My inner focus was on using my wand to bless everyone: the fundamentalists, the marshals, and the parade supporters. As I first began to move my body, dancing brought back feelings of how it was when I first made love with a member of my own sex. At moments it felt as if I were swimming in thick molasses, and I had feelings of breaking free from a mold of clay and gradually rejoicing in the beauty and vitality of my own being for the first time.

What was most important to me was that I didn't allow another's judgment to curtail my own essential and loving nature. I was determined to lovingly manifest my own beauty and not allow external factors to thwart my highest vision. As I danced, a hush settled over the demonstrators. I am sure some were stunned and perhaps horrified. But what mattered most was that I had refused to be limited by someone else's limits. I claimed and became one with my power in a joyous and healing way.

A few months after the parade, Jess's mom came to visit Jess's sister, Cathy. Ruby wanted to see Jess, but didn't want to meet me. Jess refused to meet with her alone. After a few phone calls, Ruby consented, and the four of us went out for dinner. While things were tense at first, I decided that the best approach was to just be myself. Realizing that most people enjoy talking about themselves, I began to ask her questions about her life. I spoke with her about the difficulty of being a widow, inviting her to share as much as she wanted about her relationship with Walter. Her desire to talk about her husband overshadowed her uneasiness in opening up with me. We managed to have a fairly pleasant evening, and the ice had been cracked. Jess felt good about this first personal contact with her in five years. She confided to Jess later that, although she disapproved of his lifestyle, she really liked me and was only sorry that I wasn't a woman.

Chapter 8

The Shy Boy from Pacific Gas and Electric

He who has gone, so we but cherish his memory, abides with us, more potent, nay, more present than the living man.

Antoine de Saint-Exupéry

In November 1984, the San Francisco premiere of *The Times Of Harvey Milk* debuted at the Castro Theatre. The film premiere coincided with the tenth anniversary of Shanti Project, and film directors Robert Epstein and Richard Schmiechen selected Shanti Project to be the beneficiary of the proceeds. Bobby Reynolds, Jess, and I attended the sold-out event.

It had been a mere six years since Jess and I had walked by the closed caskets of Supervisor Harvey Milk and Mayor George Moscone. As I watched the film, I recalled that I was just beginning my work with Shanti when Harvey and George were assassinated. Now, six years later, Shanti Project had as much name recognition in the Bay Area as our beloved supervisor had had—and both man and organization were held in the highest regard for their positive impact on our community. The film went on to garner an Academy Award for best documentary, and Shanti Project was the frequent recipient of community benefits and civic awards for outstanding community service.

Bobby, the shy boy from Pacific Gas and Electric, had played a pivotal role in helping Shanti Project become highly respected as a premier AIDS model organization. He had also become my closest friend. No longer worried about speaking before sixteen gay men, Bobby was now seeking my assurance before leading several hundred thousand people in a visualization in front of the Nation's Capitol. He was to speak at a demonstration requesting more federal funding for AIDS. I simply reminded him to speak from his heart. He did. And, as in San Francisco and many other cities throughout the country, his gentle voice and message touched the hearts of all who heard him.

Bobby was so endearing. He was a boy in a man's body. His best friend had been his mother, until she died when he was seventeen. His father partly blamed his wife's death on the stress of having a gay son, and Bobby's only sister remained estranged until the last few months of Bobby's life. Bobby longed to be loved and accepted. Bobby and I talked about the rejection that he felt in his life. We both found it curious that now, with his AIDS diagnosis, he would again be dealing with people's rejection. Perhaps this time his own self-acceptance would make it easier, his focus having shifted to helping others with their fear and ignorance rather than quietly hurting alone.

Bobby had lived with his lover, Mark, for five years. Bobby and Mark shared a cheerful home in the hub of San Francisco's busy Castro District. They idolized one another and had developed an intimate and sensual relationship. Bobby's gentle and unassuming nature also provided a balance for Mark's highly-strung personality. Mark was a caterer and could be quite persnickety. Everything in Mark and Bobby's home had its place. There was a proper way and time to do everything. If you screwed up, you could count on catching hell from Mark. Mark was not one to hold grudges, though; he would just level you with a zinger that made his point and move on. Everyone tried to avoid being his partner in pinochle because he got very prissy if you misplayed a card! Mark also managed a gay softball team and, of course, the whole point of playing was to win!

Mark came from a large and very supportive family. Mark's family didn't meet Bobby until after he was diagnosed with AIDS. Mark decided that when he took Bobby home to meet his folks, he didn't want them to know that Bobby had AIDS—Mark wanted them to get to know Bobby first. Mark's family loved Bobby, and Mark told them about Bobby's diagnosis soon after their visit. Mark's family remained intimately involved in Bobby's life throughout his illness.

I had plans for Bobby after the first time we met. Bobby often referred to his shyness, and that was something I didn't want to accept. My plans for Bobby included breaking down the stereotypes regarding people with AIDS and solidifying Shanti within the community of people with AIDS. Bobby was aware of my expectations and the role I wanted him to fill. One of Bobby's most powerful abilities was his willingness to put himself in emotionally charged situations and speak his feelings.

A number of other spokespersons with AIDS were angry, and in many situations, their anger was completely justified. But Bobby's was a quiet voice. He had the gift of knowing that the most important people to reach were those who were in front of him. He wasn't striving to become a national spokesperson or a poster boy. Bobby felt compelled to share his own personal experience as a way of healing and affecting change in others.

Bobby and I roomed together at the second National AIDS Conference in Denver, Colorado, in 1983, where we were presenting. We had spoken together on numerous occasions at hospitals, city health clinics, and community forums. I had been asked to conduct a workshop on the psychosocial impact of AIDS. I was scheduled to present with a slightly arrogant representative of New York City's Gay Men's Health Crisis. When I had called my co-presenter to plan the workshop, he proclaimed, "Well, you and I are the only ones in this country who know what the psychosocial issues are. It makes sense that we are doing this workshop together." I was left with the feeling that the only reason he included me in that statement was that I had been asked to present with him. I told him what format I thought would work well for our two-hour segment. I suggested beginning with a visualization as a way of helping people get in touch with their feelings. "Oh, that Marin County, California, stuff," was his retort. I also told him that I wanted to have a person with AIDS speak at our workshop. He was concerned about whether that person would be an effective speaker and how much time he would take. I told him not to worry, and I said that Bobby would present with me in my time allotment and that what he had to say would be relevant.

Except for my unintentional reference to Gay Men's Health Crisis as Gay Men's Health Collective, which many found humorous and more to their liking, the presentation was a huge success. Bobby and I worked on the visualization together. It helped people get in touch with their feelings and be open to how AIDS was affecting their lives. My New York co-presenter was crying when Bobby finished reading it. He later told me that in New York, they just don't deal well with feelings. He thanked Bobby and me for helping him to learn an entirely different approach to coping with the stress and grief of the epidemic.

I remembered a time when Bobby and I spoke at a San Francisco health clinic, and the first six rows of chairs were empty. Bobby began, "It could just be me being overly sensitive, but when I see these empty rows up front, I think you must be afraid of me. You are not going to get AIDS from sitting closer. I need your support." The empty seats were immediately filled.

At the conference, other people with AIDS warmly embraced Bobby. They gravitated to his simple message. "I am a person and not a statistic. I hurt like you. I will tell you what it is like to live with this disease if you will listen." In Bobby, people with AIDS had found a voice that contained the presence of mind and the presence of heart that was necessary to educate others. During the national conference, Bobby met with others and formed what was to become the National Coalition of People with AIDS.

Bobby and I also had a chance to play together on that trip to Colorado. We checked out a few local gay clubs, went to an amusement park and rode the roller coaster, and drove south to Colorado Springs to visit the Garden of the Gods. I felt so grateful to have time with my friend as we walked through the giant rock formations. We, too, were pillars of strength, God-like beings that taught and played together.

Bobby lived and breathed Shanti. He devoted almost all of his time to supporting people who were newly diagnosed, serving on the project's board of directors, and organizing the fun squad. He sent birthday cards to all the clients, wrote the monthly *People with AIDS* newsletter, and helped with updating files. He was always thinking of ways to improve our services and to create new services that would be meaningful to our clients.

Bobby was not one to wear jewelry, but one year for his birthday, I bought him a crystal to wear on his neck. When I arrived at his house for his birthday party, I realized that I had not taken the time to get fully in touch with what giving him the crystal meant to me. I circled the block a number of times, asking the power of God to join with me in that moment and bless the crystal and Bobby. I called on the spirits of Buddha, Jesus, Mother Earth, and every other spiritual teacher I admired. I asked that Bobby be imbued with the power necessary to fulfill the tasks that lay before him. Bobby loved the crystal and wore it every day for the next three and a half years.

The diagnosis of Bobby's lover, Mark, was a shock to all of us. We had thought that it would be Mark who would be present to care for Bobby when his time came. Mark quickly succumbed to the devastating effects of the illness. His neurological system was greatly impaired, and he lost his ability to walk. Mark spent considerable time on a respirator with Bobby at his bedside. While

Bobby was so involved with Mark, I handled many of the speaking engagements and training sessions with other people with AIDS. I asked Bobby how he felt about me forming close relationships with other people with AIDS. He said he was jealous, but he realized that was what I needed to do.

During this period, I did a fairly effective job of setting limits. I reminded myself that Bobby had an emotional support volunteer and numerous friends. While I could offer him supplemental support, I was not his primary support person. I also didn't want to compete for his attention, because I knew that we had a deep respect for one another. Quantity of time together was not as important, for it was the quality of our connection that mattered most. Regardless of the chaos that might be happening when Mark was in the hospital, Bobby and I would find a corner where we could sit and check in with each other.

Mark's death was very difficult for Bobby. Bobby returned to Mark all the support that Mark had given him in those two years prior to Mark's diagnosis. He was left now wondering who would be there to hold his hand when his death came.

Bobby, Mark's family, Jess and I, and a few friends went to Yosemite National Park to scatter Mark's ashes. The chips of white bone stood out on the clear floor of the lake in which we scattered them. Bobby blew bubbles and spoke of rainbows. But his bubble of safety in knowing that Mark would be at his side had burst, and the end of the rainbow which Bobby believed would reunite him with Mark was still nearly two years away.

Shortly after Mark's death, Bobby began another relationship with a dear man with AIDS. Bobby enjoyed the intimacy for a while, but he came to realize that his new relationship was only intensifying his grief over Mark. Bobby decided that it was best to end the relationship and focus on working through his grief.

I hired a new staff member to take over a lot of the volunteer projects that Bobby was involved in. Bobby supported the hiring, as he admitted that he could no longer assure that the newsletter would be published on a regular basis. Bobby was involved in the hiring interviews, but a friend whom he wanted to fill the position didn't have a green card, and the position was offered to another person. Bobby was disappointed that his friend couldn't be hired. He began to frequently criticize the person we had hired to others on staff. As a board member, these actions were inappropriate.

Other staffing problems began to arise, and I was swamped. I was dealing with an employee in upper management who had a serious cocaine problem. The employee was not honest. Since it was difficult to trust him, I had to undertake a long process of information gathering regarding his drug use and his poor work performance. Eventually, I made the decision to fire him. Interpersonal problems arose among the residence program's staff, and there were serious morale problems with the Shanti staff at San Francisco General Hospital. My relationship with Bobby became strained as I found myself relating to him less as a friend and more as a bothersome board member.

More people began to complain about Bobby behaving inappropriately with staff. I met with Bobby to see whether we could address his concerns, but, after a number of meetings, it became clear that Bobby's real issue was an inability to accept that he was no longer able to run the activities program the way he wanted. He wasn't able to do this emotionally or physically. He was losing his sense of purpose. I suggested that some of the frustration and anger he was experiencing was his unresolved grief over Mark. This suggestion seemed to resonate with him. Bobby didn't like getting irritated at staff and feeling that staff was avoiding him. I think that seeing his behavior as a result of repressed grief allowed him to be softer on himself and others.

When Bobby's grief began to lessen, dementia set in. He became forgetful of conversations and things he had agreed to do. Bobby assured me that whenever he had a complaint regarding a staff member, he would take it to the assistant director in charge of that employee's program. Bobby also agreed not to talk to one staff member about another. Yet he continued to do these things and I kept on hearing complaints from staff regarding his actions. I found myself wanting to avoid him.

The information and referral staff asked to have Bobby's desk relocated to another part of the building. It was awful; the man who had given so much to so many was deteriorating daily. I realized that my desire to avoid him was not because he had become a nuisance but because I wasn't ready for my friend to die.

At board meetings, Bobby increasingly became the lone dissenting member because he didn't understand the issue. No one quite knew how to handle it. Carol Tocher, a close personal friend and our wonderful board chairperson, and I were in close communication regarding how best to handle Bobby. There certainly didn't seem to be any easy answers.

A previous board member, Gary Walsh, who had died from AIDS, had resigned when he recognized the first signs of his altered clarity. Now I was asking myself, *Should Bobby be asked to resign from the organization he had devoted the last four years of his life to?* Would we be able to see through our own denial and address what we witnessed happening to him?

I met with him in December 1986. I told him about the changes I had observed in his mental clarity, and we talked about his need to let go. Bobby told me that he wanted to be remembered as a teacher and a healer. He said that he would like to make a video with me before he died, and I assured him that I would set it up. I also told him that I felt he needed to refocus his involvement with Shanti. His attempts to oversee staff members' work were unhelpful; he needed to trust the management of the project to handle staff supervision. I suggested that he focus on what he could now do best, speaking during training and through the speakers' bureau. Bobby was relieved to have a clear sense of how I wanted him to continue to contribute.

My friend needed to know that he was still wanted. I don't think Bobby ever stopped looking to me for direction. Bobby asked me what I thought about him remaining on the board. I told him that I felt his disease was affecting his clarity, and that perhaps the board was not the best vehicle for him to offer what he had to give. Bobby said it would be very difficult for him to leave. He considered everyone there his close friends, and he was proud to be a member. I told him if he did decide to leave, he would always be an honorary member and that he had made a tremendous contribution. Before leaving my office that day, Bobby resigned from the Shanti board of directors.

I had once again learned the importance of being honest and telling the truth. It was far more painful experiencing the months of frustration, confusion, and avoidance than telling him the truth of what I was feeling. I forgave myself because I realized that I had not been ready to look at the cause of my friend's behavior. I had not been ready to accept that he would soon die. For years, I had thought that I might leave Shanti after Bobby's death. I felt that I had to see my friend's illness through. In Bobby's death, an era would end.

Six weeks later, Bobby and I made the video. It was difficult because Bobby had deteriorated greatly. He had a hard time concentrating and remembering what he wanted to say. He wanted so much to continue effecting change in people regarding their attitudes toward people with AIDS. Bobby knew that he had played a primary role in educating people about the emotional impact of an AIDS diagnosis. Now that he knew he was dying, he wanted to leave whatever he could behind. A small part of the video's text follows:

Jim: How do you want people to remember you in five years?

Bobby: Well, there are several things that are going through my mind. I want to be remembered as somebody who was loving and who was a teacher, someone who was an activist and an advocate. I guess "loving teacher" is the bottom line.

Jim: What are your thoughts, Bobby, for humanity, something you might want to share with people around the world?

Bobby: I am so impressed with the way in which the gay and lesbian community in particular has responded to this epidemic. Here in San Francisco where I live, we have been there at the grassroots level making decisions that had to be made because our government and our leaders were not making them. We had to develop support services because our leaders were not providing them to us. I have witnessed such a togetherness of spirit.

Jim: Do you have a specific message for people with AIDS?

Bobby: I think one of the most important things for them to realize is that a diagnosis of AIDS does not mean that you are automatically going to die in three months. Hiding yourself away in your room accomplishes nothing, except you becoming self-absorbed. There is a life to live after AIDS. There is a quality of life that you can enjoy. I am talking in general here because there are going to be some exceptions. But you can spend time with your families and with your loved ones. Some people have even found lovers after they have been diagnosed. Each person who sees this tape is going to have a different experience of his or her illness, a different way of handling it mentally. It is important for you to find your own path through this journey, do it your way, and follow your own inner voice. Be well as much as possible. Enjoy life as much as you can, and until we meet again in another place, good-bye brave brothers and sisters. I love you.

A few months before he died, Bobby received an award for the outstanding contribution he had made to the lives of people with AIDS. The award was presented at the sixth National AIDS Conference. Bobby flew to Los Angeles the day he received the award because he was too sick to attend the entire conference. More than sixty people with AIDS lined up in front of the stage and stood before a packed auditorium. The ovation was thunderous as Bobby slowly moved to the stage. There was hardly a dry eye in the auditorium. His own community was recognizing the shy boy who never really understood his powerful effect on others. Bobby was deeply moved and read his now familiar visualization. As he shuffled by me in the front row, I thought, _You have affected_ *people in ways that you and I will never know. This is a well-deserved moment Bobby. Soak it in!*

Jess and a number of other close friends took turns spending nights with Bobby as he became progressively weaker. Jess had told me that Bobby was disoriented most of the nights, and he had frequent bouts of diarrhea and some paranoia. The last time I saw Bobby alive was Easter Sunday. He was disoriented and rambling. He recognized me but didn't know who other visitors were. He was frightened and asked me to stay close. I talked to him about our trip to Denver and what a good team we were. I mentioned his lover, Mark, and he started to cry. Bobby couldn't understand why he didn't have Mark to help him through this time, particularly since Bobby had helped so many others. I wiped his tears and told him that I knew nothing could comfort him as much as Mark. I told him I loved him very much. His sister arrived, and I decided to leave them alone together.

Bobby died a week later. Friends tried to reach me but I didn't arrive at his home until a few hours after he passed. I bent to kiss him. I went to lift his neck but it was as stiff as wood. I was startled at the contrast between the softness of my heart and the hardness of my friend's body. I bent down lower to kiss his body for the final time. Bobby had asked me what I wanted when he died. I had told him I would like one of his jackets and the crystal I had given him more than four years earlier. When the undertakers arrived, the crystal was returned to me.

When Bobby died, many people talked about what a teacher and healer he had been. I was confused as to who Bobby Reynolds was to me. A few weeks after his death, I decided to request a Shanti emotional support volunteer. I had never worked with a counselor in my nine-year involvement with Shanti.

In the months that I worked with my counselor, Rick, I found my friend Bobby again. Bobby's teaching and healing were achieved through his willingness to talk about the things that frightened him, were painful to him, and moved him. Bobby, in many ways, was an ordinary man whose trust and faith in those close to him supported him in risking self-disclosure. Bobby was willing to share his own vulnerable process of dealing with the ignorance, rejection, and grief that stem from an AIDS diagnosis. Bobby shared first of all for himself, because he realized that his own ability to cope rested in his willingness to face what he felt. Secondly, Bobby shared because he knew others would grow and learn from it.

Bobby and I had walked an incredible journey together. We also walked separately. I am grateful for both.

In October 1987, Jess and I attended the second National March on Washington for Gay and Lesbian Rights. We stayed with my parents, who then resided in Alexandria, Virginia. This event also marked the national unveiling of the Names Project AIDS Memorial Quilt, which was started by Cleave Jones and a dedicated group of volunteers in San Francisco. In the months prior to its unveiling, many of our Shanti volunteers and clients had worked on the quilt; now, many of our deceased clients, volunteers, and board members had panels on display. It was a cathartic and overwhelming experience to witness the quilt displayed on an area the size of two football fields between the Capitol and the Washington Monument. Many visitors openly sobbed as they remembered loved ones and opened themselves to the magnitude of the tremendous loss we had and continued to experience.

The march itself was attended by over five hundred thousand. My parents, Jess, and I were joined by our good friend, Shanti Project's senior assistant director, George Voigt, in marching with thousands of others by the White House. Two days after the March, Jess, George, and I joined six hundred others in participating in mass civil disobedience at the United States Supreme Court. The demonstration was to protest the Supreme Court's recent decision to uphold the Hardwick decision, which held that individual states had the right to determine their own laws regarding sodomy. At the time, many states had laws making it illegal for consenting adults to engage in certain sexual activities. My father helped me create my sign, which read, "Decide Sexual Positions in the Bedroom, Not the Courtroom." After being arrested and held for a short time in a gymnasium, we were released after paying a one-hundred-dollar fine. I would have liked to refuse to pay, but we needed to return to our jobs in San Francisco. Still, it felt good to be participating once again in civil disobedience and sharing the experience with those close to me.

In April 1988, I was selected, with three others, to receive the prestigious Medal of Honor from the University of California San Francisco for outstanding contribution to community well-being. My parents and the two men who had supported and nurtured me most throughout my adult life, Matt and Jess, joined me. I realized that my acceptance of this award was made possible by the thousands of dedicated Shanti Project volunteers, clients, donors, staff, and board members who had joined together and refused to allow their fear of an unknown virus cage their hearts. We had brought the Shanti model across the United States and to many other countries throughout the world. We had looked squarely in the face of fear and realized that love was all that mattered. We were all heroines and heroes. Our collective radiance had brought the world a bit closer.

In October 1988, Jess and I made significant changes. We resigned from our positions at Shanti and moved three thousand miles away to begin another amazing chapter of our lives together. Our resignations came in part in response to complaints filed with the San Francisco Human Rights Commission by a number of former and current staff members. These complaints alleged unfair hiring practices, terminations, nepotism, sexual harassment, and fiscal mismanagement.

During my seven years as executive director, I had approved the firing of several well-respected employees. There was considerable criticism and frustration from other staff and volunteers who were eager to defend these employees. Their complaints centered not only on the terminations but also on the lack of detailed explanations regarding them. As a volunteer, I, too, had been an outspoken critic of the administration when they discharged a popular volunteer coordinator. At the time, there was little anyone could say to convince me that a great injustice had not occurred. Some of the current staff and volunteers felt similarly, and I clearly understood the criticism and anger directed toward me. Yet, in my role as administrator, I realized there was little I could say publicly regarding these discharges *and* simultaneously honor the considerable ethical, legal, and confidentiality issues I was bound by.

The charges of nepotism focused on the assumed conflict of interest between Jess's role as finance director and his role as my partner. The charges of sexual harassment centered primarily on an employee whom I had mooned when she was having a stressful day. There was an atmosphere at Shanti that allowed for and treasured the occasional outrageous act as a way of balancing the work's intensity. It was my intention to bring levity into a difficult situation, and, at the time, it worked. However, when the employee was discharged several years later, she cited the incident as an example of sexual harassment. Another former employee felt that the reason he was fired was that he had not responded to what he perceived as a sexual come-on. Another former employee, who had been passed over for an interview, shared similar feelings.

The Human Rights Commission's several-month investigation yielded no evidence of mismanagement. However, the project's funding suffered because of the numerous, primarily anonymous, allegations that had been reported in the press. The board felt that the situation had escalated to the point where the future of the project would be best served by my resignation.

I took comfort in the continued love and support of many dear board and staff members and the knowledge that I had always held the good of the project in my heart. That support and awareness sustained me greatly. In retrospect, I would have done a few things differently. Like each of us involved, I was going through my own maturing and learning process in the midst of an epidemic that had forever altered our lives.

It was time to let go.

Jess and I had never owned a home together. Our personal lives had always taken a backseat to our professional ones. It was now time to concentrate on being lovers and supporting one another with our own diagnoses, which were just around the bend.

First support group with Bobby Reynolds, (right
of plant) and me, (left of plant) (1982)

San Francisco Mayor Dianne Feinstein
approves Shanti funding (1982)

Robin Rose and Sam at San Francisco Gay Pride (1984)

Jess and me at San Francisco Gay Pride (1987)

Jim Geary

Mark Wood and Bobby Reynolds (1985)

Me receiving 1988 UCSF Medal of Honor; UCSF
Chancellor Julius R. Krevans, left; and UCSF School
of Medicine Dean Rudi Schmid, MD, right

Chapter 9

Choosing My own Sheets

*Whoever you are, some evening take a step outside of your
home, which you know so well. Enormous space is near.*

Rainer Maria Rilke

My parents had driven through Daytona Beach, Florida, on
their way to Miami to visit an ailing aunt. From the little they
observed, they liked the area. My folks and I had wanted to be
geographically closer for some time. While Jess and I loved the
San Francisco Bay Area, the thought of residing in a warmer
climate was appealing. After living in San Francisco for fourteen
years and being so enmeshed with AIDS, our move to Florida felt
like entering an entirely different life.

For the first year, Jess and I rented a small two-bedroom condo
overlooking the Halifax River. The sunsets were spectacular, and,
from our balcony, we could watch the graceful flight of the great
blue heron and the occasional play of porpoises. The Atlantic
Ocean was just a short walk from our front door. It was a perfect
place to heal and to recharge ourselves.

Jess's mother, Ruby, called to tell us that she was making plans to visit us in March 1989. This would be her first visit to Jess's home since he had come out, and only my second visit with his mother. We were both apprehensive but also hopeful that her time with us would lead to some healing. Jess developed a week's itinerary, complete with our favorite restaurants, a trip north to historic St. Augustine, dinner with my parents, and renting a pontoon boat to explore the inland waterways. He also scheduled a few days alone with her, toward the end of her trip, at Disney World. The week went fairly well. The pontoon boat was a great success. Jess was a wonderful captain, utilizing all the boating skills he had learned from his father while salmon fishing. We had a thrilling time viewing alligators, manatees, and the myriad colorful birds Florida has to offer.

Ruby liked my parents immensely. My mom and dad were uncertain at first how they felt toward Ruby, commenting afterward on the tremendous amount of negativity she carried regarding her children. While alone with Jess at Disney World, Ruby told Jess that she had a reoccurrence of melanoma. She said that her physician had said that it was operable, but he was not optimistic about her long-term prognosis. Although she continued to make it clear that she disapproved of our relationship, her visit opened the door of communication. When she called occasionally, after returning home, I felt more comfortable talking with her if Jess was unavailable.

Matt also came to visit us that first year. Matt had remained supportive during our last difficult year with Shanti. It was a wonderful feeling to be affirmed by someone who knew us best. On the morning Matt was to return to San Francisco, I was disappointed that, during his week's visit, he had not seen the porpoises from our balcony. Without thinking, I went out on the balcony and spoke the words, "Porpoises, Come!" three times. Instantly, three porpoises surfaced! I was more than flabbergasted as I went to get Matt so that he could enjoy their command performance.

I had been given a sizable settlement from Shanti, which, coupled with back vacation pay and stress disability for Jess, enabled us to focus on play and relaxation. We agreed that neither of us would seek employment for at least six months.

For the first time in my life, I felt a profound lack of direction. Given the intensity of my involvement with Shanti, I was not surprised. The transitional period to Florida life was difficult. I found great healing in walking on the beach, consciously sending loving energy to those whom I felt I needed to forgive. The Daytona Beach area differed greatly from San Francisco in that many of its residents were retired. The gay community was much smaller and less organized. Meeting friends was difficult. I found myself relying on and discovering my love for Jess in new ways, which the following letter reflects:

October 3, 1989

Dear One,

My mind is blank except for distorted rumblings, which seem to lead nowhere. Yet the idea to write this letter to you has excited me. Prior to thinking of you, I thought of writing this letter to myself. I have been feeling a feeling a lack of anyone special in my life I desire to share with. In California, so many dear and close friends surrounded us both. I never had time to be aware of feeling alone. Being basically self-reliant, the depth of my affection now and my desire to rely on you frequently catches me by surprise. At night, sometimes when you lie sleeping, I watch you silently for a while and feel such awe that you are still in my life. We both have let go of so much: satisfying careers, friends who now walk a different path, and many loved ones who have died. It feels like we have been reborn into another life. In those silent moments, I rediscover the thrill of being in relationship with you.

Darling, at times I feel so alone, not particularly melancholy but totally self-contained and detached from the world. When I feel numb, empty, without purpose and direction, the thought of you lifts me from despair and I feel I belong again. You, sweet Jess, are the music when I have no song to sing.

What pleasure it is to relax into loving you. To realize that one, who in some ways, I previously viewed as my little brother, is now the flame of my being. I feel that I have just begun to tap into the fullness of you. You, dear gentle brother, lover, are the one I have been searching for. And the wonder is that it is you who now remain by my side. How difficult at times and yet how wonderful it is, to simply stop and enjoy this tender awareness.

I love you.
Jim

Before Jess seriously began to look for employment, we decided that we would take a trip to our favorite vacation spot, Las Vegas. When we lived in San Francisco, we vacationed in Reno and Las Vegas frequently; being there seemed to be such an effective way to let go of the world of death and dying.

Our favorite game was joker wild video poker. In video poker, you are dealt five cards and given the option of holding any or all of them. The "wild" joker offers the opportunity of getting four of a kind more frequently, which pays twenty times your bet. If you're lucky enough to get five of a kind, you win two hundred times your bet. However, the big prize is getting the royal flush, which, on the quarter machines, pays a minimum of one thousand dollars. We meticulously studied the odds on which cards to hold, and we often quizzed each other, in hopes of improving our playing skills. Since our usual vacations were for two weeks, it was important to budget our money daily, keeping close tabs on our winnings and losses. Amazingly, we usually broke even—most of the time my winnings covered Jess's losses!

I began to play duplicate bridge several times a week, forming a close and nurturing relationship with my eighty-year-old bridge partner, Margaret Pennypacker Wisner, or Peg. Peg and I shared being only children. Her mother had been a classical pianist. Peg was born in Asbury Heights, New Jersey, and grew up in Philadelphia. She fell in love at fifteen with her first husband, Ed, who was twenty years her senior. They married when she was seventeen and never had children. Ed was the love of her life; they were married for twenty-five years before Ed died of cancer. Peg married again five years later and was with her second husband, Jim, for over twenty years before he died. Peg had a degree in business administration from the University of Pennsylvania and had worked as a fiscal manager for a psychiatric institution.

After Monday night bridge, Peg often invited me home to share a few beers and to talk about our lives. She lived alone and was nearing the point where she was considering moving into a retirement home. Caring for a home was becoming a chore. She knew that Jess and I had begun looking for a place to eventually buy. One night, she half humorously, half seriously suggested getting a house large enough for the three of us.

The possibility of getting a larger home, with the three of us sharing it, was appealing to me. Jess thought the arrangement was also worth pursuing, so we began a six-month search for the ideal setting. Eventually, we found a four-bedroom, four-bath Mediterranean style home, with a swimming pool and a large fireplace made of coquina and sandstone. The house was in Ormond by the Sea, between the Halifax River and the Atlantic Ocean, about six miles north of Daytona Beach. In addition to helping us with the purchase of the house, Peg wanted to pay rent. Jess and I met with Peg's lawyer and negotiated a mutually agreeable rental agreement.

Six months prior to moving, Jess had begun working at a temp agency. Well-paid positions are sadly lacking in the Daytona Beach area, where most jobs are service-related or centered on tourism. After having a well-paid position at Shanti, the transition was difficult. However, just before moving into our new home, Jess began working as a temp for the United States Postal Service. His supervisors quickly recognized his ability to work without close supervision and he was assigned to jobs in which his many skills could be utilized. His self-esteem improved greatly.

Three months after moving to our new home, we had a housewarming party. Peg invited many of her bridge friends and Jess and I extended an invitation to all of our neighbors. Our neighbors were all retired and heterosexual. We figured that the best way to fit into the neighborhood was to just be ourselves. My parents provided our guests with tours of our home, including the upstairs bedroom, which they casually referred to as Jess and Jim's room. Everyone seemed to be comfortable with how open we were, and in the years that followed, we were invited to a number of get-togethers at our neighbors' homes.

Jess and I began to make a few friends. We had met Pete, a man with AIDS, through one of my bridge partners. Pete had recovered from a bout of pneumocystis pneumonia several years earlier, yet was still working full-time. He drank too much but had a good heart. Pete had been raised in the South and shared with us that his grandfather had been a Grand Dragon with the Ku Klux Klan. Despite Pete's past, it was he who joined me at a counter demonstration when the KKK came to Daytona Beach in 1992. The KKK had chosen Daytona Beach to launch their new campaign in Florida; they advocated the death penalty for all homosexuals.

Three Grand Dragons and about forty of their supporters met at City Hall, carrying placards advocating the death penalty. I had made several placards and Pete carried one that read, "Blacks and Jews Yesterday, Gays Today, You Tomorrow?" Pete specifically chose that placard. I was so proud of him. My banner read, "Two

Guys Under the Sheets Are Wonderful, One Guy Under a Sheet Is a Shame." My banner caused quite a reaction; even KKK members couldn't help smiling at my unabashed shamelessness!

Relocating to the South was a challenge, particularly after living in a progressive city like San Francisco. Jess and I needed to make it clear on numerous occasions that racist and sexist terminology was not welcome in our home. I found myself telling several bridge partners that I was sickened by their comments. I decided to confront their behavior directly, instead of speaking ill of them behind their backs. This approach worked miracles. Still, it amazes me how deeply rooted bigotry remains and how vigilant one needs to remain in addressing it.

One of the first improvements we made to our home was purchasing a spa. It was like having a touch of California in our backyard! I landscaped a rock and cactus garden around the spa. Jess never missed a morning soak in the warm water or a night soak, gazing at the stars.

Jess developed a love for gardening and, before long, our front courtyard and pool area were resplendent with jade, rubber, and philodendron plants. One day, Jess told me that he viewed himself as a steward of our land and not a property owner. He felt that it was his role to lovingly care for it, eventually to release it to the next owner in better condition. I was very touched by the wisdom of his words.

Ruby returned to visit our new home, and, to our surprise, she brought with her Jess's eleven-year-old niece. It was a sweet trip and a big step for his mother to share our relationship with her granddaughter. I wrote Jess the following letter for his birthday.

May 20 1990

Dear Jess,

   Happy birthday, darling! Thirty-six years old! I continue to feel that every day is a birthday celebration with you. I feel that on your birthday, it is I who have received the biggest and best gift of all—You!

How blessed I am to have you in my life. One of the best things I did in my life was to attract two wonderful men into my life. I am so thrilled and complete in the lover relationship part of myself. I never knew I would feel such happiness, contentment, and desire to continue to share my life with someone. I love you, Jess Andrew Randall, more than I have ever loved anyone in my life.

I love the daily experience of seeing more of you. Your immense talents that you manifest around the house and your drive and ability to figure things out awe me. I treasure the way you interact with people, your sensitivity, your many acts of kindness, and the way you appreciate others.

I am touched by the genuine thoughtfulness you show Peg. I admire the way you rose to talk with your brother and keep moving through your pain with your mother. You make a wonderful uncle and are such an inspired communicator with children.

I am so proud of you, specifically the way you interact with neighbors, how you meet them eye to eye and share your brightness and enthusiasm with them.

I am aware of the security that you bring to my life—no longer a younger brother whom I feel the need to take care of, but an equal in whom I find comfort and safety—-one whom I can hold onto and who will hold me back.

In this world of prejudice, it is such a comforting feeling to be with someone emotionally strong enough to stand tall and speak his truth in the face of bigotry. I feel that strength in you, Jess, and it fills me with peace and security.

And, darling, you are still my young boy stud in heat; your handsome shining face and soft but muscular body excites me wildly! Your mouth is the tenderness I melt in and the most tender that I have ever kissed.

Happy birthday, sweetheart! Life's sweetest nectar wanes in the light of my love for you.

Jim

Jess took a test, with seven thousand other individuals, for a full-time position with the United States Postal Service at the end of 1990. He scored in the top seventh percentile. We were very proud of his accomplishment, and he was eventually hired. It was a great job for the Daytona Beach area and provided excellent benefits.

I focused on caring for our home, devoting considerable time assisting Peg, and coordinating additional help for her. Part of our initial agreement was to cook dinner for her three times a week. Yet it was soon obvious that her health was declining and that she required more assistance. In the first year of living with us, she developed a very painful case of shingles, which required hiring someone to help with her physical care. She designated me her power of attorney.

Peg shared all holidays with us. She had a special Christmas stocking for the fireplace, and when speaking with her friends, referred to herself as our adoptive grandmother. Peg was a member of the local yacht club and enjoyed having us escort her to dinner weekly. She also loved going to the symphony and purchased season tickets for the two of us.

Peg, Jess, and I soon began to attend a small Quaker meeting twice monthly. It was a particularly quiet group, even for the Quakers! Usually, only one or two persons felt moved to share. Yet for the years we attended, it provided wonderful grounding. I found the absence of ritual greatly appealing, with the focus being on meditation and listening to the voice within. We took turns meeting at different members' homes and followed our meditation with a potluck luncheon.

In July 1991, Jess and I adopted a four-year-old longhaired Chihuahua from the local humane society. Patsy was particolored, primarily black with white and tan highlights. Her previous owner was moving into a retirement facility that didn't allow pets. Timid and gentle by nature, she was destined to bring such joy to our lives. Weighing only six pounds, she was the perfect traveling companion. I purchased a pet-carrying shoulder bag, and whenever she realized that we were going out, she ran to the bag, attempting to get in. She was in many of the fanciest restaurants throughout the United States and Canada, and was so quiet and well-behaved that no one even suspected we were sneaking in a dog! Patsy provided great company for Peg and did her best to share her affection equally between Jess and me.

For my fortieth birthday, Jess and I stayed at the local Marriott. My parents, Peg, Pete, and a few close friends joined us for champagne in our room before dinner. It was a fun evening, and Jess and I were enjoying a relaxed morning in bed when the hotel fire alarm sounded. We slipped into our coordinated full-length robes and made our way to the hotel lobby. To our slight embarrassment and amusement, the other guests had apparently taken time to get fully dressed. Oh well, I guess we can be the most effective instruments of change when we aren't even trying!

Jess was frequently asked to work extra hours at the post office. Although the money was good, the stress was immense, and the need for vacation time acute. In April 1992, we decided to go to New Orleans. Jess and Michael had been there for a few days while they were dating but I had never gone. We were both very excited. A few days before we were to leave, Jess called me into the bathroom. He was looking at his gums. He showed me a white pasty substance. As my fear rose, my heart sank into my stomach. We were quite certain it was thrush, but we tried to rationalize that it was a result of the tremendous stress he was

undergoing at work. We had always said that we would postpone
being tested until one of us exhibited signs of HIV infection. Jess
was able to easily brush the substance off of his gums. We decided
that we would decide what course of action to pursue during our
time in New Orleans.

My sweet darling was now manifesting the beginning signs
of one of our greatest fears. How I longed to make it go away—to
will him to health—to not give any additional power to my rising
fear. New Orleans, with her many charms, would make that
easier: there was Bourbon Street, delicious Cajun food, horse
races, and late night revelers to lose ourselves in. And yet, still
before me, the most precious person in my life lay vulnerable.
The short journey before us was a respite, the longer one at times
would be a nightmare.

Jess and I reached the decision to be tested while driving
across Lake Pontchartrain. We had seen the large lake, which
lies north of New Orleans, on a map. We felt that a leisurely
drive would give us an opportunity to weigh the pros and cons
of being tested. In the early nineties, treatment options were still
limited, but consensus seemed to support medical intervention
as a way to prolong life. We knew, however, that a definitive
confirmation that we were positive would greatly affect our lives.
We had witnessed many times how a diagnosis of AIDS had
consumed the life of friends. For so long, we had optimistically
focused our daily meditations on affirming our health. Jess had
come to believe, because we had been asymptomatic for so many
years, that we were negative. I honestly felt that it was a matter
of time. I couldn't imagine how we both could have avoided
exposure to the virus considering our past sexual activity.

Upon returning from New Orleans, we were both tested.
The results were more unsettling than either of us had imagined.
We both tested positive for HIV, Jess's t-cells were 117, and mine
were 264. The Centers for Disease Control criteria for an AIDS
diagnosis included anyone whose t-cells were below 200. Jess was

dazed and depressed. I was heartbroken that Jess's t-cells were so low and immediately became protective.

We both started medication and began the difficult process of telling family and friends. I had tried to prepare my parents throughout the years by telling them I was certain that I had been exposed. However, nothing could prepare me for having to share with my parents a confirmed diagnosis and the likelihood that I would die before them. Mom did her best to remain strong for me, but I know she was devastated. Dad was silent but supportive. It was comforting knowing that my mother had my father to rely on. Fortunately, my parents had grown to respect and deeply value my relationship with Jess, so there was no judgment about having contracted AIDS because of going against God's plan.

Ruby, on the other hand, responded by reminding Jess that she had never approved of our relationship. Her comments included, "You reap what you sow," "You've always done what you wanted to," "I'm so glad I have my religion," and "I've had so many disappointments with you kids." Jess was deeply angered and hurt by her reaction. He wrote her a seven-page letter, which he opted not to mail.

Peg responded with much love and support. She decided to redeem two certificates of deposit that she had in our names. She wanted to be sure that we would use the money while still feeling healthy. Peg's own health continued to deteriorate, as she had been diagnosed with emphysema and congestive heart failure. She required daily oxygen.

Jess and I began attending an HIV support group offered by our local AIDS service organization, Outreach Inc. At first, it felt awkward for me to be a group member and not a facilitator. However, Annya, the group facilitator, was skillful in encouraging group members to interact with one another. I soon grew comfortable giving feedback to others and sharing my own feelings and process. Jess found it helpful to talk about his difficulty with the disease symptoms, which he was already manifesting. He told me that whenever he talked in group about the diarrhea, fatigue, or night sweats, it was his way of acknowledging what he was dealing with and letting it go.

Jess and I decided that if we had a limited amount of time with good health, what we most wanted to do was travel. Since most of our financial assets were invested in our home, my parents lovingly decided to buy our home so that we could use that money for travel.

I pressed our doctor for a prognosis. I wanted a timeframe so that I could better allocate our money. After some hesitation, she said that a five-year prognosis for Jess seemed reasonable. She added that new medications could of course increase his life expectancy.

Jess's supervisor at work advised him not to tell other employees about his health condition. He was concerned about employee hysteria, and he wanted to have time to educate employees about HIV transmission. This recommended course of action greatly added to Jess's stress and isolation.

Peg was now eighty-four and dreamed of returning to Pennsylvania to visit with close friends. Jess and I made the decision to accompany her in May. I arranged for oxygen and a wheelchair both on the plane and at her friend's home. We stayed with her friend Rose, in her Kenneth Square home. The dogwoods, lilacs, and azaleas were in full bloom, and it was if all of the beauty of spring had released itself to welcome us.

Rose's neighbor's son had recently died from AIDS. Upon learning of our condition, the young man's father shared the tremendous grief and isolation he felt. Once again, I marveled that there are no accidents in life and that we are continually guided to be where we are needed.

All of Peg's five closest friends were in their eighties and each required some help in walking. Before going out to dinner one evening, I took group pictures outside. Jess and I then escorted each of them, one by one, down the path to the car. It was very sweet, and they were overjoyed at being in each other's company once again. Jess was touched by their enduring love and found great joy in assisting them.

Later that year, Jess and I returned to San Francisco. It felt empowering to reclaim the city, going to our favorite places, and on a Sunday morning stopping by the quiet Shanti office building. We visited close friends in the city, including Matt and our former roommate, Robin. We also stayed for a few days with Jess's sister, Cathy. Cathy had separated from her lesbian partner of many years and had recently married a caring man, Terry. They were living among the redwoods in Los Altos, California. It was comforting being with Jess's sister. Cathy had always been supportive and shared Jess's frustration over the lack of communication with their mother.

I shared with Cathy a recent frank discussion I had had with Ruby, in which I had confronted her on her hurtful communication with her son. I had asked her point-blank if this was the type of relationship that she wanted to have with her son in what could very possibly be the last few years of his life. I told her that both Jess and I were *very* aware that she didn't approve of our lifestyle and that it was unnecessary and immensely painful to bring this up in every conversation. She accepted what I had to say, appreciating my honesty, and began to be a bit more reflective in the way she communicated.

In the fall of 1992, as I was painting our garage door, a neighbor whom I had noticed before stopped to chat. Jean was in her early sixties and lived on the same block. She quickly confided that her "friend," A.K (Anne Katherine), was in the last stages of emphysema and that she was caring for her at home. I liked Jean immediately and invited her to lunch at our home later that week.

I learned that Jean and A.K had lived in the house they currently owned for twenty-five years. They had met in Illinois during a period when Jean was an active alcoholic. A.K had a small, jockey-like build, and, early in their relationship, she frequently passed as a man. Jean said that they had gone to heterosexual dance clubs, swanky restaurants, and hotels and no one was the wiser. Since moving to Daytona, they were not out to anyone. I had a hard time imagining living in a community for twenty-five years, socializing with close friends, and keeping my sexual orientation totally private. She told us that A.K was confined to bed and that A.K was hoping she would pass soon.

Jess felt that his job was adding to his overall deterioration. He was approved for full disability in September 1992. Because he had been a full-time employee for more than eighteen months, he was eligible for full benefits.

I decided that the upcoming presidential election afforded me a perfect opportunity to make public my HIV status. I wasn't looking forward to telling everyone individually about my condition. As an active member of three duplicate bridge clubs and an avid tennis player, I knew that everyone would eventually find out. I wanted to announce the news directly and not leave it to word of mouth. I decided to have a number of T-shirts made that bore the message, "I Am HIV Positive, Elect Clinton-Gore, Our Lives Depend On It."

Almost everyone was very supportive. However, a friend who was a board member of one club told me later that the board had discussed whether it was okay for me to use the bathroom. Fortunately, the board members were sufficiently enlightened to realize that my HIV status posed no threat. I campaigned locally for the Clinton-Gore ticket, and we had a festive election eve party at our home. Jess created banners for the party, centering on the popular campaign theme, "Not One Person to Waste."

In February 1993, Jess and I returned to Las Vegas. Jess loved skiing, and during our stay, he went skiing at nearby Mount Charleston. The night before he went, he drew a royal flush on the quarter machine and won twelve hundred and fifty dollars. We were both very excited! I had never been skiing, so I opted not to go. Jess accepted my decision, because, as an advanced skier, he knew we would not be spending a lot of time together. Jess had the ominous feeling that this would be his last skiing opportunity.

His physical stamina was beginning to slowly decline. Because of his waning energy, he was only able to ski for half a day.

From the onset of his diagnosis, Jess had only responded marginally to drug therapy. His t-cells never rose above 160, whereas my t-cells steadily increased. We found it difficult to go to our doctor and receive our different reports. While I was glad that I was responding to the medicine, my relief was overshadowed by my awareness that the drugs were not working effectively for Jess.

In March, Peg decided that it would be best for her to move into an assisted living community. She knew that Jess and I wanted to travel, and, since she had fallen and broken her arm during our recent trip to California, she didn't want to be left alone for an extended period. We had shared three years together and brought much happiness to one another's lives. I helped her move into a local facility, and, when we were not traveling, Jess and I visited her a few times weekly.

In April, we purchased an eighteen-foot trailer, which we pulled with Jess's 1986 half-ton Chevrolet pickup. For our maiden journey, we attended the Gay and Lesbian March in Washington DC. Jess wanted to stay in national or state parks whenever possible. He enjoyed sitting around a campfire, listening to birds and the rustling of small wildlife.

We were fortunate to spend some time with Pat Norman and her lover, Karen, at the march. Karen was holding their new baby, and we were carrying Patsy. It had been five years since we had last seen Pat and Karen, and seeing them and their new child brought us much joy.

Jess and I joined my parents, Matt, and other close friends in the parade's PFLAG (Parents, Family, and Friends of Lesbians and Gays) contingent. As we walked past the White House, arm in arm, carrying Patsy, we received jubilant applause. It was healing to share special moments like these with my parents.

The highlight of the weekend, however, was in attending an interfaith service and celebration at the Washington Cathedral.

The church was packed with over three thousand attendees. When one minister proclaimed, "I am here to say that we are gay and that God loves us," all three thousand people spontaneously rose to their feet and applauded for several minutes! It was the most alive I can ever remember feeling in a church.

When we returned home, Jess noticed a few suspicious lesions on his torso. They tested positive for Kaposi's sarcoma. Since they weren't severe, our doctor began freezing them with liquid nitrogen.

For the next three years, we took a three-month road trip each summer. My parents bought a pop-up trailer and accompanied us on all three trips. My folks had never traveled across the United States or visited Canada. I had never been to many of the national parks that Jess and his family had visited in his youth. It was wonderful sharing the beauty of North America and Canada.

In the summer of 1993, we drove diagonally across the United States on our way to visit Jess's home state of Washington. Our first major stop was Atlanta, where we visited the inspirational Dr. Martin Luther King Jr. museum. Jess was very moved by the inscription on Dr. King's memorial stone, "Free at last." After spending a few enjoyable days in Little Rock and Hot Springs, Arkansas, we stayed the night in Oklahoma City and visited the decimated federal building where more than one hundred sixty people had died. We prayed with onlookers at a community altar that had been created and that was overflowing with candles, teddy bears, and notes to those who had lost their lives. Returning to Garden of the Gods in Colorado brought back so many sweet memories of Bobby for me. It was exciting to share the mountains of the West and see their awesome beauty reflected in my parents' faces. We headed north to Badlands National Park in South Dakota, and drove through the beautiful Black Hills on our way to Mount Rushmore. We gambled for a few days in Deadwood, where the four of us monopolized a five-cent progressive video poker carousel. Jess soon got the royal flush and graciously split his three-hundred-dollar jackpot four ways.

Next, we headed east to Devils Tower, Wyoming, which had been made famous by the wonderful film, *Close Encounters of the Third Kind*. We spent an incredible five days in Yellowstone, where bison came right up to my parents' cabin window. Moose, bear, elk, and coyotes were at home in meadows of wildflowers, waterfalls, geysers, and extraordinary thermal activity. Driving by the majestic Grand Tetons, we followed the Snake River through the beautiful state of Idaho, but not before visiting Craters of the Moon National Park, a little-known North American volcanic wonder. We entered Washington at Spokane and took the scenic northern route through the state. It was exciting to be in Jess's home state, and I understood and appreciated him more as we traversed his native soil. Before making our way south to Seattle, we camped for several days in the North Cascades National Park, skinny-dipping in the cold water and finding solace on the wooded trails.

We stayed at Ruby's for three weeks. The first hurdle was getting Ruby to let Patsy in the house. Ruby did her best to act disinterested in the dog, but when she wasn't aware that we were looking, we frequently observed her smiling and talking tenderly to Patsy. Ruby had my folks stay in her room, while Jess and I found it more comfortable to remain in our trailer, which we parked in her driveway. We had some wonderful day outings with Ruby to Mount Rainier, Snoqualmie Falls, Ballard Locks, Pike Place Market, and lunch atop the Seattle Space Needle. My parents' influence helped to soften Ruby, although their unwavering love for Jess and me overwhelmed her at times. Their support was a stark contrast to the attitudes of some of her long-term friends, who were disapproving of gay relationships.

My folks, Jess, and I also explored western Washington, visiting Olympic National Park, where we were awed by the massive driftwood at the ocean and the lush rainforests. We drove north to Victoria, Canada, and visited the beautifully landscaped Butchart Gardens.

We returned to Ruby's, where Jess and I remained another week, while my folks returned to Florida. I took a funny picture of my dad cleaning Ruby's toilet in the nude, and when I got home, I had an 8x10 enlargement made and took the risk of mailing it to her. Ruby thought it was hysterical and responded that she wanted to hire my father to clean her kitchen in the buff as well! She was softening indeed!

Jess and I returned to Olympic National Park and completed a nine-mile hike to the ocean that held many fond memories from years past. He was concerned about whether his energy would be sufficient, and he was disappointed that he was too weak to carry in camping supplies so that we could spend the night. We still enjoyed a thrilling hike, three miles through the woods to the ocean and then three miles along the beach, filled with spectacular driftwood and grazing deer, with the three-mile return along another wooded path. It was bittersweet, in that he was fairly certain it would be his last time there. Yet his joy of sharing its significance with me made the journey a shared treasure.

During our last few days with Ruby, Jess and his mother visited a favorite spot of theirs called Troublesome Creek and had a pleasant day driving in the country, sharing memories of their earlier years. Jess and I meditated in the Japanese Tea Garden, sat by train tracks which held fond childhood memories, and enjoyed visiting a few gay restaurants and clubs. On our last night in Seattle, Jess and I attended a Joan Baez concert. We both had long admired Joan and had the pleasure of seeing her in concert numerous times when we lived in the Bay Area. It was a fitting ending to a healing time with Jess's mom.

The Oregon coast was breathtakingly beautiful. We took time to enjoy the spectacular Oregon Dunes National Recreational Area and to experience the wonder of Seal Rocks. Heading into Northern California, we got permits to visit the world's tallest redwood trees, and found that the area reflects the serenity and the sacred sanctuary created by monitoring and limited access.

We basked in the early September sun of Lake Mendocino before visiting friends in San Francisco and making our way south to the extraordinarily picturesque Big Sur area. It was there, sipping drinks on the spacious deck of Ventana's restaurant, that we met a couple who would become our special playmates for the next five years; friends who would intimately come to know the painful yet more often joyous journey of spending time with a dying friend.

Chris and David lived in Petaluma, California, had been married for ten years, and were in the Big Sur area celebrating their birthdays. David was a successful stockbroker in San Francisco but was seen as a bit of an oddity at his firm. To the dismay of his coworkers, he was prone to offering hugs to other partners on their completion of a lucrative deal. Moreover, unlike others at the firm, he felt that he was making plenty of money and enjoyed taking considerable time off, vacationing with Chris throughout the world.

In part, it was the type of vacations that they enjoyed that most startled others at his firm. They relished backpacking in Morocco and Turkey, white-water rafting throughout the United States, and viewing the Bay Area from Angel Island and its unique vantage point, where they frequently enjoyed camping with friends. Chris and David loved getting to know people, and, on their trips, they went out of their way to mingle and sometimes live with people of different cultures.

Chris was a social worker and therapist who had worked for a number of years at Planned Parenthood. She had recently started working at a hospice. Whereas David's eyes were brown and his physical appearance unassuming, Chris wore brightly colored sundresses, and her emerald eyes clearly conveyed her emotional vibrancy and empathy. She was gregarious, articulate, and very flirtatious!

They invited us back to their campground that night for a late night supper. We had them over to our campground the next morning for breakfast and a hike. They marveled how we were living our lives—holding in one hand the possibility of healing and in the other the awareness that our time might be limited. Our conscious commitment to using whatever time we had together in ways that enriched and brought joy to our lives inspired them. Their unconventional lifestyle, warm and inquisitive natures, and zest for living complemented us perfectly. Before we left the following morning on our way to spend a few weeks in Las Vegas before heading home, we made plans to celebrate New Year's together in Key West. The four of us had fallen instantly in love.

In Las Vegas, I won my first progressive jackpot. It was on a joker wild machine. Jess and I had been playing nickels for a couple of hours, and I was down forty dollars. Somewhat disgusted, I told him that I was returning to our room. As I walked past the progressive carousel, I realized that I had eight quarters in my pocket, reserved for tips for the cocktail waitress. To win the progressive jackpot, I needed to play five quarters at a time, but, against all advice, I started with two quarters; on the first hand, I doubled my money. Now I had enough quarters for two plays of five coins. On my last five quarters, I was dealt four crappy cards and the king of diamonds. The machine paid on a pair of kings or aces, so I dutifully held the king. The next four cards completed the diamond royal flush—I won seventeen hundred dollars! My screaming brought Jess and a number of other players running, as well as several security officers. It was such a thrill and such fun to share it with Jess by my side.

We followed through with our New Year's Eve plans with Chris and David. Key West was grand. Chris, David, Jess, and I rented bicycles for the entire week. Jess came up with the idea of playing follow the leader, where we took turns pedaling off in any direction with the knowledge all others would follow. We played a daily game of spades, shared wonderful meals, laughed naked in the rain, and danced at the Copa on New Year's Eve until we could hardly stand.

When we returned home, Peg had become much frailer and needed to move into the nursing wing of her residential facility.

When we were not traveling, we visited her several times a week and transported her by wheelchair to the dining room. Her mind continued to be alert, although she now required oxygen all the time.

I began volunteering with Outreach, Inc. to train volunteers for their newly formed buddy program. I was the primary facilitator for six training sessions, and Jess participated in various segments. It felt good helping out three or four times a year and being able to walk away from the daily responsibilities required of staff.

Jess and I took a week-long trip to Cancun in early 1994. Our room provided a mesmerizing view of the beach, and each day we swam in the blue waters of the Gulf of Mexico. We enjoyed awesome snorkeling, visited the ancient ruins of Tulum and Chichen Itza, and engaged in passionate, erotic lovemaking. Although the frequency of our sexual activity had decreased with the many side effects that Jess experienced from his medications, our lovemaking continued to take us to deeper places of intimacy and healing.

For our second three-month trip, we decided to explore eastern Canada and New England. We were absolutely overwhelmed with the grandeur and raw force of Niagara Falls. We boarded the *Maid of the Mist*, and, as the boat made its way near the base of the falls, we got absolutely drenched and were filled with gratitude in the healing moments of laughter that followed.

Montreal and Quebec were very beautiful and stimulating; however cities were more difficult to navigate and exacted more energy. Whereas my mother and I relished a three-hour French dinner, Jess often tired and would have preferred to enjoy a simple meal in our trailer. Still, he made a tremendous effort to accommodate everyone's desires, and I made certain that he got a nap each day. My parents did their best to understand his limitations. Yet, my mother also wanted to ensure that I, her only child, was enjoying myself the best I could. At times, it was hard for her to understand that my primary focus was Jess's energy and health.

Prince Edward Island was a welcome relief, providing us the opportunity to relax and enjoy charming country roads and the solitude of our campground overlooking the Gulf of St. Lawrence. We entered Maine and explored the beauty of Acadia National Park, the White Mountains of New Hampshire, and the Green Mountains of Vermont.

Chris flew out from California and joined us for an exciting week in Provincetown, Massachusetts. The three of us frolicked in the water at a remote gay beach and began a spontaneous harmonizing of moans and laughter, which we delighted in knowing sounded like a collective orgasm to our fellow sun worshipers on the beach.

Later that year, our friend Jean joined us for a week in Washington DC. Jean had long wanted to visit the nation's capital, and I enjoyed playing tour guide in what was once my backyard. Jess and I had been instrumental in helping Jean through her grief after A.K.'s death. She doubted that she would ever fall in love again, but she was finding joy in the company of friends and travel. She was very sweet to Jess and me, keenly aware of our energy and stress levels, and had become one of our closest friends. When we traveled with my parents, it was Jean who watched our home, handled our mail, and attended to bills that needed to be paid.

Our friend, Pete, passed away in April 1995. Jess and I had visited him often at home and in the nursing home. I was with him the day before he died. He told me that he was trying his best to merge with the Light. About six months before Pete passed, he had held a huge party at a local club. He had decided that he didn't want a memorial service following his death but a chance to celebrate with his friends one more time.

Jess's Kaposi's sarcoma continued to slowly worsen. He got several lesions on the side of his face, in his mouth, and in his groin area. On his torso and back, he had about twenty-five lesions. The freezing treatments were getting more painful. His oral thrush was getting much harder to control, and he was regularly taking medication to increase his appetite.

In the summer of 1995, we took our third three-month trip. We focused on the Southwest, visiting Georgia O'Keeffe's home in the Santa Fe area and the Tiwa Indian Pueblo in Taos, New Mexico. We took the thrilling Durango & Silverton Narrow Gauge Railway in Colorado and climbed into Anasazi dwellings in Mesa Verde National Park. Sitting in Balcony House at Mesa Verde, overlooking the canyon, I was keenly aware of the passage of time and of the beauty and impermanence of everything except the present moment.

Next, we traveled to Arches National Park in Utah. Jess and I took several stimulating hikes, including a moderately strenuous one to the awe-inspiring Delicate Arch. Our former roommate, Wendy, joined us to celebrate Jess's forty-first birthday in Bryce Canyon National Park, where we hiked through the multicolored hoodoos to the canyon floor. We camped for several days at the North Rim of the Grand Canyon before heading to the South Rim. For Jess and me, the Grand Canyon remained the most awesome and beautiful natural wonder. We spent five wonderful days in Sedona, Arizona, visiting the seven natural vortexes and opening ourselves to the healing energy of that magical place.

After being recharged spiritually, it was time for us to enter the neon world of Las Vegas, Nevada, for a few weeks before rendezvousing with Chris and David at Lake Powell, Arizona. My parents stayed in Las Vegas while the four of us rented a houseboat for a week. We had a wonderful time sleeping under the stars, playing in the cool water, and finding secluded places to camp along the endless miles of waterways.

Peg passed in November. She was ready to let go. Perhaps because of her many health problems and age, her passing was easy to accept. She did not want a memorial service, so I arranged for a luncheon to focus on the beauty of her life, and I invited twelve of her friends. I remain grateful for her friendship in my life.

In February 1996, Jess and I returned to Hawaii. Throughout our years together, it had remained one of the most beautiful and healing places to vacation. We had a wonderful condo in Kona, on the big island of Hawaii, overlooking the water. It was a sweet time of lovemaking, snorkeling, smelling flowers, and enjoying mouthwatering tropical food. We had the good fortune of observing volcanic activity at Hawaii's Volcanoes National Park before spending a week on the "Flower Island" of Kauai.

There we visited Waimea Canyon, referred to as the Grand Canyon of the Pacific. We hiked a few miles along the beautiful Na Pali Coast and enjoyed sumptuous brunches while mesmerized by distant waterfalls.

For our final week, we teamed up with Chris and David on Maui. We spent a few joyful days in the Hana area, swimming naked at Red Sand Beach and frolicking in the Seven Sacred Pools that at one time had been reserved for royalty. Toward the end of our Hawaiian odyssey, the four of us rented a condo near Makena Beach. Jess and I had visited Makena numerous times before, preferring the smaller, secluded Little Makena Beach, where clothing was optional.

It was there, on our last sunset swim in the shimmering turquoise water, that Jess kissed me in a most tender and loving way. Jess had always been more hesitant than I to show signs of public affection. On this particular evening, we were one of only a few gay couples on the beach, which made Jess's action all the more significant. As he gazed into my eyes, holding me tenderly in his arms, I had the bittersweet awareness that he knew that this would be our final time there. It is a moment that has, and will remain, etched forever in my mind and heart.

Patsy and me in Florida (1992)

Margaret "Peg" Pennypacker Wisner (1992)

Jess winning the Royal Flush, Las Vegas (1993)

Jess, Chris, and me in Provincetown, MA (1995)

Martha, Jess, and Joe on *Maid of the Mist*, Niagara Falls (1995)

Jean and Jess in Washington DC (1996)

Jess in Hawaii (1996)

Chapter 10

It has been Exquisite

The most I ever did for you, was to outlive you. But that is much.

Edna St. Vincent Millay

Jess's t-cells continued to decline. We optimistically read about each new drug that was soon to be released, hoping for the best, only to be faced with the disappointment of intolerable side effects and his declining immune system within a few months of trying each new drug. Conversely, my overall health and immune response continued to improve. I began to dread calling my parents after our joint doctor visits. Naturally, they were happy about my continued improvement, but when I weighed it against the steady decline in Jess's health, I was often at a loss as to how to respond.

In late March 1996, we received word that Ruby had had a stroke. I encouraged Jess to consider going to see her. I felt that there was still considerable healing that needed to take place in their relationship. Not knowing how long we would be gone, we took Patsy and left the next morning.

Jess's brother, Jack, and his wife, Marilyn, picked us up at the airport. He told us that when he had mentioned to his mother that we were coming, she expressed disapproval about us staying at her house. After all, what would the neighbors think! Fortunately, Jack left the decision to Jess. After getting unpacked at his mother's home, we went to visit her in the hospital. Ruby warmly welcomed Jess and told him that she loved him. She gave me a pleasant hello. I was a little guarded, prepared for anything, but when we told her where we were staying, she seemed to take it in stride. It was clear that she was glad that we had come and would be by her side.

The next morning, she was withdrawn, mostly unresponsive, and paralyzed on the right side. When she was awake, she was also having difficulty seeing and focusing, and she was having considerable abdominal pain. Although we learned from her oncologist that her melanoma had spread and was inoperable, the nurses were planning an aggressive approach of forced feeding and rehabilitation.

Ruby had long ago indicated to us that if she ever reached this state, she wanted no heroic measures. When she had a lucid moment, I explained to her that she had had a stroke, and we talked about her overall prognosis. It was very clear that she wanted to let go. I summoned the head nurse, who confirmed what I had already surmised by asking Ruby a few key questions. Morphine was ordered and plans were made to move her into the first available bed at hospice.

For the next three weeks, Ruby demonstrated amazing resolve and inner strength. Knowing of my work with Shanti, Ruby had asked me early on how she might expedite the dying process. I told her that by limiting her food intake, she could speed up the process. For the next three weeks she refused all food, often opening her eyes just long enough to ask me how much longer I felt she had to live.

Ruby had great spiritual faith and was eagerly looking forward to being reunited with her husband, Walter. Jess and I made a tape recording of her favorite music, which she found immensely soothing. I also stood behind the head of her bed and gently massaged her neck and shoulders, which she responded to most positively. Her daughter, Cathy, called daily from California for updates and to communicate her love. Her son, Jack, exhausted from caring for his mother in the months prior to our arrival, and clearly uncomfortable being with someone who was dying, visited for short periods weekly.

Ruby was temporarily transferred to a skilled nursing facility while we continued to wait for an opening in hospice. It was there that Jess and I attempted to wash her hair. We had secured a special basin for shampooing hair in bed. Midway through the process, I commented to Jess that the shampoo he had handed me wasn't producing any suds. On closer observation we realized that we were using mouthwash for shampoo! Ruby rolled her eyes and smiled, as if to say, "What can I expect next from these two!"

The Seattle hospice was a beautiful setting. Ruby had a spacious private room, warmed by the morning sun and made cheery by the bird feeders that had been lovingly placed by the large windows. For the first ten days in hospice, Ruby remained in a coma. Jess and I visited for a few hours in the morning and the evening. After the tenth day, Ruby suddenly came out of her coma. She was thrilled to see us. Ruby was radiant and almost childlike as she requested chocolate ice cream and milk. The nurses openly expressed their shock that she was eating and conversing lucidly.

After enjoying her snack, she asked Jess and me where she was and why she was there. I felt my heart sink as we oriented her and reminded her of her stroke and her decision to come to hospice. As she listened to our words, I could see her excitement about interacting with us wane, as she once again resolved to let go. A few minutes later, a chaplain who had been checking in on Ruby stopped by. Jess asked his mother if she would like to meet him. When Jess introduced them, Ruby told the chaplain that Jess was her youngest son, from Florida. Ruby then smiled at me and said, "And this is Jim, who is like my third son, and whom I love very much." Jess and I smiled at one another, warmly treasuring the healing that had occurred.

A few hours later, Ruby slipped back into her coma. For the next several weeks, she had brief moments of awareness. I kept her updated on what was happening physically and how close I thought she was to the end. She greatly appreciated my honesty, and having a likely time frame made her dying process more tolerable. I also assured her that I would continue to care for Jess until they were reunited. She responded, "Thank you, I love you, Jim."

We visited her on the Sunday evening before she passed. She was very agitated—she was continually rambling, had extreme facial twitching, and made loud, unsettling sounds because of the increasing build-up of fluid. Although her vital signs were strong, I had a feeling that she might pass during the night. Jess was very unnerved by her apparent discomfort, although the nurse assured him that she was receiving everything possible. After about thirty minutes, Jess told me that he couldn't handle seeing his mother in that condition and he wanted to go home.

I told him I would drive him home and then return to be with his mother, calling him if it seemed her death was imminent. At 7:30, I called Andy, Ruby's brother, and his wife, Toni, and told them I felt that it was likely that Ruby would pass during the night. They had told us that they would like to be with her at the end, and I wanted to be sure they were prepared to receive a late-night phone call. Andy told me to call.

For the next four hours, I sat beside Ruby's bed wearing earplugs, so that I could tap into a place of calm within myself. I thought that it was amazing that, of her three children, it was her gay son and his lover who were caring for her during the last three weeks of her earthly life. In addition, the head nurse of the hospice unit, who was intimately involved in overseeing her care, was lesbian. Moreover, her nurse that evening was a gay man who had never worked with her before. I believe that this scenario had been divinely orchestrated so that in her last days of earthly life, healing could occur. I was proud of her for rising to the task.

As I held her hand, remembering the hurt and pain she had consistently leveled at Jess and her other children, I forgave her. She had come to see the Light and to realize it is only the love that we hold in our hearts that matters. I am sure that those final hours together were designed to allow our hearts to meet as one. It was our time to make amends, to thank one another for the gifts we had given and received, despite the challenging nature of our time together.

As I let go of my need for further interaction or additional awareness of the unique paths we had walked, her limbs began to go cold. I summoned the nurse and asked him to take her blood pressure, which he was unable to measure. I called Jess, Andy, and Toni, and within thirty minutes, we were all gathered at her bed. Jess was at her side, with his hand on her heart, as Toni gently touched her leg, and I stood at her head softly caressing her forehead. Andy stood rather stoically at her side. I knew he wanted to touch his sister, but his Swedish and family background made touching more difficult. I encouraged him by saying, "Andy, it won't be long, now is the time for touching." As she began to take her final breaths, Andy began to stroke her shoulder, telling her that he would see her again soon.

Jess spoke at his mother's church the following Sunday. He told of the many camping trips that the family had enjoyed when he was younger and the tremendous healing that had taken place with his mother in the last few weeks. At the end of the service, his mother's minister approached us and told us that his daughter was lesbian. He said that when he first found out, he was concerned for her eternal soul. But in time, he had come to believe that gay and lesbian people are placed on earth by God to teach others how to open their hearts to the wondrous diversity and inclusiveness of God's love. If only Ruby had been able to open up to this dear man years earlier.

In June, Jess and I returned West to visit our friends Chris and David. We spent a relaxing week at their home, playing cards, soaking in their hot tub, hiking amid the wildflowers on cliffs overlooking the Pacific, walking among the Russian River redwoods of Armstrong Woods, and enjoying our first limousine excursion. Chris and David had bid on a four-hour limousine rental at a local AIDS auction. They had been saving the experience for a special occasion. On our last night, we were driven to a wonderful Mexican restaurant in Tiburon, overlooking San Francisco Bay. We toured Sausalito, enjoying the breathtaking views of San Francisco while making the most of the cocktail bar inside the limousine.

After leaving Chris and David, we met Jean at the airport and spent two weeks showing her the sights of San Francisco. She had always wanted to visit the "City by the Bay," and it was a lot of fun introducing her to our close friends and playing tourist in a city where we had lived for fourteen years. We attended the yearly Gay, Lesbian, Bisexual, and Transgender Parade. Jean had only read of such sights and was dumbstruck as over a thousand Dykes on Bikes went zooming by at the parade's start!

Later that summer, Jess experienced increased difficulty swallowing his pills. When I examined his throat with a flashlight one afternoon, I was horrified to see a yeast-covered lesion, about the size of a grape, on the back of his tongue. We had talked previously with our doctor about how internal lesions could damage his organs. But, after weighing the pros and cons of chemotherapy, we decided against it because of his overall poor health. Instead, we focused on staying positive, praying, and affirming that the new medication he was taking would work. Jess began a series of radiation treatments that destroyed his saliva glands, resulting in extensive tooth decay. However, the radiation destroyed the lesion, and we turned our focus again to being as optimistic as possible.

Jean, who was now our closest local friend and primary support, suddenly became plagued with severe headaches over her left eye. In November, she was diagnosed with advanced brain cancer and told there was little recourse. Everyone was in shock. I couldn't believe that my primary support person in coping with Jess's illness would now pass away before he did. Jean accepted her situation amazingly well and made the necessary arrangements with her lawyer. As her condition worsened, she was increasingly concerned about being alone. Jess and I moved in with her for several weeks prior to taking her to hospice. Once she accepted that there was nothing that could be done medically, she announced, "I just want out of here!" In April 1997, two weeks after being admitted to hospice, Jean passed away. Several close friends, my parents, and Jess and I were by her side.

Just prior to Jean's passing, Jess and I won twenty thousand dollars in the Florida Fantasy Five Lottery. To celebrate, we returned to Provincetown in May for his forty-third birthday. Despite the suffering pain in his esophagus and considerable reflux, we spent a tender time together. Again, we rented bikes and explored the wonderful trails and dunes. We shared sumptuous meals, delighted in the view from our balcony of Cape Cod Bay, and took a four-hour whale-watching excursion where we were blessed with seeing more than forty whales.

Shortly after we returned home, Jess was hospitalized for severe esophageal thrush. He remained in the hospital for a month and was treated with the powerful and toxic amphotericin B. Jess needed to have a port placed in his chest, which delivered the drug directly into the artery. The drug was administered over a four-hour period, producing high fevers and severe shaking. His doctor said it was the worst case of ulcerative esophageal thrush he had ever seen. Since the hospital where our doctor had admitting privileges was over an hour away, I rented a room in a nearby hotel, spending most of the days and evenings with Jess.

When Jess was well enough to come home, we arranged for visiting nurses. We were told that he might need to continue the amphotericin B treatments three times weekly for the rest of his life. I soon learned how to do his treatments so that his ongoing care would be more cost-efficient. More important—the more that I was able to do, the less intrusion we had in our daily lives. On the weekends, I was able to remove the needle from his port so that we could enjoy our pool and spa together.

Despite the considerable physical difficulty that Jess endured during his last months, he was determined to try every new drug, regardless of its side effects. He told me frequently that he didn't want either of us to be left with regrets that he hadn't given his all in combating his disease.

Sensing that our time together was more precious than ever, I arranged a three-week trip to Las Vegas in August. We stayed at our favorite casino and had a local clinic fax Jess's lab results to our doctor weekly. Our wonderful pharmacist, Randy, shipped all the supplies that we needed for Jess's care in insulated containers packed with ice.

I had purchased walkie-talkies at Radio Shack, in case Jess had a problem while we were separated. On two mornings, prior to receiving his amphotericin treatments, Jess rose early and went downstairs to the casino. On one special morning, I awoke to his excited voice, fourteen floors below, letting me know that he had gotten the royal flush and won a thousand dollars! Despite all that we were going through, I found myself feeling increasingly grateful for moments like these and the way we continued to make the most of very difficult times.

In September, Jess developed acute pancreatitis. He was no longer able to eat and was started on liquid nutrition, which I gave him daily through his port, over a twelve-hour period. Except for beverages, which he continued to enjoy, and a few bites of food here and there, Jess remained on liquid food for the rest of his life.

In October, he was admitted to the hospital because of sepsis. His temperature had hovered around 104 for twenty-four hours. Once he was admitted, they were able to bring his temperature down to 102. However, I remained concerned; the following day, he was to receive his amphotericin treatment, which always increased his temperature. Two hours into his treatment, his temperature was 104 and he became increasingly disoriented.

The well-meaning nurses on duty were unfamiliar with him and thought that the way he was acting was normal for him. Frightened, I called his doctor and left word on his voice mail that I was greatly concerned and felt that Jess needed to be transferred to a more intensive unit. When our doctor called the hospital thirty minutes later, I listened helplessly as Jess's nurse said that he felt that things were under control. The next four hours, until his doctor made rounds, were excruciating for me. Jess's respirations were consistently rapid and shallow. I fully believed that it was possible that Jess could die at any moment. I prayed to God to please give Jess the strength to hold on until our doctor arrived. When his doctor finally arrived, ours eyes met, and I simply said, "This is not right." He took one look at Jess and immediately wrote an order transferring him to intensive care.

When Jess was admitted to ICU, the nurses told me that there was an extremely high likelihood that Jess would go into respiratory arrest in the next few hours. They wanted to know if I wanted them to resuscitate him. Without much thinking, I said, "By all means, yes!" They told me that they needed to work on him for a few hours. I decided to use the time to find a hotel, since I couldn't sleep in his room while he was in ICU. I drove around in circles for an hour, crying, praying, and trying to adjust to the possibility that my precious angel might not be long for this world.

Finally I located a hotel, called family and some close friends, including Chris, who said she would fly out the next day. When I got back to the hospital, the nurses told me that Jess was still very likely to have a respiratory arrest. I told them that I needed to talk with his doctor. When I heard our doctor's voice on the phone, I fell apart. I repeated what the nurses had said, and I added that I didn't want to prolong Jess's agony if he felt it was only a matter of a few weeks. He said that he wanted to treat the sepsis infection as aggressively as possible, and that we should know in a few days if Jess would respond. He said that he couldn't give me an overall timeline on Jess's prognosis, but he felt that it was very possible that we could pull him through this episode.

Jess and I had living wills and durable powers of attorney. We had talked a lot over the years about what measures we wanted and which ones we would refuse. Since he was now completely disoriented, all decisions were solely up to me. Despite his long illness, Jess had still enjoyed a good quality of life a few days prior. He had told me recently that as long as he still had five minutes a day of quality time with me, his life was still worth living. I was now caught off guard. I had felt that when the time came to stop struggling, it would be a conscious decision made in unison.

By the next morning, the crisis had passed. Jess was no longer a high risk for respiratory arrest, and he was starting to respond to the massive amounts of antibiotics they were giving him. They had inserted a gastric tube through his nose, and he could have nothing by mouth. The next day, a consulting physician reordered his amphotericin treatment. Convinced that giving Jess this treatment would lead to respiratory arrest, I told them there was no way I was going to allow it. Because of my power of attorney and health care surrogate status, my words were golden. Jess remained in ICU for ten days before being transferred to another floor.

It was wonderful to be able to sleep in his room again. Chris had brought all sorts of wonderful "California stuff"—incense, candles, rainbow mobiles, and the notorious remote-controlled fart machine! She told us that, during a recent picnic, she had put the machine under the picnic table and, as guests lined up to fill their plates, she had pushed the remote. The machine had five very distinct and authentic fart sounds. Of course, everyone at the picnic thought it was hysterical when they finally figured it out.

Jess had great fun hiding the machine under his sheets, and, when unsuspecting physicians, nurses, and staff entered his room, Chris or I would push the remote. Nearly everyone was too polite to comment. Finally, we couldn't contain ourselves and broke into raucous laughter. It was great therapy, and the machine and our antics were soon the talk of the ward.

In preparation for his upcoming discharge, Jess began working with a physical therapist. The therapist was somewhat arrogant and really pissed off Chris and me. After his initial assessment, and in front of Jess, he commented that it was quite likely that Jess would never walk again. Three days later, Chris and I had Jess walking in the hall. On his first day home, after three weeks in the hospital, Jess insisted that Chris and I help him walk about thirty feet and up five steps to the hot tub. What a wonderful sight it was!

In early December, Jess developed CMV retinitis. His ophthalmologist said that his retinas were beginning to detach, and she performed a series of laser treatments to protect the retinas. Jess started on another intravenous drug, which I administered five days a week. He was frequently nauseous and began taking strong anti-nausea medication every eight hours. Cathy visited in early December, followed by Jack and Marilyn, later in the month. Chris and David, Matt, and my parents joined us for Christmas.

Jess was working at home with a physical therapist and was soon able to walk by himself with the help of a cane. He developed another case of sepsis in February, but we caught it early enough that we could treat it at home. Somewhere amid all the rapid changes in Jess's health, Patsy had gone deaf and was showing signs of fading health.

It was awful at times being aware of my limitations. In the last several years, my father had suffered a minor heart attack and my mother had had a double mastectomy due to pre-cancerous cells. As their only child, I had wanted to be more supportive both emotionally and physically. Yet Jess required so much of my attention. I frequently felt that, for my own well-being, I needed to limit the extent of my involvement with others.

I wanted to get Jess to Las Vegas one more time. The in-home nursing coordinator thought that I should wait until we had Jess's sepsis completely under control, but intuitively I felt that I needed to move now. *After all,* I thought, *who knows what new trials tomorrow will bring.* My parents joined us, and with Patsy under the airline seat in front us, we flew to Las Vegas for three weeks.

We had a great trip. Jess played his quarter video slots and won a number of sizable jackpots. The largest came when we were playing side-by-side on the third day of the trip and I got a royal flush for two thousand dollars. We went to my parents' room and tossed the hundred-dollar bills on the bed and gave them each fifty dollars in quarters to play with. Fortunately, Jess's health remained stable, and I was glad that I had trusted my intuition and that we had gone for it once again.

Except for groceries and occasional doctors' appointments, that was the last time Jess or I ventured out of our home for the next five months. I began to wonder what would be the state of my own health at the time of Jess's passing, and I questioned whether I would have any emotional and sexual vibrancy left to share. At times, I experienced guilt because of this pondering, feeling that I was in some way quickening Jess's passing by entertaining these thoughts. However, most of the time I was blessed with knowing that my thoughts and desires were natural. I also continued to hope and pray that Jess's health would be restored.

Whenever possible, Jess met my emotional and sexual needs. He fondled me as I masturbated, holding me close while kissing me tenderly. While this was different from the form of sexual play we had been accustomed to, I found myself deeply satisfied by this connection. Jess also encouraged me to meet some other HIV positive men online with whom I could share intimacy, however, with the time demands of his physical care and because I was essentially housebound, it was difficult to manifest that possibility.

Jess began to find a lot of comfort in images of the Divine Mother and Mary. He was raised in the Methodist faith and was unfamiliar with the Hail Mary prayer that I had often recited while growing up. I slightly revised the words and taught it to him. He found much peace in saying it. The revision is:

Hail Mary, Full of Grace
The Lord is with us
Blessed are you and all women
And blessed is the Fruit of thy womb, Jesus
Holy Mary, Mother of All
Pray with us, now and forever. Amen

Before long, friends started to send rosaries and small pictures and statues of Mary and of the Divine Mother. Jess said that the image of resting his tired body in the arms of a tender and loving mother image was both powerful and healing for him.

During this period, I was mostly filled with gratitude. I felt that we had been given a second life since we had left San Francisco ten years earlier, and where we had experienced the passing of so many dear friends. In addition, I viewed the last year as a special gift. Ever since Jess had avoided respiratory arrest in the ICU, I felt that each passing month together was a blessing from God. I had also begun to find comfort in the writings of Neale Donald Walsch. The first two books of *Conversations with God* were in print at the time, and both Jess and I found inspiration in reading a few pages each morning, discussing the text, and then meditating together. The second volume was the last book that we completed together.

As I let go of all outside activities and focused on Jess's care, my mother was particularly concerned about how I was holding up. I explained to her that the best way to support me was for her to be here more for Jess. Seeing people I loved getting more involved with Jess was a double gift for me. It gave the person I cared most about more attention, while allowing me to step back and breathe. Fortunately, she understood what I was saying and my parents focused more on being with Jess than on trying to get me to take care of myself.

Patsy became progressively sicker, developing a heart murmur and fluid buildup in her lungs. Both she and Jess were on diuretics for fluid retention. I couldn't believe that my lover and my dog were both dying at the same time. Increasingly, Patsy fainted and sometimes remained unconscious for several minutes. When it first occurred, I thought that she was having a heart attack and was dying. I called for Jess, and, with much difficulty, he got down on the floor to hold her. When she rallied, Jess had to crawl to a nearby couch to support himself in getting up.

In August, Mom and I took Patsy to a specialist, while Dad stayed with Jess. The specialist did a number of tests, including an ultrasound. She told us that it was just a matter of time before Patsy would die; it could be as short as a few days or possibly two months. Patsy was so weakened at the end of the tests and had so much difficulty breathing that I asked the doctor to put her to sleep. They put her small body in a box, which I brought home to my unsuspecting lover and father.

As soon as I walked in, Dad asked, "Where's Patsy?" Jess's and my eyes met and I told him of the decision I had made. Jess had been on antidepressants for several years. While effective in dealing with his anxiety, the drugs had made it almost impossible for him to cry. He had missed the healing release of crying greatly. When I brought Patsy's body in and placed her on the pillow at the head of our bed where she always slept, Jess cried and wailed for about fifteen minutes. Our little dog had provided him with a release that was essential. I held Jess in my arms as he petted her soft hair.

Later, when Jess had fallen asleep and I was alone in our living room, I opened myself up to the finality of not seeing Patsy again.

It was now my turn to sob as I questioned whether I had made the right decision. The veterinarian had assured me that she would have made the same decision. Before making the decision, I had wondered whether, if I was stronger, not simultaneously caring for her and Jess, if I could have nursed her for another few months. But then I questioned whether it would be the best thing for Jess to watch her become progressively sicker and die at home.

I came to fully believe that on some higher level, Patsy decided to pass before Jess. She knew that I was exhausted by my daily care for both of them and that my focus needed to be entirely on Jess. She knew that we loved her, and it was an act of selfless love on her part to pass before Jess. Our beloved companion would now be on the other side to welcome Jess into the Eternal Light.

Patsy remained on her pillow, between us, that last night. Jess and I shared a few prayers in the morning before I buried her in a special garden in our yard. Jess was too grief-stricken to take part.

Several weeks later, in early September, Jess began developing increasing edema in his legs. His body was no longer able to process the liquid food. His doctor wanted to put a feeding tube in his stomach, but Jess hadn't eaten any solids by mouth in a year. I was wary of the procedure and began wondering if it was time to consider letting go. Jess's nausea, diarrhea, and neuropathy pain had been increasing daily.

I prayed and meditated for several days before deciding to broach the subject with Jess. I turned the matter over to the Spirit, asking my Higher Power and guides to come to a decision with Jess's Higher Power and guides. When I still felt the same after a few more days, I tenderly looked into Jess's eyes and asked him, "Do you feel that we are nearing the time for some type of hospice care?" He responded quickly, "No. I feel that the quality of my life is still sufficient to continue living."

I was relieved and fully supported his decision. He had struggled bravely for so long, and he was not ready to stop. I trusted his inner wisdom implicitly. Still, I had broached a most difficult subject, trusting again in my need to communicate my feelings.

During the days that followed, as he continued to physically decline, I concentrated on enjoying the few good hours he had each day. Everyday events, such as watching a favorite show, listening to music, soaking in the spa, or holding hands on our loveseat were all the more special.

Another week passed. It was a Saturday, and his symptoms had continued to worsen. I decided it was time to broach the conversation again. As he sat in his wheelchair by the pool, I asked him if he had thought any more about our conversation of a week ago. He said he had and he felt that it was time to stop fighting. He said he wanted to stop all medications and the liquid food. I asked him if he was certain, and he assured me that he felt it was time.

That night, I called my parents. My mother was shocked, still holding out for a miracle. She wanted to be sure that I hadn't pressured Jess and that it was fully his decision. I called Chris and David. Chris asked me if I wanted her to come now rather than later. I told her that there was a lot of stuff to arrange and having her come would be very helpful. She said she would be here in a few days.

The following day, I called Jess's doctor. Jess's care had been transferred to a new physician a few months earlier to make traveling to appointments easier. From friends, I had heard that this doctor had a particularly hard time with patients deciding to let go. I told him of Jess's decision. He said that he didn't know if he was ready to stop treating but that he would arrange for what we needed if this was the direction we wanted to take.

Chris arrived Monday, and a hospital bed was delivered Tuesday. As Jess expressed his gratitude for the bed and was helped into it, my heart ached as I realized that we would never again spend the night together in the same bed. Similarly, when he was catheterized, I realized that my sweet lover would never again soak in our hot tub or feel the healing water of our pool.

It had only been four days since his decision when I entered our bedroom the following Tuesday night. Already, I could see the drastic signs of weight loss and the death mask taking form on his face. I told him that I couldn't imagine how I was going to continue on without him. I said it was not too late to change directions, to restart him on his liquid food. As he restated his comfort with his decision, my heart ripped open, and I sobbed profusely. My sweet, weakened Jess held me in his arms, too weak to continue talking but holding me until I felt the strength to carry on. I cried more deeply then, than in all of our twenty years. Not once did his grasp of me noticeably tire; his silent but oh-so-present care and love sustained me. I shared with him my feeling that it was one thing to make the decision to allow him to die but quite another to witness the daily process of seeing him slip away. I shared how much I was going to miss him and my feeling of the inevitability of the locomotive coming our way. I couldn't believe that he was holding me, loving me, for it was he whose face death was claiming as its own. He was the sick and weakened one, but it was his strength that was so alive and present in that moment. I was awed by the tender gifts he continued to give me.

I would revisit that conversation several times in the weeks that followed, a large part of me hoping that he would change his mind. He never wavered. Amazingly, much of the discomfort and symptoms brought on by forcing his body to process the liquid food vanished. His edema left, he was pain free, and he had no nausea. Embarrassed, he said that he felt guilty for feeling so well and being the source of so much attention.

During the first week, I got a call from my doctor. He informed me that my lab work concerned him and said that I should come in to discuss changing my medication. I was naturally alarmed that he had called me at home; he had never done that before. I told my doctor that Jess had decided to stop his medications and said that since I was providing his home care, I couldn't leave him. I told him that it would be several weeks before Jess passed. He said that a couple of weeks wouldn't make a difference and told me to call his office when I could schedule an appointment. I put the conversation out of my mind, since I was committed to being totally present for Jess.

Jess began the process of saying good-bye to friends. I made a list of about forty people. Jess decided which ones he would like to see one more time, talk with on the phone, or have me talk to. I felt that we would have about three weeks from the time Jess stopped his food and medications until he would be ready to pass. Not wanting to overly tire him, and not wanting his every waking moment to be an exercise in saying good-bye, I did my best to space out the interactions.

Matt said that he wanted to visit but that because of work obligations he couldn't arrive until October 3. That was more than two weeks away. I told him that I wasn't sure if Jess would live that long but that I had talked with Jess and Jess had said for him to come. Some friends we saw in small groups or individually for short durations. Jess always welcomed them with tender arms, thanked them for coming, and expressed his love to them. He said his good-byes by phone with his brother and sister and with many of our closest friends in San Francisco. He told his brother that he would be thinking of him when he passed.

One late morning, as he sat with me in his wheelchair by the pool, I softly sang to him the words to a favorite song, "May the longtime sun shine upon you, all love surround you, and the pure light within you guide your way home." As Chris and I brought him back into the house to put him in bed, we stopped for a few moments in the dining room. Part of him already seemed ready to let go. I told him that I would manage and somehow be okay. I said that he didn't need to continue living for me, because I was full of his love and that it would always carry me. I assured him that our friends whom he had not yet said good-bye to would understand. I talked about what a remarkable relationship he and I had shared, to which he intently responded, "It has been exquisite."

He spoke volumes of love to me in those four words. His eyes then lifted upward, and I was flooded with a surprising wave of peace. I sat in awe of his beauty and holiness. Just twelve hours earlier, I had been in such pain and grief while opening to his dying process. Now, I was filled with peace and acceptance of his dying. I felt my own spiritual energy rising in my spine, out the top of my head and joining with him throughout the universe. As I felt my spirit begin to soar with his, I yearned to follow him. I closed my eyes, completely content to ascend together in that perfect moment. Eventually, the need to have him rest reentered my consciousness, and I helped him to bed. However, I was left with a level of acceptance I had not previously felt and a taste of the bliss that awaited him.

Toward the middle of the second week, Chris and I were taking a quick dip in the pool as a thunderstorm began to pass overhead. Sitting in his wheelchair at the side of the pool, Jess was watching us. I commented, "Well, this certainly would be a lovely sight, for someone to come in and find Chris and me electrocuted in the pool and you half-dead in your wheelchair!"

"Good," Jess replied, "then I will be the one who gets the life insurance!" We all broke up!

It was at the end of the second week that Chris was finally able to voice her grief to Jess. She thanked him for the incredible times they had shared, and, through her tears, spoke about her sorrow over his passing. Jess chided her gently as he responded, "I've been wondering where you've been."

The last several weeks, we played much of Jess's favorite music. He nearly broke our hearts as he tried to sing the words to Bette Midler's "The Rose," a song that he had sung many years ago at the funeral of a dear friend. Chris had also brought with her the beautiful duet by Sarah Brightman and Andrea Bocelli, "Time to Say Goodbye." Upon hearing it for the first time, Jess uttered, "I want to live until I hear all the beautiful music there is to hear in the world."

I feverishly searched the house for our recording of the Broadway musical, *Sunday in the Park with George*. Jess loved the musical, but I apparently had left the tape in Las Vegas on one of our trips. Fortunately, Chris was able to buy it a local record store, and when I told Jess that Chris had found a copy, he covered her face with many tender kisses.

Mom and Dad came over often with food, to lend a helping hand, to pray, or simply be with Jess. They would have gladly stayed with me, but with Chris present, they realized that there would be too many people in the house. Mom was also a little squeamish about cleaning up frequent episodes of diarrhea, although toward the end, she did her best to overcome her discomfort.

I was very protective of Jess's feelings. One day he became apologetic about having no control over his bowels. I assured him that to me, it was a very sacred task, serving him in that way, through all the bouts of diarrhea, each day, I saw more clearly the absolute holiness of who he was. I kissed his sweet mouth and lips, which now were regularly trembling from the dying process. For a few minutes, having my lips to lock on to, his trembling abated.

Jess loved to identify the numerous calls of mockingbirds. The week before he passed, Chris, Jess, and I were astounded by the sound of a mockingbird singing by our window between one and two in the morning. Chris or I were usually awake, changing the bed pads and turning him. Jess would have a few sips of a beverage as we listened to the bird's serenade. It sang by our bedroom window, at this unusual hour, for four consecutive days. I never had previously observed this unusual occurrence.

On Thursday, his last day out of bed, Jess told Chris that the seat next to him on our loveseat was reserved all day for Jimmy. The next morning, he slipped into a coma. Since Jess was unable to take liquid Tylenol, we switched to suppositories, but his temperature was consistently over 104. All of our friends had made closure except for Matt, who was to arrive at 6 PM the following day.

I continued to talk with Jess while he was comatose, telling him a few times each day how long it would be before Matt arrived. I assured him that Matt would understand if he needed to let go. I called my parents on Saturday and suggested that they spend the night. They were still thinking that he might have a week or so to live, but, intuitively, I felt that he was preparing to let go. They were on their way. When my folks arrived, I took them in to see Jess. After a few moments, my dad started to sob uncontrollably as he told Jess how he would miss his buddy and how unfair it all seemed. My mother was concerned that my father's emotions would upset me, but I was deeply touched by Dad's outpouring of grief and grateful that he had found his voice.

Later that day, when my folks left to pick up Matt at the airport, I was uncertain if Jess would be alive when they returned. Amazingly, he held on. After Matt arrived and had some time alone with Jess, we all took up vigil around his bed for the next six hours. Candlelight and soft music filled our bedroom, as Chris, Matt, my parents, and I sat quietly. An hour or so after midnight, I asked people to go to bed.

As soon as I lay down, I heard a change in Jess's breathing. He stopped breathing for about twenty seconds. Exhausted, I listened for a few minutes, waking a half-hour later to the sound of silence. His apnea was now lasting about forty-five seconds, and, as I kissed him, I told him that I was willing to share this special moment with others. I thanked him for giving me the option to be alone with him. I told him that I could never say I was okay with letting him go, but that I did want him to move toward his ultimate happiness. I then woke Chris and asked her to wake the others. When we all had gathered, Jess began taking his final breaths. I softly whispered into his ear the transcendental meditation mantra that he had been given by Maharishi Mahesh Yogi in Vittel, France, twenty-three years earlier. He passed at 2:00 AM on Sunday, October 4, 1998.

The mockingbird did not sing that night, and I have not heard its early morning song since.

I went outside for a dip in the pool and a short soak in the spa, as I opened to Jess's spiritual body while reclaiming my physical body. Chris, my mother, and I then bathed his body, rubbed him with lavender and sage oil, and dressed him in his Yellowstone wolf shirt and his string pants. I slept my last night in the room with him, before calling the mortuary in the morning.

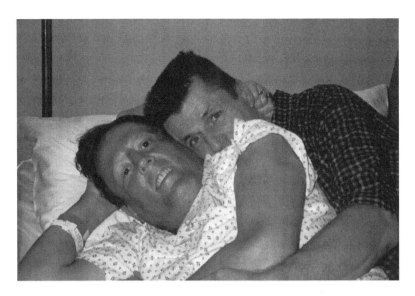

Jess in the hospital (1997)

Jess in Las Vegas—"Let's go for it one more time" (1998)

Chris and Jess, "I have been wondering
where you've been" (1998)

Calming his trembling lips (1998)

Chapter 11

Harvest Moon

*I am here to go on, to carry the legacy of my relationship into
the days ahead, to make bright my loved one's memory, to see
it as a fire from which I can forge a future.*

Carol Staudacher (*A Time to Grieve*)

The remaining chapters chronicle my grieving process following
Jess's passing. I have decided that the best way to convey my
feelings from that period is through my journal entries. I began
keeping a journal a month after Jess's passing. I have included
the original journal entry dates in these chapters. Interspersed
among the journal entries are chronological accounts of after-
death communications that I have had with Jess. My contacts
with Jess have taken many forms: sensing a presence, symbolic
and synchronistic occurrences, hearing a voice, dream encounters,
visions, and physical phenomena.

The first one occurred within thirty-six hours of Jess's physical
death, and I have been blessed by their continued occurrence
in my life. Prior to Jess's passing, to my knowledge I had never

experienced an after-death communication from the many clients, friends, and family members I had known who had passed.

During the last two years, I have read many books explaining the phenomenon of after-death communication and about many people who have experienced them. I consider myself fortunate to be one of them. The communications have made my grief bearable and have helped me immensely in fulfilling my purpose in this world.

Jess's favorite albums were Neil Young's *Harvest* and *Harvest Revisited*, which featured the song "Harvest Moon." The album's cover depicts an orange-colored full harvest moon. I played the song "Harvest Moon" often in the last week of Jess's earthly life and found myself crying to words that had taken on deeper meaning. The lyrics of the song acknowledge the fleeting nature of time and the desire to dance together one more time while seeing the moonlight reflected in each other's eyes.

The day following Jess's passing, I called my doctor's office to schedule an appointment. I was concerned about what he had told me earlier about my lab results and figured that it could take some time to get an appointment. To my surprise, there was an opening later that afternoon. Although I was hesitant to venture out so soon after Jess's passing, I decided that it was best to take the appointment. It was an hour's drive to the office, and Chris and Matt accompanied me. When I met with my doctor, to our mutual surprise, he discovered that he had been in error when he called me. My lab work was fine. He said he must have been reading someone else's results! I found myself using our time to share with him a little about Jess's passing, and, as it was nearing dinner time, to discuss local restaurants he could recommend.

I hadn't been out to eat in more than five months. Although it was difficult being out without Jess, through the tears, the three of us shared a good meal and enjoyed the company of each other.

We returned home about 6:30. As I turned the car onto my street, which runs between the Halifax River and the Atlantic Ocean, directly and perfectly centered in front of us, hanging over the Atlantic Ocean, was a full and brilliantly colored orange harvest moon! In the ten years that I had lived in the area, I had never seen an orange-colored harvest moon or such a magnificent sight. The three of us were speechless.

Jess was very attuned to and had a great deal of respect for nature. While Matt ran into the house to get a camera, I basked for a few minutes in the beauty of the orange moon, and I felt an inner peace begin to well. I was overwhelmed by the synchronicity of this event.

Everything had worked together to get me out of the house to observe this phenomenon. I knew that this was a miraculous gift of God and Jess's way of reassuring me that he was fine. At the time, the rawness of my grief only allowed me to feel the sense of peace briefly. Yet the image of that harvest moon is one that I will continue to hold and be healed by throughout my life.

For the one-month anniversary of Jess's passing, I decided to go to Joshua Tree National Park, outside of Palm Springs, California. The park was a favorite place of ours, and we had visited it several times in our travels. I felt that being in the desert during the full moon would be healing. I also thought that Joshua Tree would be a special place to scatter a few of Jess's ashes.

I decided that the time was right to begin a journal. The following is my first journal entry, which I wrote at the Atlanta Airport on my way to Palm Springs.

November 3, 1998

Oh sweet Jess, how hesitant I am to write my feelings about you. Can words and my limited grasp of them begin to express the heaviness in my heart? Oh sweet darling, how I miss you so. How

I long to push your wheelchair up the gate ramp again, to have my sweet angel Jess to care for, to assist, to protect, to help empower once again. Nearby, I hear the cold metal clank of a wheelchair's footrest; it reverberates briefly against my emptiness, as my longing swells to aid you once again.

In the adjacent food court, an African American couple now occupies our place; unaware of the sacredness those plastic seats hold for me. I remember how we enjoyed early morning subs and how happy I was to see you eat and enjoy your food. A porter passes by, wheeling two empty wheelchairs; how I long to see the back of your head, to be rendezvousing with you at a distant terminal. Yet now I sit at the next gate, alone, with this pen and page to comfort me. Oh sweet darling lover, to have you watch my carry-on once again, while I use the restroom before boarding. How I long to feel your warmth next to me, to share the excitement of our final destination, and to experience the joy from knowing that we once again conquered all obstacles and went for it. To seize the moment, to go against medical advice, to be sustained by one another, to flourish in the process of making our dreams come true, once again my darling, once again.

The month's anniversary trip began when I met a man named Bill, who was staying at the same Palm Springs resort. Bill's lover had passed from AIDS six years earlier. Bill and I shared our mutual losses, and I told him of my plans to go to the park. He said that visiting the park was also on his list of things to do. I decided to invite him to join me, even though my original plan had been to be alone. The synchronicity of meeting him that particular morning assured me that it was the right thing to do.

Although I had driven to Joshua Tree numerous times before, and had refreshed my memory that morning by referring to a map, I somehow managed to miss my turn and ended up fifteen miles out of my way. To my surprise, I found myself at an Indian casino. At first, the thought of playing slots on this special day seemed sacrilegious. But then I opened to the feeling that Jess was orchestrating the whole thing. I could sense his loving, smiling presence saying, "Well, I bet you didn't think you would be doing this today!" It was his way of reminding me to continue to enjoy the things we had shared together. While it was painful being in the casino without him physically, it was also healing for me to begin to reclaim familiar activities that we had enjoyed together. After about forty-five minutes, and forty dollars lighter, Bill and I continued on our journey.

We entered the park from the northern entrance, and it was a section of the park I had not previously seen. It was a gloriously sunny day, and the rock formations and shrubbery were illuminated with a golden light. In the early stages of my grief, it was hard to be fully open to the beauty of nature; I so much wanted Jess to be physically present to enjoy it. As we drove through the park, I began to look and intuitively feel for a spot that seemed appropriate to scatter some of Jess's ashes. After riding for about fifteen miles, I came to a flat clearing. About two hundred yards off the road, there was a section of hills that were about forty feet high and looked fairly easy to climb. I felt compelled to see what lay beyond. When we reached the top, there was a wonderful hidden valley that was surrounded by a circular wall of rock. (I later learned that Hidden Valley is its actual name.)

Everything was still and picturesque. I sat down on a cliff overlooking the valley and quickly found myself merging with the surrounding landscape and feeling an inner sense of peace. Part of me still wanted to fight settling for less than being with Jess physically. Yet there was no denying that I met my beloved again in that silence—I so clearly felt his presence, and it was reflected in and all around me. A few pinches of his ashes were all I could part with that day, and it felt right that part of him would remain where grandeur resides and waits for all to encounter it.

Jess and I were both fascinated by coyotes. We had been lucky enough to view a few coyotes on our trips, but, since they are cautious animals, it was always from a distance. Before going to Joshua Tree that day, I had mentally communicated to Jess how wonderful it would be to see a coyote. I told him that I would interpret its presence as a sign from him. However, in our previous visits to the park, we had never seen one.

About ten miles down the road from Hidden Valley, I was stunned to see a coyote coming toward me along the side of the road. I stopped immediately, thinking that it would surely dart into cover, but instead, it continued to walk, passing within six feet of my window! I could hardly breathe as I asked Bill to hand me a small piece of string cheese, totally forgetting any admonitions about feeding wildlife! Before I knew it, another coyote came out of nowhere and they both began circling the car as I feverishly snapped pictures. They circled the car about fifteen times. It was thrilling to be this close to animals in their natural habitat. I was certain that Jess was instrumental in arranging the whole thing.

About ten miles down the road, a coyote ran across the road about forty feet in front of us and stopped and turned to study us before continuing his journey. And if that hadn't been enough to convince me of the miracles I was receiving that day, just as I left Joshua Tree to turn onto Interstate 10, yet another coyote bolted right in front of my car! I had to slam on the brakes to avoid hitting the coyote, which stopped about twenty feet away and looked back at us. I could swear it was smiling. I knew beyond a shadow of a doubt that the events of that day were a gift from God with the loving input of Jess, who knew what symbols would reflect his ongoing energy and most heal my heart.

After we returned to the hotel later that evening, I asked Bill if he would like to join me for dinner. The owners of the resort had recommended a restaurant called Shame on the Moon, which they said was a little expensive but very good. I had thought about saving it for the end of my trip, but Bill suggested that we go there that night, and I thought, *why not?* We got dressed up, and, I must admit, Bill looked very handsome in dress clothes. We had to wait about forty-five minutes before being seated, but they had a lovely bar area. Bill offered me the last remaining chair, and it felt so good to be out with an attractive man at a nice restaurant having a drink. However, as with the casino at the day's beginning, this was the last thing I had expected to be doing on this particular night! We were seated at a corner circular booth that looked out over the restaurant. Although the booth was large, they had our set-ups shoulder to shoulder, with a card on the table that read, "Warm Greetings to Bill and Jim." All I could do was laugh at how this magical day continued to unfold, now complete with a romantic dinner. Talk about being accelerated through one's grief! I laughed to myself as I thought that "Shame on Jess" would be a more appropriate name for this restaurant than Shame on the Moon!

November 7, 1998

Talked with Mom and Dad yesterday about how things were going here and shared the incredible events of November 4. They were very attentive. Dad agreed that the coyotes had a very special message. I shared with them how I have been crying frequently and that I feel it is a healthy thing. At the very end of our conversation Mom said, "Keep your chin up." I recall her saying that to me once before, when things were getting progressively worse at Shanti. It was more helpful then. I don't want to keep my chin up, darling. I want to feel my feelings of loss regarding you. When my heart rips, the pain at times is overwhelming, but my love for you exists so fully in those moments, sweet angel.

Yesterday, at the Living Desert, so much beauty surrounded me, the glory of the plants, children, visitors, elder guides, big horn sheep, and stillness. I was also aware of my own strength, my ability to walk five miles, something I haven't done in quite some time. I claimed my health, my endurance, and my ability to walk alone. I cried as I reclaimed these gifts, gifts that I had put on hold while caring for you.

Oh darling, I cried at what was lost and what was being found. You opened up the world to me, your eyes now live within my heart. I can see new sights but can never see apart from you. Our relationship is far from over, because you will continue to speak to me; when I simply pause to remember and feel your love, your pulse vibrates in my every cell. I love you, sweet darling, and I feel your love. Do I dare say more today than yesterday?

November 8, 1998
     I worry some that if I don't keep up my feverish attempt to write down my feelings about you that they will be lost to me. I wonder how many can understand that I would not trade one bit of the pain and tears I have experienced, for they are, in part, my way of connecting with you. I know there will be a time when the pain is less sharp, or at least experienced in less frequency and duration. I think focusing on your risen spirit may in time comfort me, although there remains a part of me that says that is all a bunch of bull to make our experience of loss more tolerable. Perhaps there is a part of your ascended self that, even now, wishes me peace and envelops me. Yet, it waits for me to be free enough from my grief to sense you here and be ready to be held by you again.

November 9, 1998
     Yesterday was the Gay Day Celebration in Palm Springs, my first parade without you in so many years. I am doing well, sweetie; I am able to cheer and cry. I think the more I can open to God again, the more I will open to you. If I can find comfort in a loving all-encompassing Spirit, then I am certain you will meet me there. You add a whole new wonderful piece to God, sweetie. You did in life and now you do in death. God is becoming more personal now, as I begin to surrender to Spirit, I sense you waiting there. Is this the beginning of finding you again, sweet angel? Can and will I find comfort in knowing that my two great loves are now united?

November 10, 1998
     Oh, sweetie, how many wonderful, sensual parts of you I found myself having to let go of throughout your illness. Last night while

masturbating, I caught a glimpse of my stud boy, before the Kaposi's sarcoma lesions, the oral thrush, the change in body odor, the chest port, the fragility, the dick that couldn't produce cum. Now, I find myself grieving my lost lover, yet also excited about remembering you apart from the terrible illness. While you were alive, I wouldn't allow myself to grieve over the loss of your sexual attractiveness, choosing instead to focus on how we could continue to connect in mutually pleasing and satisfying ways.

I would push away thoughts that would have me recoil at the scent of yeast in your mouth, a constant reminder of your illness and impending death. Pressing against your lips, I would block out the large lesion on your gums in the front of your mouth. Lying on you, I would try to be mindful of not pushing your needle deeper into your port while, at the same time, trying to love you in a manly, abandoned manner.

Oh darling, now that you are gone, I can remember you before the symptoms of AIDS and not feel guilty. In my fantasies, I can rediscover you as my lover again. I can lay claim to my young boy stud in leather, who was oh-so-delicate with his feelings, and who made love to me so well.

November 11, 1998

Grief is a much bigger word than death. Death is a brief moment in time, whereas grief is all that follows—and much of what transpired before. I have read several books on grief which have been helpful. Others' experiences of grief is similar, yet it remains so uniquely mine. My grief at times feels like a mountain, and all I can do is stand in the shadow of it. Slowly, I am able to traverse its trails, even now and then rejoicing in a newly discovered vista, yet the mountain's vastness remains heavy on my heart at the same time. I want no skilled guide to take me quickly to its peak, it is not something I feel can be rushed, or even want to conquer. If anything, I want to stretch my heart's arms wide enough to hold it, to love it, to make it my own. My grief is my love for you, sweet darling, I am very protective of it. I cherish

*it now, the way I cherished you. A part of it is scary, while, at the
same time, very comforting.*

November 12, 1998

    *Part of me thinks that I could shoot myself as a way of sharing
eternity with you. It is just the damn unknowing that makes any
decision so hard. Where are you, Jess? Do you still think of me? Do you
want to be with me again? Or are things so different, so wonderful,
do you see things so clearly, so differently that you have moved on,
leaving me emotionally as well as physically? Do you exist as I knew
you at all anymore, darling? Is there a "you" to still care about me
the way I care about you?*

November 14, 1998

    *I woke up tonight wondering if I had thanked you for what a
wonderful teacher you were to me regarding your dying process. I
wondered if you knew, in those last three weeks, how much you were
helping me prepare for my own eventual death? If you were at all
conscious of how your dying process was a gift for me?*

    *I then remembered a conversation we had the last week of your
life, where I cried with you again and thanked you for the strength,
dignity, and beauty with which you lived your life and which you
brought to your dying process. When I spoke my heart to you through
my tears, you held me in my process; you opened up to me and loved
me in my expression of grief, doubt, pain, and love for you.*

    *I spoke to you of your holiness, dear angel, and told you how the
angels would sing their welcome to you, of what a good and holy life
you had led, and of God's joy in welcoming you home. I told you
that the love you demonstrated on earth so well was now going to be
exalted in heaven, and that you would be reunited with your mom
and dad, not with any of their judgment but with their new eyes,
filled with divine love and pure joy at seeing you again.*

November 17, 1998

Early this morning, between 3:00 and 6:00 AM, there was a meteorite shower. From what I hear, it was the most meteorite activity in seven hundred years. It was somewhat overcast, but in an hour's viewing, I saw about twenty. Some were incredibly bright, but as the clouds covered the stars and skies, making it difficult to see, it became a metaphor for how the cloud of your death has made it so difficult to know where you are. Is there just a thin veil that separates your radiance from me? Is part of you looking over my shoulder as I write these words? Are you sending your love to me now? Oh, darling, if you can hear me, watch over me, sweetie, help me to sense you in the divine again. Continue to be my special friend, as long as that doesn't hold you back from where you need to go and what is for your highest good. If at all possible, burn the veil of clouds of doubt from my heart and let me know that my sweet angel is whole again.

November 21, 1998

Your preciousness envelops so much of what remains in my world. I know, in time, many physical objects will break, be discarded, lose significance— but now they speak of you in so many tender ways; the pair of rubber shoes you wore to the hot tub is more precious than a thousand other things.

Chapter 12

Call on Me

Would that life were like the shadow cast by a wall or tree,
but it is like the shadow of a bird in flight.

The Talmud

The last time that Jess and I were arrested for nonviolent civil disobedience was in 1987, on the steps of the Supreme Court in Washington DC. We were protesting against the Hardwick decision, which upheld the rights of individual states to determine their own laws regarding sodomy.

After Jess passed, I mentioned his arrest at this demonstration in his obituary. My parents were uncomfortable with the reference to states' sodomy laws, despite the fact that that is what they are called. They felt that the word "sodomy" was too charged. I agreed, but I argued that, for these laws to change, people have to be able to use the word and understand how much it encompasses. Webster's first definition is "copulation with a member of the same sex or an animal" and its second definition includes anal and *oral* copulation with a member of the *opposite* sex. Many people are unaware that many state sodomy laws prohibited heterosexual oral sex as well as homosexual sex. However, I agreed to say that Jess was arrested protesting state laws that prohibited sexual relations between consenting adults.

Thanksgiving was the first major holiday I had to face alone. My parents and I had discussed how we could spend the holidays to make the time as easy as possible. We decided that getting out of town would be a good idea. Before Jess passed, the four of us had talked about going to Savannah, Georgia, a place we had never visited. Jess's declining health had prevented us from making the trip. I suggested that Savannah would be a good place to go for our first Thanksgiving without him. We decided to make it a four-day holiday, and we stayed at a charming bed-and-breakfast inn.

When I came downstairs the first morning, the owner of the inn was very excited. He was on the phone talking about a front-page story. I glanced at the paper and couldn't believe the headline, "State Supreme Court Throws Out Sodomy Law." The innkeeper, who was involved on the state level working for gay and lesbian issues, said the vote came out of nowhere. There had been no special lobbying, and no one knew that the court would be voting on the issue. Of all the places that I could spent my first Thanksgiving without Jess, I had ended up here. I knew instantly that I had been directed to be in Savannah. For the remainder of our mini-vacation, I felt Jess's loving presence all around me. It made my first holiday without him much easier to bear. I was able to be part of the celebration that stemmed from overturning a bad law. I was grateful to God and Jess. Once again, they had orchestrated where I needed to be to make my grieving easier and savor a victory that Jess and I had fought to achieve.

Several years before Jess passed, we had seen a made-for-television movie called *Substitute Wife*. The movie had made quite an impression on Jess, and he recounted the plot frequently to friends. From my recollection, it took place out West in the late 1800s. The story line revolved around a mother who was dying of cancer. She felt driven, before she passed, to find a new wife for her husband and a mother for her two children. She eventually was guided to the town's red-light district where she met a prostitute (played by Farrah Fawcett), whom she convinced to come and meet her family. The dying woman was amazingly selfless. She encouraged her husband to connect sexually with this woman to see if the new relationship was viable. She ultimately passed with the love and support of her family and the knowledge that this "substitute wife" would help care for her family.

Jess frequently expressed his concern and hope that I would meet someone who would value and love me after he passed. A few months after his passing, I decided to get together with a man whom I had met on the computer about a year earlier. He also had AIDS and, although I didn't know a lot about him, he seemed like a nice guy. I knew that he worked as a theater director. Since my grief was still raw, I was concerned about getting together so soon. I asked Jess to watch over me. Something told me that it would be fine; meeting the man felt like something important for me to do.

About thirteen years earlier, Jess had taken singing lessons. Jess had wanted to learn a favorite song of mine so that he could sing it to me. I had seen Angela Lansbury on Broadway in *Sweeny Todd*, a great and macabre musical about a couple who make meat pies filled with cats—and with a number of people who eventually get in their way! I fell in love with the song "No One's Gonna Harm You." Jess learned the song and was excited to share it with me. Jess's favorite musical was *Sunday in the Park with George*, based on the life of painter George Seurat. I played the title song, "Sunday," many times during the week before he passed.

When I arrived at my new friend's home, I learned that he had worked on the production of *Sweeny Todd*. In fact, he had a bronze meat pie on his living room table that Angela Lansbury had made for several of her favorite crew members! He then proceeded to show me a promotional tape of his work as a director. The tape featured *Sunday in the Park with George*, with the title song playing in the background. The synchronicity of these circumstances was astounding! I felt Jess's guiding and watchful energy all around me, as I was flooded with my awareness of his ongoing love and support.

December 9, 1998

Oh Jess, I miss you so much, darling. What a perfect match we were, and how we complemented each other so. It has been just a few days over two months since you passed. I have decided against antidepressants for now. Although I think of you every day and cry on most, I feel that I am moving along well. I have played some tennis and am doing yoga daily. I cleaned the garage and changed the message on the answering machine. I carried your plastic trash can in from the garage that you used to spit up in, and that did me in. I had nowhere to put it, darling. I sat on the bed and clutched it to my heart, my most sacred possession, for about ten minutes.

I then emptied a dish that contained the last pair of foam earplugs you wore. I remembered how your earplugs had fallen out the last few days of your life, as you were too weak to put them back in. I came apart again, recalling how close you had been to death. My sweet Jessie, whose last act before he fell asleep was putting in his earplugs. Oh darling, how I love you and miss you so.

December 12, 1998

Oh angel, a yucky day today, depressed and little motivation. I am still experiencing a let-down from Thursday, when Mom and Dad came over and we shared our grief together. It was a cathartic time, as I shared a little from my journal of stories of you and me. Mom asked me to sit on her lap, she wanted so much to comfort me the way she had when I was a child. Dad shared afterward that she had wanted to do that for some time.

December 16, 1998

Oh, darling, occasionally I have thoughts of you suffering on the other side. These thoughts feel dark, fear-based, rooted in myth, yet for moments, they cause me great distress. Some of these thoughts took hold after a conversation with our friend Gail. She was telling me how her psychic told her that after people pass, they sometimes wander about in a similar weak and frail form for several years on the other side. She added that sometimes people continue to drain them from this plane by not releasing them.

The thought of you continuing to suffer is unbearable for me. That you should have to endure more physical anguish makes me angry with a God that would allow such a thing. The thought of you being confused, alone, weakened—and me being unable to assist you—seems devilishly cruel. At times, even thoughts of old deep-rooted religious indoctrination give power to images of you suffering because of you being gay. Even having a trace of these dark thoughts in my consciousness embarrasses a larger part of me.

I want to run to your side and do battle, to slay any force that would cause you additional pain or condemn you. These fears gain power by the 1 percent of me that ponders, what if God is antigay? My estrangement from the Spirit at times doesn't help with these fleeting images and thoughts. But even in my unknowing, a much larger part of myself recoils at this treacherous possibility, believing these feelings to be remnants of a culture that has embedded us with self-hatred, sin, and guilt.

In this moment, I see myself as an impenetrable shield surrounding you, sweet angel. Within this shield, you and I embrace in perfect love and light. And as we join there as we did here, the need for any protective space dissipates as our love becomes a radiating gift for all around us.

The first Christmas came in less than three months. Christmas had always been a special time for us, and we usually went all-out with presents for family, friends, and one another. It was not unusual for us to spend more than four hours opening gifts! I had decided that for this first Christmas alone, I would forgo as much of it as possible. I invited my parents to join me in South Beach, Florida.

Whenever I left home for more than a night after Jess passed, I took several of my favorite pictures of him, a small container of his ashes, incense, and a few crystals. I would arrange these on an attractive scarf on a small table in my room. I also had a small box of inspirational cards that had sayings from *Conversations with God* by Neale Donald Walsch, which I had taken with me on several previous trips. As time unfolded, I cut back on the number of pictures and assorted items that I took to give me comfort. I really thought about leaving the box of cards at home, but at the last minute, I decided to bring them.

One issue that remained difficult throughout my grieving was wondering if my daily thoughts of Jess were somehow keeping him bound to this plane. I found myself often telling him that I did not want to interfere with what he was supposed to be doing on the other side. However, I also needed to be one with my grieving and express it as often as necessary. Additionally, I felt that I needed to honor my desire to call on him to help me with the tremendous pain and emptiness I often felt.

After getting set up in my room in South Beach, I told Jess that the next few days were going to be especially difficult. It would be the first Christmas in twenty years that we were not together. I again mentally shared with him that my biggest dilemma was my uncertainty over whether it was okay to continue calling on him when I was feeling low. I looked at the box of over one hundred inspirational cards. I told him that I was going to pick only one card to look at while in South Beach. I asked that it be a message from him that would help me get through the next four days and one that would shed light on my ongoing uncertainty.

The message read, *"Call on me whenever and wherever you are separate from the peace that I am."* Tears of joy streamed down my face as I felt my lover's tender concern all around me. I realized that I had been given permission to do exactly what I needed. I could not have been given a more perfect message. I had never picked that card before. It made that first Christmas so much easier, and during times of doubt and difficulty, it continues to fill me with peace.

December 26, 1998

I have just put down the third volume of Conversations with God, *which I purchased earlier today. Although exhausted when I returned to my room, I felt compelled to search the index for references to life after death. I found a number of them, and the synchronicity of the passages and the card I drew a few days ago are exhilarating and most comforting.*

"If somebody from the 'other side' has something they want you to know, they'll find a way to cause you to know it, don't worry. If part of what they want to do is to come back to you—to see how you are, to bring you an awareness that they're all right, whatever—trust that they'll do that. Then, watch for the sign and catch it. Don't dismiss it just as your imagination, wishful thinking, or coincidence. Watch for the message and receive it. The slightest thought having to do with a being existing on what you call the other side brings that being's consciousness flying to you."

Reading this, darling, has given me such a sense of peace!

January 5, 1999

"You will have choice—always you will have free choice—to go anywhere you wish to go, do anything you wish to do, in your re-creation of the experience of God. You can move to any place on the Cosmic Wheel. You may 'come back' as anything you wish, or in any other dimension, reality, solar system, or civilization you choose."

(*Conversations with God, Book 3*).

After sitting and reflecting on this passage, in which God is talking about our unlimited free choice *after* death as well as in this life, I wrote the following:

Oh Jess, I claim my ability to dance through star-brilliant galaxies with you. I meet you whole, more whole than we have ever been. I am flooded by the continuous emanations of our expanding love. We are free of disease and aging, war and poverty, homophobia, sexism, and racism. We visit spheres where all entities emanate love for one another and join consciously with the Absolute. We materialize things at will. I swim with you and feel our oneness with the water, sky, sun, and everyone and everything around us. We breathe each breath in conscious, joyful sacredness. We laugh frequently, fully, in harmony because of the pure joy of being together and seeing each other's eternally unfolding magnificence. Our extraordinary love vibrates and heals the whole universe. As we kiss, we see the planets spinning, the flowers growing, the radiant celebration of the One Self. We visit different realms at will, rejoicing together consciously in the effects of our healing, playing without tiring. I hold your hand, feeling your heart as one with mine, as we bask in the light of the Absolute.

Take my hand, darling, and lead me there.

January 31, 1999

The last few weeks, I have been looking more squarely at the question, Do I want to continue to remain on this planet? Most people reserve this line of thinking for a time when death is imminent. Asking myself the question now is at times uncomfortable, fearful, exhilarating, and spiritually freeing. While you were alive on this earth, darling, there was no question that I wanted to remain here. In being with you, I found great joy, purpose, adventure, and peace.

I now find myself opening to the possibility that my human form has served its purpose. Part of me is both thrilled and frightened by this prospect. In addition to my ongoing grief process, I have simultaneously been experiencing a spiritual awakening. My intensive reading of Conversations with God *has prompted this awakening. I have read how there are thousands of places more evolved than this earthly dimension—planes where beings choose to live in conscious oneness, respect, and love. However, finding clarity in how I should proceed in this earthly dimension seems beyond me much of the time.*

Oh darling, I love you so. In many ways my heart continues to open to the beauty of who you are and the blessings you brought to my life. Your gentleness, mindfulness, and love for me I appreciate on new and deeper levels when I think of you. Just as one in life grows in awareness of the splendor and glory of God, I grow in my awareness of your splendor and glory.

Never in my life, sweet darling, have I been suicidal, but, for the last month, images of ending my life are commonplace. Thoughts of remaining here without you lead to feelings of despair, emptiness, desertion, and wasting precious time that I could share with you in another dimension. I know we cannot go back, but I believe we will go on together in another realm. It is only my uncertainty over whether there remains a purpose for me here and a better way for us to be reunited that prevents me from ending this earthly existence.

Oh darling, I remain here for now in this earthly turmoil, but if it is for our highest good, let's choose consciously now to dance together again, to manifest ourselves in a world of conscious loving connection with one another as companions, soul mates, and cosmic lovers. Join with me in bringing that thought into reality, sweet darling. I give you my complete permission to manifest our shared vision <u>now</u>. Help me, darling, to wake from this earthly dream, to soar with you to conscious loving and conscious remembering of who we really are, two parts of one, both expressing and creating the majesty of God. Lift me, darling, to heights far greater than either of us experienced together in this earthly realm. Reveal the shortest path to you, sweet darling. May our highest good be manifested and revealed.

I release any ties which bind me here—family and friends, who I am one with forever; money and possessions—for mine is eternal abundance; sexual pleasure for a greater love I am yet to realize. I release this world and all her beauty for a higher beauty and a simpler truth that awaits me now. Help me to pass from this earthly existence now, *to play with you again. I call to you, awaken me, lead me home, darling. I welcome and embrace your summons, I release my body and the illusion of a separate self, and I release my fear of death. I choose to remember that I am one with God. I release taste, I release smell, I release touch, I release sight, and I release sound. I choose being. I choose knowing. I choose continuous awareness that all is one. I open to knowing that your glory is my glory and together we are One Being, One Self, and Co-creators, now and forever more.*

Chapter 13

Opening to Glory

Her absence is like the sky, spread over everything.

C. S. Lewis

March 24, 1999

Oh, sweet angel. It is getting easier to engage in life again; yet at times the awareness of this pangs me so. I fear that we are moving away from each other, and that frightens me. Oh darling Jess, perhaps I just need to pause and call on you, and you will come rushing to my side once again. I just completed a week with a new friend from Iowa; my focus was naturally on showing him a good time. When he left, however, my grief about you poured through me again. I want to feel it (you), so I intentionally played music, which made crying easier and thoughts of you more conscious.

I feel healthy and have increased my joy of daily living. I feel more resolved, and yet there remains a large part of me that still longs to join you, darling. I fear that perhaps you, too, are looking for a way, and yet, as you see me going on with life, you will stop and move away. Oh, Jess, I do want to join you. I gladly would release everything now to be with you again. I feel your presence, darling, and it is comforting. Walk with me awhile, I miss you so.

March 26, 1999

Oh darling, do I allow and accept that you are blending into God or do I hold onto thoughts of your form and essence? Is it an either/ or? Can it be both?

April 3, 1999

Well, angel, tomorrow is six months since you left your body. I have felt your healing presence throughout the day, and a significant shift is occurring in my grief. I now no longer feel that I need to end my life as a way to commune with you. I can turn that decision back to God and my Higher Power. I now realize that I can connect with you in meditation whenever I choose and join your ascended spirit there.

Tomorrow is also Easter, which for me is very symbolic. Easter was the first time we shared intimate lovemaking, many years ago. To have this first Easter fall on the six-month anniversary of your passing provides me special comfort. It is also symbolic to me in that Easter is April 4th, the fourth month, the fourth day and that forty-four was the age of your earthly transition.

This week, I thought a lot about how crazy and limiting this "letting go" concept is. I realized that when people speak of the need to let go, they are often locked into dimensional seeing. They view the departed as a body and lose sight that we are spiritual beings encased in a physical form. I now recognize that my determination to resist the gentle prodding of others for me to let go, as well as society's often more blatant message to move on, is rooted in sacred ground. It is centered in my refusal to believe that Christ Consciousness died on the cross, or to live under the illusion of my separation from God on earth.

Just as my life's journey on a spiritual level is in remembering who I am and choosing to consciously connect with my Creator, so is my daily journey about joining you, sweet Jess, more consciously in Spirit. My goal and sacred intention is to continue to hold and love

*you more, my darling, joining you whenever I choose in meditation,
on an even higher level of manifested love than that which we realized
on earth. Just as parents release their infant's changing forms to
embrace them anew in the many moments that will span their lives,
so do I, sweet lover, realize it is but your form that has changed. Our
love for one another increases moment to moment as we continue to
grow in self-awareness.*

*I revel in your spirit now, sweet darling, for you are the resurrected
Christ this Easter, as much alive this moment as you were six months
ago, as real and as much a part of me as you were two thousand years
before. Each moment, as I move toward conscious communion with
all of who I am, the illusionary barriers that separate myself from
God and separate myself from you evaporate. You and I now behold
one another in an even more glorious and awakened manner than
when our earthly bodies saw each other last. Hallelujah, sweet Jesus!
Hallelujah, sweet Jess! Hallelujah, sweet Self!*

April 19, 1999

*Well, darling, tomorrow I leave for Amsterdam, my first big trip
to a city that you and I talked about visiting but never got to. I know
you will be with me on another level.*

*I got so high doing a walking meditation this morning, sweetie. I
was by the pool, soaking up the rays before the cooler temperatures that
await me. As I walked around the pool, twenty or so times, naked,
with hands and arms extended fully upward toward the clouds, I said
aloud, "I consciously choose to be with you now, Jess. And I am, for
we are the great I Am for all eternity." This affirmation brought me
such joy and strength. So powerful were these words, sweet darling.
How wonderful it feels to move more consciously toward you. If you
were to have chosen to physically manifest, it would have seemed so
natural. The quiet that followed and the sense of peace I now feel
is pregnant with you, sweet angel. My eyes are longing to close as I
surrender to that awareness now.*

May 20, 1999

Hi, angel. Well, your birthday is almost over and it's nice to be spending the last few minutes of it thinking of and talking to you. Walking on the beach this morning was a good way to begin the day, and the time allowed me to focus on you.

I recalled my first day with Chris and David in Amsterdam. We had set off biking in North Amsterdam to explore the countryside on a bright, crisp, sunny day. I was suddenly flooded with such happiness. The thought occurred that I couldn't remember a happier time but that was quickly followed by the thought, "How could this be? Jess is not here!" But then the awareness that yes, I can continue to grow in happiness. You would want me to experience happiness greater than I ever had before, just as I want the same for you, sweet darling. I want you to continue to grow in love, laughter, happiness, and awareness in the realm that you are now experiencing.

What a gift that was, that I was able to open, receive, and accept that awareness—that I can say and desire that this is your best birthday yet. And that even for me, here without your physical form, I can now begin to open to the same truth for myself as well. I can claim that this is the best birthday I have spent with you, since I am more myself today than ever before and that my love for you is more today than yesterday. I love you, sweet darling. Happy Birthday, Jess!

One day in late June, I found myself talking aloud to Jess with a great deal of energy and emotion. I told him something that signaled for me a very big shift of thought regarding my feelings: I admitted that I could remain on this planet if I were certain to see him again. No sooner had I completed this thought, I heard his voice. He said very distinctly and in his own intonation, "You bet!" His voice was audible, and there was no mistaking that it was Jess. My whole being lightened as I opened to this connection with him and accepted what he was saying. Tears of happiness ran down my cheeks.

"You bet!" was an expression I then recalled hearing him say on a few occasions. It was not an expression that I ever used. Jess had chosen two simple words that conveyed the essence of him. From that day on, my thoughts of suicidal ideation lifted. I continue to find such comfort in trusting the sincerity and simplicity of his words, which confirm that we will be together again.

July 7, 1999

Hello, darling, up in the clouds again, on a plane to San Diego with Mom and Dad for a six-week adventure to Southern California and Las Vegas. I have been feeling particularly close to you the last several weeks. When watching television, I frequently find myself reaching out and placing my hand on your picture. I feel a tangible connection with you that brings me much peace.

Recently, I have been working with affirmations that state my clear intentions:

I am intending to consciously commune with you, sweet darling.

I am intending to be a continual transmitter of light and love.

I am intending to be consciously aware of my oneness with all things.

It is my intention to express my love openly and offer it freely to my parents on this trip.

It is my intention to manifest and maintain perfect health in body, mind, and spirit.

It is my intention to hold sacred, and joyously celebrate, the God/Goddess within all.

It is my intention to have joyous and spiritually healing sexual relationships.

It is my intention to hold you, Jess, in my heart and my mind's eye throughout eternity.

I love you, sweet darling; it is good to be traveling with you again.

It wasn't until ten months after Jess passed that I clearly connected with him in a dream. Before going to bed, I had lovingly chastised him for not coming to me in a dream. In my dream, I was fully aware that he was on the other side and that I was being given a very special opportunity to connect with him. We met in a secluded area, and, while the image of Jess was very vivid, the surrounding scenery was obscure. My focus was completely on Jess and the emotions that I felt emanating from him. He was a little younger and very healthy. But more significant than his physical being were the feelings of gentleness and love that emanated from him. The wonderful thing was that we were able to hold one another, and, while the physical contact was thrilling, he was also holding me emotionally. His very presence and loving embrace were healing me.

I told him how difficult it was remaining on earth without him. He didn't try to placate me by saying we would soon be together. Jess simply allowed me to express my feelings. I was also aware throughout the experience that I would have to return to the waking state, but I never felt rushed by him. In fact, it was I who seemed to be so caught up in time and how much time we had remaining to communicate. I knew that we had come together so that I could be soothed by his presence. He was incredibly gentle and tender with my grief. He didn't try to explain it away. We both knew that simply being together and feeling his unconditional love was healing me. At one point, I felt the time approaching for me to return to my physical body, but Jess reached out to hold me again. I can understand what people mean when they say that your sense of time on the other side is completely different, because when we embraced again, it was as if each nanosecond was eternity itself!

July 22, 1999

It is our last day in Santa Barbara, where you worked in a health food restaurant many years ago. It is such a beautiful area, Jess. I can see why it held such wonderful memories for you.

I told you a few days ago that I was going to consciously call on you more. I stipulated that if it was not for your highest good, then you should ignore these calls. But, darling, I want to commune with you more, to have you visit me in my dreams, and to feel your ongoing presence in my life. You were such expanded sweetness and nurturing light when we last connected in my dreams. You felt so complete in yourself, and for that, I am very grateful. Hold me in your heart, sweet darling. I love you, honey. Forever, Jim

We were nearing the end of our six-week trip. I found Las Vegas especially hard. Gambling didn't hold the same interest without Jess, so I decided to go to one of the major bookstores and purchase some good reading material. I had read that they offered a large collection of gay and lesbian literature. The bookstore was huge, and I wandered around for over twenty minutes looking for the gay and lesbian section, but, try as I might, I was unable to locate it. I kept circling the New Age section, which had more than one hundred shelves of books. Mentally, I asked Jess to help me find some good reading material. Not knowing quite where to begin, I sat on the floor and started on a bottom shelf. Directly in front of me were books on afterlife. I selected four books within a very short time.

As I began reading during the next few days, my excitement grew about all the research that has been done through time on after-death communication. I read with interest Raymond Moody's *Reunions*, in which he presents a historical perspective on different cultures' attempts to connect with loved ones who have passed. In Elsie Sechrist's *They Still Live*, she highlights Edgar Cayce's work on life after life. Sechrist shares numerous stories from others who have made contact with those on the other side. Harold Sherman's *The Dead Are Alive*, provided similar interesting accounts of individuals who have communicated with loved ones. Reading this material increased my desire to have contact with Jess. Reading about full visual appearances and even conversations with loved ones who had passed filled me with much awe and anticipation.

On the ten-month anniversary of Jess's passing, I decided to visit Mount Charleston. Mount Charleston is about forty-five minutes northwest of Las Vegas. This was the last place that Jess had gone skiing. When we were last there together, we had taken a hike to a small waterfall. My parents joined me for the outing, but Mom was not feeling well, so she opted not to hike. Dad accompanied me on the trail, but after tiring midway, he told me he would wait for my return. When I reached the small waterfall, I was flooded with pleasant memories. I was the only one there, so I had time to quietly recollect my last visit with Jess and enjoy the stillness.

While the reading I was doing had greatly increased my desire to continue to connect with Jess in spirit, I was still uncertain if I was clinging to him too much. Whenever I asked for a sign from him, I would always qualify it by adding that I only wanted one if it was for our highest good. I told him frequently that I didn't want my grief or my desire to connect with him to hold him back from freely pursuing his path on the other side. Yet, I also knew that I had to follow what felt right for me and furthered my own healing. At the waterfall, I told him half humorously that I wanted a clear, yes or no response from him. I wanted to know definitively (but sensitively!) if he was okay with me trying to connect with him more.

As I started to leave the waterfall area, I stumbled and fell to the ground. When I started to rise, I slipped and landed on my bum. It felt as if an outside energy was forcing me to sit for a while and take in the stillness. I began looking at the narrow canyon walls to see if some graffiti contained the words, yes or no. Fortunately, I saw no graffiti on the walls, so I began looking at the actual rock formations to see if I could decipher a message there. Disappointed, but also amused, at this seemingly impossible test I had created for myself, I stretched back on the earth to better view the beauty of the sky.

It was a gloriously bright day, and several large cloud formations filled the heavens. As I looked upward, two very small clouds were moving rapidly together. As I watched them overlap directly above me, I could hardly believe my eyes as they formed the letters Y-E-S!

I was instantly reminded of Jess's love for nature and how he would often use the words God and Nature synonymously. I recalled my other signs from him involving nature and realized that this was yet another incredible testament of his love and conscious link to me. I was flooded with feelings of peace and gratitude. After about forty-five seconds, I watched with wonder as both the clouds and the letters Y-E-S completely evaporated before my eyes.

The first week in Las Vegas, I avoided our favorite casino where we had played video poker. Since I knew I would be staying there for a second week, and since it contained so many memories of happier times, I felt it best to approach it slowly. Of all the cards in the deck, I saw Jess as my jack of hearts. For some reason, I associated that card with him. Maybe it was because his name began with the letter *J* and hearts are a symbol of love.

While in Las Vegas, I decided to carry a small picture of Jess in my fanny pack. Having his picture with me made me feel like he was somehow closer and joining me in the fun of playing the slots. The first afternoon, after checking into our favorite casino, I went to my favorite nickel machines. I had Jess's picture in the slot tray as I was playing joker poker. I thought of how much fun it would be to get five of a kind and watch a thousand nickels cover

Jess's picture. I was visualizing a waterfall of abundance falling from the heavens through the top of my head, flowing through my body, into the machine I was playing, and covering him with coins. After about twenty minutes of this visualization, I hit five kings and watched Jess's smiling face being completely covered with fifty dollars' worth of nickels.

Later that afternoon, I felt it was time to try the quarter machines. I asked Jess and Spirit to guide me to a machine. Soon, I found myself popping in five quarters at a time into a joker machine. I was feeling very peaceful and connected to Jess, and I was thinking that it would be fun to get another five of a kind, specifically five jacks. I had Jess's picture in the tray, and, again, I was visualizing my waterfall, when I was dealt three jacks. I was missing the joker and the jack of hearts. I smiled at the possibility at hand and felt my lover's presence around me; I pushed the draw button and up shot the joker followed by the jack of hearts! One thousand quarters now fell into my tray, this time covering Jess's picture with two hundred and fifty dollars.

Two days later, on my last night in Las Vegas, I was back at the nickel machines, again with Jess's picture in the tray. I had been playing this one machine for a while and had over four hundred credits. I was feeling very connected to Jess and my inner sense of abundance when I was dealt two jacks and the joker. I said to myself, *Well, here is your chance, baby! I would love to see you showered with fourteen hundred nickels!* I pushed draw and was dealt the jack of clubs, followed again in fifth position by the jack of hearts! As the machine pumped out all those coins, I basked in watching my baby being surrounded by coins yet again.

A few hands later I was dealt four 4s, straight up. All I needed now was the joker for another thousand coins. I looked at Jess's picture, barely visible under all the coins in the tray, and said, "Come on baby, let's do it again!"

No sooner had I formed that thought then I clearly heard Jess's laugh as he followed with the words, "Give me a break!" I broke up. I am sure the people sitting around me were convinced that I was crazy. Needless to say, I didn't get the joker. Yet I received much more than a jackpot in hearing my lover's laughter and knowing he was enjoying the slots with me once again.

As with most people, I am certain that specific songs hold a significant place in relationships. On the morning that they came for Jess's body, I played Sarah Brightman's duet with Andrea Bocelli, "Time to Say Goodbye," as his body was wheeled through our front door for the last time.

On one of our last visits to Las Vegas, my parents joined Jess and me to attend Cirque du Soleil's *Mystere*. The four of us had never seen a show that we enjoyed more. On this trip, the night before I returned home, my parents and I had bought tickets to see Cirque du Soleil's new show, *Oh*. The show was held at the grand new casino, Bellagio, which has outdoor water fountains choreographed to music. The music varies throughout the evening. I was very aware that this was our last big night in Las Vegas, and the way that I was feeling, I wasn't sure if I would ever return.

We decided to have dinner at the Bellagio before the show. We hoped to get a chance to see the fountains from the outside terrace of the restaurant we had chosen. We were seated at a wonderful table overlooking the water. I was very aware of Jess and was feeling both vulnerable and melancholy. I was focused on him not being with us for this wonderful meal and view, as well as realizing he wouldn't be joining us for the show afterward. We were seated at the table just minutes before the first water show commenced. My dad and I gasped when the music began. It was none other than "Time to Say Goodbye." We knew that Jess had once again decided to communicate that he wasn't far away.

While I felt ready to return home, I was also apprehensive. I wondered if I would still feel my lover's presence and how I would feel walking into our house. I had decided to return home a week earlier than planned. I had a very long plane trip, with two stopovers, totaling more than eleven hours. After getting my baggage, I wandered around the Daytona Beach airport trying to locate a taxi. In my fatigue, I had walked right by the taxi stand, eventually ending up at the security desk seeking help. They directed me to the taxi, and, since it was after midnight, I was the last customer to secure a cab.

The first album Jess ever bought was Neil Young's *Harvest*. "Old Man," from that album, was one of his favorite songs, and we had played Neil Young's music often during the last weeks of Jess's earthly life. After helping the driver load my bags, I collapsed into the backseat. While giving the driver my destination, I was absolutely stunned to hear Neil Young's "Old Man" on the radio. I asked the driver if it was a tape or a radio station. He said it was a rock station, but at this time of night, they often played oldies. Such an incredible peace and calm settled over me as I felt Jess's presence and the wonderful gift he had arranged for my homecoming!

When I entered my home thirty minutes later, all of my earlier apprehension quickly vanished. There was a translucent light throughout the house and I felt Jess's presence everywhere. I stood by our kitchen sink gazing at a picture of Jess and me, which had been taken twelve years earlier at the San Francisco Gay and Lesbian Parade. Jess's energy was beaming out of the picture, and I was filled with his light and love. I had never experienced that picture in this way before. I found myself laughing and crying at the same time, as I once again realized that my sweet lover was making my return as joyous as possible. I realized, as I looked at the picture, that this was the way that he looked now, free from the ravages of a long AIDS illness, his gentleness and open heart sending me his gift of healing and love.

As my suicidal ideation continued to lift and be replaced by the certainty that I would eventually be reunited with Jess, I had a dream. It was a little over ten months since Jess had passed when I dreamed of being with our dear friend, Robin, on Maui. Jess, Robin, and I had shared one of our most memorable vacations together on Maui. Robin shared our love of Little Makena Beach, where we would frequently swim at sunset.

In my dream, I was aware that Jess had passed. It was Robin's last night in Hawaii, and I realized we had not yet visited Makena Beach. It was about an hour before sunset, and I told Robin to hurry up and get in the car. I felt excitement rise as we made our way to the beach, knowing the serenity that awaited us.

Suddenly, above me, materializing out of the heavens was Jess's radiant face! He was beaming total love, and yet his eyebrows were slightly raised as he teased, "And you thought you were ready to join me!" I laughed and replied, "Well, I guess not until I see Little Makena once again!" He gave me a wry smile and shook his head slightly. His smile filled my soul. I know he had entered my dream to tell me that there were still a few wonderful things for me to do before joining him again.

It was approximately eleven months after Jess had passed and I had settled in bed for the night. I was meditating and opening to the joy that Jess must feel being out of a body. I was thinking and feeling how he was free from the struggles of an earthly existence. I was sensing how joyous it must feel to be surrounded by the loving energy of our many friends who had passed. I felt an incredible wellspring of happiness as I visualized them with Jess.

On our last Christmas together, Jess's sister, Cathy, had given us a number of presents. Included among them was a small brightly colored ceramic sun and moon piece that you attached to a pull chain. I had it on the fan over our bed. One side depicted a sun face and the other a moon face. Both faces were smiling, the only difference being the eyes were open on the sun side. As I opened my eyes from meditation, the ceramic piece was swaying with great momentum and very rhythmically. The eyes of the sun were focused directly at me. The blissful smile and the radiance of the sun perfectly mirrored the happiness that I was feeling internally, and what I believe Jess was experiencing on the other side.

The fan was turned off, no windows were opened, and no air conditioner was running to make the piece sway so wildly. I had never observed this phenomenon before or since. I saw a bluish aura around the piece extending a few inches as it swayed. I could sense Jess's fingers around the chain. For at least fifteen minutes the swaying continued. I was flooded with the joyful awareness that Jess was confirming his agreement and acknowledgement of the happy state he was now experiencing.

Eleven months after Jess passed, I was on my way to a doctor's appointment about an hour away. When alone in the car, I often found myself thinking about Jess. On this particular day, I was recalling a few events that had occurred when he was last hospitalized. When he had sepsis and was admitted to the ICU, they inserted a nasal tube to keep his stomach empty. It was an awful procedure for him and caused him much anxiety.

For the next few days he was only allowed chips of ice. Due to previous radiation to shrink his oral Kaposi's sarcoma lesions, he had developed dry mouth, and being denied fluids was very difficult for him. On his second day of ice chips, Jess excitedly confided that he had managed to open the ice bags that were being used to cool his body. He now had plenty of drinking water, and he was thrilled with his discovery! Because of his disoriented state, I felt like I was talking to a six-year-old. It had been hard to share his secret and inform the nursing staff of their need to watch him more closely. Thoughts such as these ripped at my heartstrings. I was crying quite hard as I remembered his gentle spirit and the many difficult times we had faced together.

Suddenly, right above my windshield, as I traveled seventy miles an hour on the interstate, a beautiful yellow butterfly fluttered by. I experienced such awe and felt Jess's love reaching out to me. In the next thirty seconds, three more yellow butterflies passed above my car. It was an odd area of the interstate for this to occur, since the road was lined with tall trees. It was not a location where you would expect to see such a sight. I had seen similar butterflies near my home during the preceding week; they had also showed up just as I was thinking of Jess and feeling my loss most acutely. But here they were, appearing at the depth of my pain and in seventy-mile-an-hour traffic! I knew that my darling was reaching out to me in his gentle way—and what better way to convey that tenderness than four fluttering yellow butterflies!

As I was driving home from my doctor's appointment, I wondered if Jess had connected with Jean and Peg on the other side. Instantly, I felt that I had been joined by the presence of three additional people. Jess was in the front seat, Jean was seated directly behind Jess, and Peg was seated behind me. It was peculiar to have the distinct feeling of four separate energies in the car.

Jean had liked luxury cars. Jean and her lover, Ann, had owned a number of Lincoln Town Cars and Cadillacs in their thirty-five-year relationship. When Jess's mother passed, we had used some of our inheritance to buy a Lincoln. It was extravagant, but I never regretted it. It was great to have a comfortable car for Jess during the last two and half years of his illness. Jean had been excited for us. On her last car trip, when we had escorted her to hospice, she had asked to be driven in our Lincoln.

I told Jean that I was glad to have her in the car again. I could hear her laughter as she mentally conveyed that she didn't think she would ever be in it again. I felt as if the three of them had been waiting for an invitation to drop in and see how Jim was doing! After enjoying their energies for a short time, I thought of turning on the radio. I had a sense that Jess wanted me to hear a song.

In the singing lessons that Jess had taken early on in our relationship, the song he had decided to practice and learn first was "The Rose," by Bette Milder. It was no surprise for me when, after a minute, "The Rose" came on the radio. My sweet lover had decided to communicate his love to me again. More than that, he had decided to bring two dear friends along for the ride!

I was standing in front of the fireplace mantle, looking at a picture of Jess, which had been taken when he was in his late twenties. His skin was so beautiful. He had a sweet little mustache and a slightly open-mouthed smile. I was thinking that this was perhaps how he now looked. I was feeling a growing sense of inner peace that stemmed from realizing that his body was no longer wasted by AIDS.

I began to feel an increasing sense of his presence, and I noticed some white vapors wafting above the picture. I decided to close my eyes in meditation. Instantly, I got an image of a sunrise. I could see the rays extending from a brilliant gold and red center. Something seemed very familiar about it, but I couldn't place it. I just allowed myself to bask in its warmth and beauty, knowing that it was a communication from him. This vision spoke to me of his ascended glory.

An hour later, as I was getting into bed, I was overcome by remembering a tattoo that Jess had on his chest. It was an eagle with a rose in its claw. The addition of the rose had been my idea, to soften the image of the eagle. The tattoo's background was a sunrise, brilliant gold and red, with rays extending outward. I knew this was the vision I had seen earlier, in a more vivid and radiant form. Now, before sleep, I was filled with such sweet peacefulness and my awareness of Jess's desire to convey his love through this powerful vision.

September 23, 1999

Been missing you, darling. Before going to bed last night, I affirmed that I wanted you to come in a dream (or, even better, my waking state!) I prayed to Spirit. Toward morning, I had a dream of you and me outside a museum, and we were on a path that was cumbersome. You were having difficulty walking and needed my assistance. When I awoke, I had mixed feelings, because, while I was glad to have you in my dream, I was saddened by not seeing you physically healed.

Later today, while showering, I caught some brilliant flashes of white light, which I feel are the result of your attempt to break through. Over the last few months, I have seen a number of gray misty swirls. I have felt that these, too, are your attempts to make contact and descend to this plane. The swirls resemble ripples in a pond. I am grateful to have these fairly common occurrences of light, which help me to realize how close you are.

⊗ ⊗ ⊗

Almost a year after Jess passed, I was watching a Cher special on HBO. Jess and I had seen Cher live and always enjoyed her as a unique personality and performer. The HBO special was recorded at the MGM hotel in Las Vegas. Just as Cher was about to begin her finale, "I Believe," I saw Jess begin to materialize about fifteen feet away. I struggled to surrender to the brilliance emanating from his ascended state. It is hard to explain, but it was like suddenly coming face-to-face with a very spiritual being, such as Jesus or Buddha. How much of their magnificence could you let in?

Jess was radiant; he was not completely formed, but I could see his face and luminous smile. Effulgent white light encompassed him, almost giving the impression of angel wings! Tears of joy streamed down my cheeks as I opened myself to his transcendent beauty and consciousness. I became aware that perhaps part of the reason it is so difficult to communicate with our loved ones after they pass is that we are in such different states of awareness. Perhaps our grief prevents us from perceiving the glory of their new life. I was full of gratitude that Jess had come to share himself with me in this manner. I was also very thankful that I had moved through enough of my pain to behold him in this light.

Chapter 14

Our Love is Here to Stay

I don't want to locate myself only by geography (however strongly I acknowledge its power and point), or books, or beliefs. I want to be located in every breath I take.

Padma Perera

October 2, 1999

Well, here it is, almost a year later, and I am reaching out to you to enter my life again, sweet darling. I really love the book, The Eagle and the Rose, *by Rosemary Altea. Thank you for bringing it into my life. The title, of course, reminds me of your tattoo. A discussion group about her book begins on October 4, the anniversary of your passing. I plan to attend. Once again, I marvel that I will spend a special day in a way I couldn't previously imagine.*

Tomorrow, Mom and Dad are coming over, and we will share communion and devote some time to thoughts of you. Drop in and join us, darling. I love you, darling. Please stay close these next few days. If it serves us, darling, I would love to see you in my dreams or to feel, hear, and see you anytime.

It was the day after the one-year anniversary of Jess's passing. I had just finished *The Eagle and the Rose*, in which Rosemary Altea describes her early years and eventual acceptance of herself as a spiritual medium. Toward the end of the book, she writes about the spiritual healing in which she is currently involved. I was reflecting on the book's message of healing and wondering what role healing would play in my life. I recalled that when I did massage, I had always focused on channeling healing energy to my clients.

I was sitting on the loveseat where Jess and I had spent many hours together. I had not received any communication from Jess on the anniversary of his passing. I was intentionally not sending energy that I needed to hear from him on that date. I was learning to trust that, if it was for our mutual highest good, I would have contact with him.

The thought occurred to me that what I really needed at this moment in my life was to focus on receiving healing energy rather than sending it. As soon as I formulated that thought, I felt Jess standing behind me. I could see him clearly in my mind's eye. He was extending his arms and hands above my shoulders and sending me healing energy. He had a sweet smile on his face, and he was glad to be giving me what I needed in that instant. I felt no sadness that he was on another plane, just tremendous gratitude that he had responded so quickly to my desire.

The funny thing was that he was wearing thick-rimmed glasses. On earth, he had put a lot of energy into choosing and wearing attractive frames. Several times, he had purchased expensive glasses frames, only to determine later that the glasses were not properly made. Then he would get upset with himself for spending too much, and he'd become frustrated that, because of the shape of the frame, he was unable to get them satisfactorily adjusted. I couldn't quite figure out why he appeared with unattractive glasses—or any glasses at all! Maybe it was a subtle message about my need to relax, or a message that, on the other side, things that matter on earth are viewed very differently.

A few days after the anniversary of my lover's passing, I awoke around 5:00 AM. This was several hours earlier than I wanted to arise, so I decided to stay in bed and meditate. I thought of how drawn Jess had been to Mary and the Goddess energy before he passed. It had been a while since I had called on Mary. I repeated the revised Hail Mary prayer that I had taught Jess, asking Mary to keep the lines of communication open between Jess and me if it was for our mutual highest good.

After meditating, I became tired and drifted back to sleep. Suddenly, Jess was lying next to me. I was overjoyed at seeing his entire body, and I reached out to touch his chest. I could hardly believe it when my hand rested on his skin. I felt the smoothness of his torso and the softness and warmth of his flesh. I was clearly aware that we were meeting each other in another dimension and that this reunion was in direct response to my request to Mary. I savored the touch of his skin for a while, and then I removed my hand. My focus shifted to Jess's face. Jess was smiling and beaming his love to me. I could tell he knew that the experience was extraordinary for me and that there was no need for words.

After a short while, I reached out to touch his chest again. This time, my hand began to pass through his body. I realized that Jess was showing me another aspect of his ascended self. The feeling of joy and peace remained constant as I touched both his physical and spiritual body. It was wonderful to feel this physical and spiritual closeness again. I awoke with the realization that I had been given a precious gift, a gift I will carry until we are reunited.

Since Jess had passed, I had kept the notorious remote-controlled fart machine that had brought Jess so much pleasure on a small table next to our loveseat. I had not operated it in over a year except to test it several times. Also on the table was a favorite picture of Jess that had been taken in Hawaii. A few days after the anniversary of his passing, I was sitting on the loveseat watching *Jeopardy.*

I was rooting for the two-day champion to win again. When *Final Jeopardy* arrived, the former champion needed to wager over ten thousand dollars to secure her win. When she got the answer right, I jumped up and yelled, "Big money! Big money!" I looked down at Jess's picture and felt ridiculous yelling out like that, alone in the house. I grabbed his picture and gave him a big kiss, as I said, "Well, sweetie, I am still a crazy ass!" Immediately, the fart machine accentuated Jess's agreement by going off twice! I had not touched the remote control. The machine had never done that in the entire year that I had had it there. I knew that Jess was enjoying the moment with me. I was filled with sweet and tender feelings. Once again, Jess had given me the healing gift of laughter.

October 13, 1999

Good morning, darling. I was blessed with such sweet thoughts of gratitude last night. I was aware that when you have made your presence known to me, you have always been so attuned to the place that I am in. This really is an extension of the way you were with me the last several weeks of your earthly life, how, despite all that was going on for you, you made such sweet, caring room to comfort me.

And so you, dear Jess, bathe me in harvest moonlight, surround me with wildlife that we admired, and allow me to hear your simple enthusiasm at the thought of being together again. You continue to tease me with your humor, hold me in my grief, listen quietly to my process, and trust in me to get through. What a teacher you remain for me, darling. How I love you, Jess.

I prayed last night and affirmed my desire to always tap consciously into the ongoing presence of our love. I choose that you always remain a guide for me, and for that, I am eternally grateful. I feel that we are both waking up. In some ways, it seems, you may have it easier where you are now, and for some reason, I apparently need to be here a little longer. Be my guardian angel, sweetie. Help me to awaken to the light. Let's keep our dance alive.

October 29, 1999
Oh darling, I love you so much; how blessed am I to have you in my life. Now reading George Anderson's Lessons from the Light, *and so far, I am completely enthralled.*

Before becoming ill, Jess had loved to spend time at home caring for our many potted plants. Our front courtyard and the pool area were always abundant with beautiful, healthy foliage. On our last visit to Muir Woods, California, in 1996, Jess had purchased a redwood burl. He told me that he was going to try growing it at home. I thought it was a waste of four dollars, but such was his way with plants that it grew to a height of three feet. As his condition worsened, I did my best to care for his beloved plants.

A little over a year after he passed, I decided to purchase a new spa. The old spa's skin had several cracks, and the frame had rotted. When we had purchased our first spa, Jess and I had placed it on twelve-by–twelve-inch cement squares. I decided that, for the new spa, I would like to have a concrete slab laid. After removing the seventy-five squares, I was in a quandary as to how to use them. I used about half of them as a new foundation for the woodpile. After racking my brain, I called on Jess to inspire me how to use the remainder.

Suddenly, out of nowhere, a beautiful yellow butterfly fluttered around the plants by the pool, about five feet in front of me. Since yellow butterflies had appeared in several previous communications from Jess, I knew this was a message from him. The squares made perfect bases for the plants. As I placed them, I realized that the plants were in need of water, fertilizer, and some loving care. After I worked on about five plants, the yellow butterfly suddenly reappeared, fluttered happily around the plants, and then vanished in the blink of an eye. I had an immediate warm wave of emotion—Jess's love. I knew that my sweet lover was not only caring for me but for the plants he loved as well.

One evening, I was talking to someone in a local chat room on the computer. He told me that he was very taken with my computer profile and that he was also HIV positive. We talked on the phone later that evening and agreed to meet at my home the following night. Throughout the day, I had a mixture of emotions. I was excited about the prospect of meeting someone with whom to share intimacy but also felt that things were progressing too fast. He did not have a computer picture to send me, which was a factor in my uneasiness.

I prayed that day for protection, asking Mary and the Goddess energy to assure that our connection was mutually healing. I also told Jess that I would welcome him to drop in and make sure that everything was developing for our best interest. I added that he was welcome to hang out in the event that we made love, although it humorously occurred to me that he probably had better things to do!

Joe was very nice; however I felt little physical attraction to him. I gave him a complete tour of the house, and we talked for several hours. I then half-heartedly said that we could go to the bedroom if he wanted. Despite my intuitive misgivings about being physical with him, I thought that maybe passion would develop and that touch would be soothing.

As we were walking upstairs, I heard four distinct beeps. I turned to Joe and asked if that was his medication reminder. He said that he had heard the beeps but it wasn't him. I immediately got a feeling that Jess was somehow involved. When we got upstairs, we heard the beeps again. Joe suggested that it might be a clock, and it occurred to me that it might be the batteries in the smoke alarm. As I approached the alarm, it suddenly began to shriek! I had an especially difficult time opening the unit to remove the battery. I was now thinking that this was a clear message from Jess that I should stop what I was doing.

I don't mean to imply that Jess was being jealous, for that was not his nature. But I do believe that he was aware that I was entering a situation in which I was not comfortable. The alarm was his way of saying, "Stop." It was just too uncanny that at this precise moment so much chaos was manifesting. When I had earlier shown Joe the upstairs bedroom, everything was calm. Perhaps to avoid embarrassment or still hoping that magic would prevail, I discounted the message and joined Joe in getting undressed.

The next hour was difficult. I didn't enjoy being physical with Joe and came close at several points to suggesting that we stop. I did try to be as present as I could, but my overriding thoughts were about what I was going to eat after he left! Although, in retrospect, I wish I had honored my intuition both before and after the alarm, I believe that the experience was a lesson for me. Just as I often ignore the voice of my inner guides or Spirit, I can also discount the helpful messages that my loved ones on the other side deliver to me.

One of the most striking features of our home is a large coquina-and-sandstone fireplace, in which Jess and I enjoyed many fires over the years. Lighting the fireplace for the first time each year brings to mind many special memories and warm feelings of our time together. A little over a year after Jess passed, it was time to build a fire. Just as I went to light the fire, the lamp next to where he often had sat in the living room flashed on and off several times; the lights in the rest of the house were unaffected. I knew that Jess had come to enjoy the first fire of the year and to bring me the gift of his warmth on a chilly November night.

Thirteen months after Jess passed, my parents and I attended a workshop by a spiritual medium, John Edward. Edward is author of *One Last Time*, which I enjoyed very much. I was excited about seeing him in person. Although I wasn't chosen for a special message, the event far exceeded my expectations. After lecturing for an hour on the different ways in which our loved ones communicate, Edward went to about ten people to deliver messages.

His ability to communicate with those on the other side was astounding. He was led to a specific area of the audience where the intended receiver sat. In almost all cases, he was able to give the name of the person who was communicating through him, the intended's name, the manner of death, and a report of observed behavior of the loved one by the spirit. It was utterly amazing.

He went to one woman whose brother had been murdered. John told her the circumstance surrounding the murder, her name, and the names of other deceased family members. He went to another young woman, directly next to me, whose husband had passed seven months before. He told her the name of her husband (Jim) and said that Jim was with his parents on the other side. He said that Jim's father had been an alcoholic and that Jim was one of three siblings (Jim had two sisters). He next went to a woman in front of me, and after telling her the name of her mother, he asked her if she had kept her mother's tooth! After shaking her head in disbelief, the woman confirmed that she did have her mother's tooth in a jar and had been looking at it that morning. John explained that the mother chose to mention that directly observed behavior so that her daughter would have no doubt that it was she.

At the end of the workshop, John led us in a short visualization in which he instructed us to ask our loved one for an indisputable sign. He said we should think of something very specific, some communication that would convince us that our loved one was closer than we thought. Jess loved yellow roses, so I asked him to send me yellow roses. I then quickly modified the request, asking for only one rose, thinking that would be easier. Afterward, I thought to myself, *How is he ever going to manage this, unless he materializes one out of thin air!*

When I got home, as I was walking into the bedroom where he had passed, I thought how wonderful it would be to find a yellow rose on the bed. Unfortunately there was none, but I was thankful for an extraordinary day and for the many other previous communications I had been blessed with by Jess. I put the thought of yellow roses out of my mind. The next day, I was at my desk, sorting papers and responding to some mail. Imagine my surprise when I opened an appeal from the Cystic Fibrosis Foundation and saw personalized address labels, fifteen of which bore the most beautiful yellow roses! Mind you, not one, not a dozen, but fifteen glorious yellow roses! A sign, which had seemed so difficult to manifest, I now held in my hand—less than twenty-four hours after my request. Once again, my sweet lover had found a way to reach me and let me know that I am far from forgotten.

While dreaming one night, I was aware of my desire to make contact with Jess. With a push of will, I found myself suddenly flying. Although I had a body while I was flying, I had broken free of the limitations of my earthbound physical body. The feeling of flying produced pure elation. Before returning to my physical body, I thought I would try to trick Jess. I started to telepathically summon Jess, telling him that I had "died." He could now come and greet me! Although part of me realized the playful mischievousness of this, I still relished the idea of calling him to my side no matter what the actual circumstances where.

Suddenly, I found myself wrapped in his arms. I had forgotten the pure joy and feeling of comfort and safety that comes from being embraced by someone who is physically larger. It felt wonderful to run my fingers through his hair, to feel his solidity and his loving embracing presence. I found myself crying in his arms as I opened myself to the pain of missing him on the earthly plane.

It was so odd to be feeling such playful elation one moment and to be releasing my accumulated grief a few moments later. But once again, as he had in the weeks immediately preceding his passing, he knew what I needed most—simply to be held in his loving arms. I felt a little guilty calling him away from the joy and peace that I believe he now experiences. However, as in life, there was no admonishment from him or advice for me to get over my hurt. His gift was his continuous, caring presence holding me, allowing me the gentle gift of healing release.

When I awoke, I thanked him for the communication and acknowledged that being held had been so very healing. However, since his focus was on holding me in this encounter, I had missed the opportunity to see his radiant face. The next night, I had forgotten about my desire, but fortunately he had not. In my dream, I found myself in a large casino. As I was walking through the slot machine area, Jess approached me. I knew immediately that he was entering my dream from the other side to grant my request. His face was radiant and happy, and his body was the picture of health. He smiled at me, and in his hands, he held two rolls of silver dollars that he told me he had found in a slot tray! What could be better than playing with someone else's money! He was beaming with excitement. He was off to find the dollar video poker machines and was having the time of his life. I was thrilled to see him overjoyed and to see his face so clearly. When

I awoke, I realized again what a dear spirit he is to have answered my request so quickly.

I was at my parents' home for Thanksgiving. I took an early nap before dinner. When I awoke, I looked out the bedroom window, beyond the porch, to a small, brightly sunlit hamlet of trees. I became very nostalgic, for the scene reminded me of Lake Mendocino, California, where Jess and I had camped in a grove of manzanita trees. It was a very picturesque setting. We had been very happy to be in the warm California sun after a rather foggy week on the Oregon coast. The sunlit trees at my parents' home brought back those warm feelings. I was unexpectedly flooded with bittersweet memories of Jess.

At the precise moment that I felt the twinge of missing Jess, a large, radiant yellow butterfly fluttered right next to the screen porch, in full view of the bedroom window. It was the only yellow butterfly that I saw that Thanksgiving. Its timing was perfect. I felt Jess's love and care reach out to me. What could have been lingering sadness quickly turned into thankfulness for the many ways Jess finds to communicate his ongoing love.

A few days before Christmas, I decided to wrap some gifts for my parents and my dog, Jasper. I had gotten Jasper three months earlier. Jasper resembles a small fox, and his loving and playful Pomeranian energy was a warm addition to my home and life. This was the first time since Jess's passing that I found myself wrapping gifts. Wanting to include Jess in our Christmas celebration, I decided to address some gifts to my parents and myself from Jess. Throughout the day, I had felt his presence around me. I saw several flickers of light and vapors. Later, as I was preparing for bed, I had the comforting thought of writing in my journal.

It had been more than four weeks since my last entry, and the thought of spending time communicating my thoughts to Jess was very soothing.

To create a mood, I decided I would light a candle and burn a stick of incense. As I entered my bedroom, right on the corner of my bed was one of my favorite pieces of incense. I had made the bed a few hours earlier and knew for certain that there had been nothing on it. Instantly, I was filled with the awareness that this was a Christmas gift from Jess for the time we would now be spending together. Once again, and in a most significant way, he had manifested his presence at an important time of year.

December 21, 1999

Oh darling, it feels so long since I have paused to write you. You certainly have been on my mind, as I have begun praying for you daily. So much of what I read in George Anderson speaks about the value of prayer for those in the spirit world. So I have asked the Spirit to reveal to me how to best pray for you. My prayers change form, but for the last month I have been repeating the following:

Jess and I are one with the lush green fields of Jesus's healing love.

Jess and I are one with the morning glory blue of Mary's universal compassion.

Jess and I are one with the silver clouds of Maharishi's infinite peace.

Jess and I are one with the mauve mist of Buddha's gentle wisdom.

Jess and I are one with the purple skies of Krishna's circular joy.

Jess and I are one with the ruby jewels of Allah's abundant ecstasy.

Jess and I are one with the rose-colored quartz of Tara's harmonious nature.

Jess and I are one with the golden rays of Jess and Jim's eternal love.

Jess and I are one with the pure white light of God's shared glory.

Today was such a full day. My doctor told me that my t-cells are over six hundred; the highest they have been since I was first tested. My viral load continues to remain non-detectable. I was happy but also a little sad as I thought how long it might be before we are together again. But then I remembered how short another ten or twenty years on this plane is and that it is not my conscious choice to pass from AIDS. As far as I know, I might ascend tomorrow! In the meantime, I will continue to do my best to be here now.

On January 3, my parents and I celebrated my forty-eighth birthday. We opened gifts at their home and went out to a superb Chinese dinner. I had not had any conscious encounter with Jess since before Christmas, and I was not feeling a strong need for him to make contact for my birthday—but, apparently, he was.

We first connected that night, while I was dreaming, in a crowded terminal. I was seated and many people were passing by. Soon, I saw Jess approaching me. I was excited to be making contact with him again. I knew that my body was asleep and we were connecting in another dimension. He looked very healthy but a little rushed. I asked him what was up, and he said, "I have just been skiing and was having a marvelous time!" He said he couldn't stay long, as he had something to complete, but he would be back. As he began to leave, part of me wanted to follow him, but my inner voice told me to trust and accept him at his word. All through the night he playfully and lovingly interacted with me. What a wonderful birthday gift it was to know that he was enjoying the thrill of skiing once again!

About fifteen months after Jess passed, our former roommate, Wendy, came for a week's visit. Wendy had been in Australia when Jess had passed, and this was our first visit since his passing. The day after she arrived, I was meditating on the loveseat in our living room. At one point, I found myself thinking of Jess and that I would never see him enter or leave through the front door of our home again. I wasn't aware of being particularly sad, I was just remembering how the mortuary attendants had wheeled his body out the front door at my request. I had wanted Jess to leave by the door he had first entered when we purchased our home, rather than a door that might have been more convenient for the mortuary attendants.

The following day, I thought that it would be a good time to share with Wendy some of the after-death communications I had had with Jess. I had not shared any of the communications with friends since typing them, and I was feeling vulnerable. When I had finished sharing a few of them, I walked through the living room, passing the front door, to let my dog, Jasper, out the side door. In a few minutes, I came back in to find the front door wide open. I was immediately aware of Jess's presence, but I dismissed the feeling, thinking that Wendy had gone out through the front door. I walked outside and called her name. As I came back in, I realized that the door had been locked—the button on the handle was still in the locked position.

I went into the dining room, where Wendy was still seated, and told her what had happened. I continued to feel a strong sense of Jess's presence, and we both knew that Jess had been with us for the readings. I also knew that his leaving through the front door was a direct response to my thoughts the previous day. He had reminded me again that all things are possible and of the importance of never saying never.

Wendy was nearing the end of her week's visit. We had just finished watching an excellent HBO special, *Life after Life*. In the documentary, many people shared accounts of communications they had had with their deceased loved ones. After viewing the video, the time felt right to share with Wendy the pictures I had taken of Jess during his last two weeks of earthly life.

It had been three years since Wendy had last seen Jess. The sixty pictures reflected, in part, the physical ravages of the disease. As we were nearing the end of them, the power in the house decreased—everything dimmed but nothing went out. I found myself getting irritated since we were looking at the pictures taken the night before Jess passed. I was concerned that the flickering lights would disturb the cathartic impact Wendy would feel from viewing the pictures.

After we finished looking through the album, I went to return it to the room where Jess had passed. The lights remained dim and were flickering throughout the entire house. Suddenly, it occurred to me that the reason the power was dimming was that Jess was present. As soon as I had completed that thought, everything returned to full power! As I placed the album on the dresser, I realized that Wendy and I had been blessed with another communication from Jess. What could have been a lingering sadness from viewing the pictures was now transformed into joyful awareness. We realized that Jess is not only free from his battered body but that he remains very present in our daily lives.

February 2, 2000

Oh darling, I worry at times that you will stop communicating with me because you feel that by continuing, I will have a harder time connecting with someone else here on earth. Tonight, I pray and thank the Spirit for keeping our hearts connected as I complete my purpose here.

I choose to walk through this life loving you anew each day, while at the same time being open and choosing to love those who also help me to see my higher purpose. While fearful at times as to my ability

*to pull this off, I remember that it is always a choice between love
and fear. And I choose that love of you now, sweet darling, as I also
choose that love of another.*

*Thank you, God, for assisting me in remembering that it is simply
a choice to love and to let go of fear. I know there is an infinite amount
of love within me. My love for you, sweet Jess, complements and
strengthens my love for another, as my love for another complements
and strengthens my love for you. My choice is love. All else will be
revealed. Blessings to you, sweet Jess.*

Nearly a year and a half after Jess's passing, my mother was
diagnosed with shingles. A week later, we made plans to have
dinner together. Both Mom and Dad are Catholic and attend
church regularly. I offered to go with them to Mass after dinner.
I wanted the three of us to do something as a family to affirm my
mother's health and state our intention for her well-being. On
the same evening, there was a local forum on issues pertaining to
same sex partnerships, sponsored by PFLAG (Parents, Friends,
and Families of Gays and Lesbians) that my mother wanted to
attend.

The forum was informative. There was a reporter there from
our local newspaper, *The News-Journal,* which, in general, is very
supportive of issues pertaining to gays and lesbians. However,
when Jess's obituary had first appeared in the paper, they had
purposefully omitted any reference to our relationship and my
name. This was most upsetting to me, particularly since I had
contacted the newspaper years earlier, when first writing our
obituaries, to see what relationship term they deemed appropriate.
At that time, I was told that "lover" was taboo but that "significant
other" or "life partner" was acceptable.

When the obituary first ran, Chris called the newspaper to
complain. She was told that the person in charge of the obituaries
was new and hadn't encountered the situation before, so he had

taken it upon himself to delete my name. After much persistence on Chris's part, the paper agreed to run a correction the following day. However, in the next day's obituary they entered my name but referred to me as a "companion." After a number of stressful conversations with the newspaper staff, Chris eventually talked to the president and chief executive officer. He apologized and said he would appoint a special committee to review the policy. That was the last we ever heard.

I brought this incident to the attention of the reporter at the forum. Even though it had been a year and a half since it had occurred, I was surprised by how emotional I still was when talking about it. The reporter clearly didn't grasp how vitally important it is for gay and lesbian couples to have their relationships described in affirming and appropriate language. Instead, she hid behind the excuse that it was a matter of journalistic style and said she was sorry.

When I returned home, I was still feeling vulnerable, and I was irritated with myself that I had not been able to better state my case. I sat on the loveseat and tried to calm myself. Almost immediately, a gray, rippling mist materialized about ten feet in front of me. It was about seven feet above the floor and its dimension was about two feet by four feet. Jess had used this method of communicating before, and I was instantly calmed by my awareness that he was once again reaching out to comfort me. It only lasted about ten seconds, but the feeling of peacefulness remained with me throughout the night.

The next day, I was wondering why spirits use darkish vapors to make us aware of their presence. Jess had also manifested in specks of brilliant white light, which, in some ways I find even more comforting. It is almost as if the grayish materialization is caused by spirits' attempts to enter the physical world. When they break through, this swirling movement occurs. As I was writing in my journal about Jess's most recent contact, I looked up and saw a flash of brilliant white light appear directly in the center of the horseshoe above the front door. I knew immediately that Jess was accommodating my preferred method of contact, and once again, I was flooded with his sweet, eternal love.

I hadn't planned anything special for Valentine's Day. In my meditation that morning, I was intentionally not putting a lot of energy into receiving a communication from Jess. Although his communications are always welcome, in my moments of fear, I continue to wonder if I am holding on to the special tenderness of our love too tightly.

I decided to go to Home Depot to buy a replacement door for my shed, an errand that I had been putting off. Jess had always handled these types of tasks, and I was feeling somewhat overwhelmed. It was difficult to get anyone to assist me at the store, and purchasing the door and parts took much longer than I had anticipated. After a few other errands, I returned home and made lunch. By the time I lay down for a nap, I was feeling spent.

Just prior to waking, I was aware that I was still asleep and singing the words to a song. I didn't realize what song it was, but it sounded very familiar. Suddenly, I was aware of Jess. He told me that he liked to hear me sing and that when I woke up he wanted me to continue singing the song to him. I opened my eyes and sang the words aloud. It was then that I realized the song was "Love Is Here to Stay". I remembered how much I had loved the lyrics, and I had practiced and sung the song to Jess a few days before he passed. I hadn't thought of it in over a year, and now, on Valentine's Day, Jess was asking me to sing it to him again!

I went into the living room and put on Ella Fitzgerald's rendition. While holding Jess's picture in my arms, I sang it to him three times! It felt wonderful to be affirming those sentiments with him again on this special day. Jess had found the perfect way to validate the special tenderness of our love. Never again will I doubt the appropriateness and timeliness of expressing my eternal love for him.

Later that night, I decided to write about this experience in my journal. I lit a large votive candle that my parents had given me for Christmas. I had the candle on my bedroom dresser, where I also have Jess's ashes. As I was writing in my journal, I noticed that the wick had fallen onto its side, and two brilliant flames were burning side by side. I felt Jess's presence and realized that he had decided to spend much of this Valentine's Day with me. The two flames burned side by side for nearly an hour before I blew them out. What a special day my lover had orchestrated for me.

Love Is Here to Stay

It's very clear, our love is here to stay.
Not for a year, but ever and a day.
The radio, and the telephone, and the movies that we know,
May just be passing fancies, and in time may go.
But oh, my dear, our love is here to stay.
Together we're, going a long, long way.
In time, the Rockies may crumble, Gibraltar may tumble, they're only made of clay.
But, Our Love Is Here To Stay.

(George and Ira Gershwin)

Jess at Grand Tetons, Wyoming (1993)

Epilogue

On May 10, 2000, I had an appointment with a renowned psychic medium, George Anderson. I had found comfort in Anderson's books and had been impressed when I saw him on television several times. Before his sessions, Anderson knows nothing about his clients. He asks that they respond with only yes or no answers to the information that spirits provide him. The discernment, as the session is called, lasted for an hour and took place in Long Island, New York. Jess wasted no time in coming through.

In the first minute, Anderson informed me that a young male had come into the room and was embracing me with love. According to Anderson, this young male said that he had passed fairly recently and "he blesses you for taking care of him." Anderson also related that the man said that he and I had had a marriage of the heart and that we had shared a long-term relationship. The visitor added, Anderson relayed, that he had come to me in dreams and many comforting visitations. Anderson finished, "Your partner thanks you for your prayers and wants you to know that he is still around you because, frankly, you are fun to be with!"

Anderson also told me that Jess had passed from AIDS and said that he had a very rough time before he passed. Anderson continued, "Your partner says that he wouldn't wish it on anybody.

He acknowledges how heartbreaking it was for you to watch him wither away. However, he adds that his illness was part of his spiritual fulfillment of his own choice, and that he is quite proud of himself for making it to the finish line."

Anderson interprets messages from spirits through symbols and pictures that he sees. He shared with me that it is often difficult for him to identify a spirit's name. However, he is aware of how comforting identifying the spirit's name is for those who seek his help. Jess then conveyed to Anderson that his name was short, containing four letters, with the last two letters of his name doubled. To communicate his name, Jess provided Anderson with the mental image of the book *Friendly Persuasion*, written by Jessamyn West. Jess communicated that there was a character in the book who shared his name. Anderson then correctly identified Jess's name, adding that the father in the book was also named Jess. It is interesting that Jess provided the image of *Friendly Persuasion*, since it deals with a Quaker family in the Civil War and their conflict over fighting. At the time, I was unfamiliar with the book or the movie version.

Both of Jess's parents also came through and referred to the inharmonious relationship that they had experienced on earth and their lack of understanding. Anderson also identified by name my maternal grandfather, George, and said that my maternal grandmother had met Jess on the other side and welcomed him, along with a small pet, to the light. Both my grandmother and Jess communicated that they were acting as my guardian angels.

Anderson said that Jess told him that I had written about many of my communications. Jess communicated that he was going to assist me with my future writing, adding that my efforts would be rewarded.

Anderson also identified Jean and Peg by name. Peg identified herself as an "adoptive grandmother" and thanked Jess and me for taking care of her. Peg communicated that "family by choice is the best kind." Anderson identified a number of my friends who had passed, by name, including Paul, Mark, Steve, and Jess's first lover,

Michael. Michael communicated that because of the number of loved ones I have on the other side, at times I seem like "the last of the Mohicans."

Anderson said that he could tell that Jess had quite a sense of humor, and that Jess had joked, "They are not quite ready for you over here yet!" Anderson told me that Jess says, "You are a survivor and that is one of the many things that attracted him to you. He knows that you have suffered in silence, in that most people do not take a gay relationship as seriously as a heterosexual one. They see it as primarily a sexual connection and not as a spiritual union." Jess had added that I should not hold that against them, they don't know any better; it is a lack of understanding. He told Anderson that we know what was uniquely shared and that is what I (Jim) should reflect upon. "Certainly he knows that I love him and that he loves me," Jess had told Anderson. That is all that I should be remembering.

I was more than satisfied with my session with Anderson. When I returned to my room after the discernment, I was blessed with a number of bright flashes of light, which I knew was Jess's way of easing me back to the present and assuring me that he would continue to be part of my life.

It is interesting to note that after my session with Anderson, I focused intensely on completing this book. True to his word, I felt Jess's loving guidance throughout the process. Whenever I questioned whether I should address a particular point, immediately off to my left side a swirl of grayish mist materialized. I knew this was Jess giving me his approval.

Before I saw Anderson, I had one other session with a spiritual medium named Patrick Mathews. I had learned of Patrick Mathews from Bill and Judy Guggenheim's wonderful website. I used the site frequently to talk with other people who had experienced the passing of a loved one. Patrick was facilitating a weekly support group and I later reviewed his web page and made an appointment with him by phone. As with George, Jess came through immediately.

Patrick also had no information about me prior to the session and only wanted me to respond yes or no. He quickly told me that he had made contact with a young man who was "literally jumping up and down to communicate with me." Patrick then began to cry as he allowed Jess to communicate his love for me through Patrick's heart. Jess told Patrick, "Jim calls me his angel, but I want him to know that he is my angel."

Ruby came through and thanked me for caring for her son. Ruby communicated that she "now realizes that love is all that matters and that she now appreciates the beauty of my relationship with her son, which she was unable to acknowledge on earth."

Jess said that he "has been with God and that he wants me to remember that he wore his illness like a badge of courage. He is very proud of how he handled his illness and he wants me to always remember that." Jess correctly told Patrick that I had organized some of Jess's files the night before my session with Patrick, as a way of showing me how connected he remains to my life. He assured me that he has "no problem being in two places at the same time and that I don't need to worry about calling him away from something."

Jess communicated that he is quite proud of the many ways in which he continues to manifest his love for me, verifying the way he reveals himself in flashes of light, dreams, and numerous visitations. Jess said that he sings with me in the car but he humorously teased that, as on earth, he is able to reach the notes better than I am!

He said that he would help me with my writing, that I was an excellent teacher, and that I would continue to help many people before it was our time to be together again. He ended by reminding me of the importance of celebrating life, of all that we had fought to achieve, and, most importantly, to enjoy myself and have fun!

I feel very fortunate to have had both of these sessions. While it remains immensely joyful to have direct experience of Jess's communication, it was validating to have Jess come through

George and Patrick in such a personal and loving manner. While there still are a few mediums whom I greatly respect, and who I would treasure a session with, I don't feel compelled to seek contact with Jess through this form any longer. I continue to trust that when it is for our highest good, Jess and I will make contact.

More than ten years have passed since Jess let go of his earthly form. For eight of those years, I have been fortunate to be in relationship with another dear man. My current lover, Jeff, is a long-term AIDS survivor who has also experienced the painful passing of a lover.

Jeff and I first met in 1996 at a buddy training that I was doing for Outreach Inc. Jeff told me years later that when he observed me the first night of the training, he was very much enamored. However, when I brought Jess, who was in a wheelchair, with me the next day to speak at the training, he was both saddened by what we were dealing with and disheartened to have to let go of what he had fantasized as possible between us.

I remember meeting Jeff again in 1999 at our annual pride picnic. Jeff was walking with a cane and had just come through a prolonged period of an AIDS-related illness that brought him very close to death. We had a great connection, but he was still too ill to consider pursuing a relationship. We met again about six months later, when he came to a support group I was attending. In May 2000, we decided to become intimately involved, and we dated for over three years before moving in together.

In our relationship, we have been able to heal places of hurt and experience abundant joy. We are able to freely talk about our past loves and to incorporate the treasures we received from past relationships into the present moment. We are grateful for good health and many new friends, marveling at how our lives continue to become grander with each passing day.

I recall, in the early days of my grief, that I was conflicted over being here now and my ongoing thoughts of Jess. I mistakenly had thought that being in the now required that I somehow not think of Jess, since he was not physically present. Yet I have come to realize that being in the present is to be with all forces—seen and unseen. In addition, being in the now moment is honoring whatever I am feeling and trusting in the absolute perfection of what I am experiencing.

I also realize that there is no need to "let go," but a desire to continue moving forward. My love for Jess was not a love "until death do us part" but an eternal love that continues to nourish and provide me strength. I do not seek to find Jess in the past but to merge with him in the present moment, in the same manner that I merge with the Spirit. It is through the grace of this conscious union that I am able to be fully present and to extend love to all I encounter.

In my most trying and my most joyful moments, I am sustained by gratitude for a strong and delicate courage that has manifested in my life and forever leads me home.

Me and Jeff on a cruise (2004)

For personal correspondence with Jim Geary or information relative to *Delicate Courage,* please contact Jim at JimGeary@delicatecourage.com or visit his website at www.delicatecourage.com

Manufactured By: RR Donnelley
                     Momence, IL USA
                     November, 2010